Sing Through the Day

Eighty Songs for Children

Compiled and Edited by Marlys Swinger

Illustrated by Nancy and Brenna McKernan

The Plough Publishing House

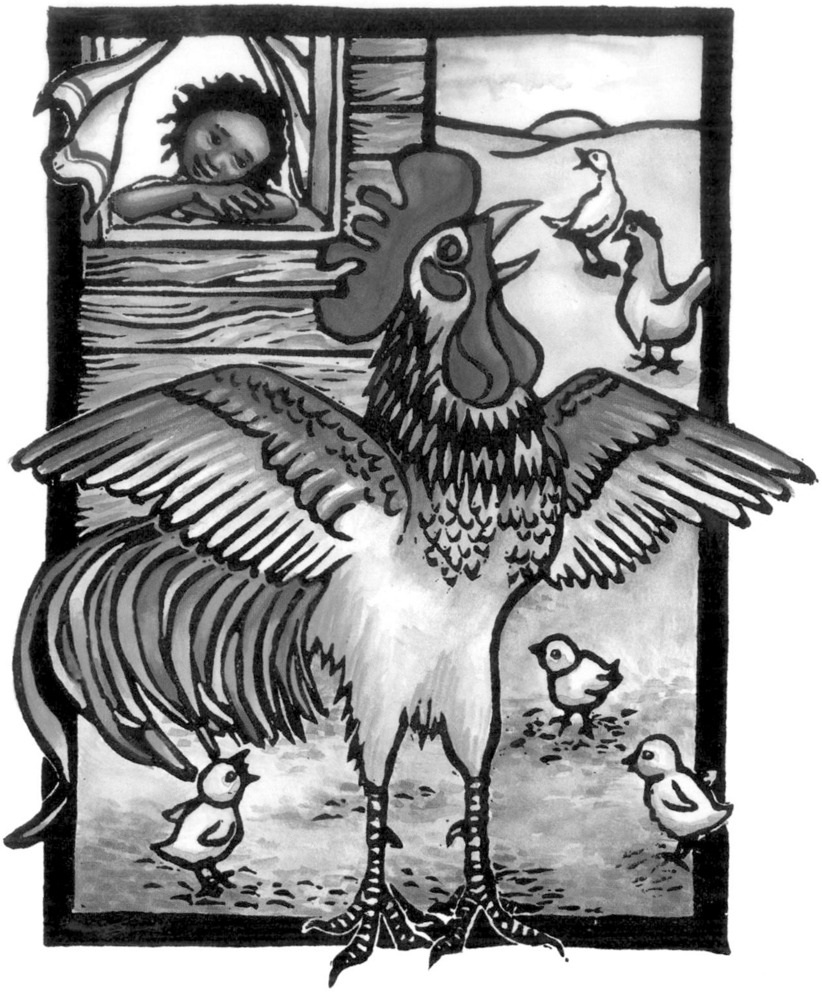

©1999 by The Plough Publishing House
of The Bruderhof Foundation
Farmington PA 15437 USA
Robertsbridge, East Sussex TN32 5DR UK
All Rights Reserved

1st Edition: 1968, 1969, 1971, 1972, 1973, 1976, 1981, 1986
2nd Edition: 1999, 1999

A catalog record for this book is available from the British Library.

ISBN 0-87486-917-4
Printed in Hong Kong

Introduction

I can only think of music as something in every human being – a birthright. Music coordinates mind, body, and spirit. That doesn't mean each person must have a violin or piano: the greatest service to society would be if every school day began with singing. If people sing or play together, they have a feeling of individual coordination as well as coordination within the body of the group.
Yehudi Menuhin

The language of music is a stepping stone to the heart of a child. It can be as natural as the beginning of speech. I have known children who hummed or chanted recognizable tunes before they said words! When parents or teachers encourage their children's musical development by singing to them and with them, it will only be a matter of months before the children know dozens of songs – tunes and words that will stay with them for the rest of their lives

The best way to build a child's appreciation for music is singing. Almost everyone has at least one fond memory of singing around a campfire with a guitar, or standing at the piano – after all, there are few activities that bring people together so closely. It is the same with the lullabies sung by mothers the world over.

Many people claim they or their children are "unmusical." I still believe music can speak to every heart and enrich every life. In a sense, it is a universal language that, according to the great Japanese teacher Shinichi Suzuki, lies hidden in every child. In some it may be apparent already in the cradle, and in others it may show itself only in adulthood; yet it is there. Whether a child grows up to be "musical" has perhaps less to do with inborn talent than with the time and care taken to develop and nourish him or her.

That is why music education in the first years should be approached as naturally as possible – that is, through singing – simply as a means of providing stimulation through beauty. The issue at stake here goes beyond music. To quote Suzuki, it is a matter of nurturing children with love: "Children in their simplicity seek what is true, good, and beautiful…based on love."

Marlys Swinger
April 1999

Note: Songs marked with the symbol 💿 *are included on the sing-along CD.*

Contents

Singing Time

Rose Fyleman   Unknown

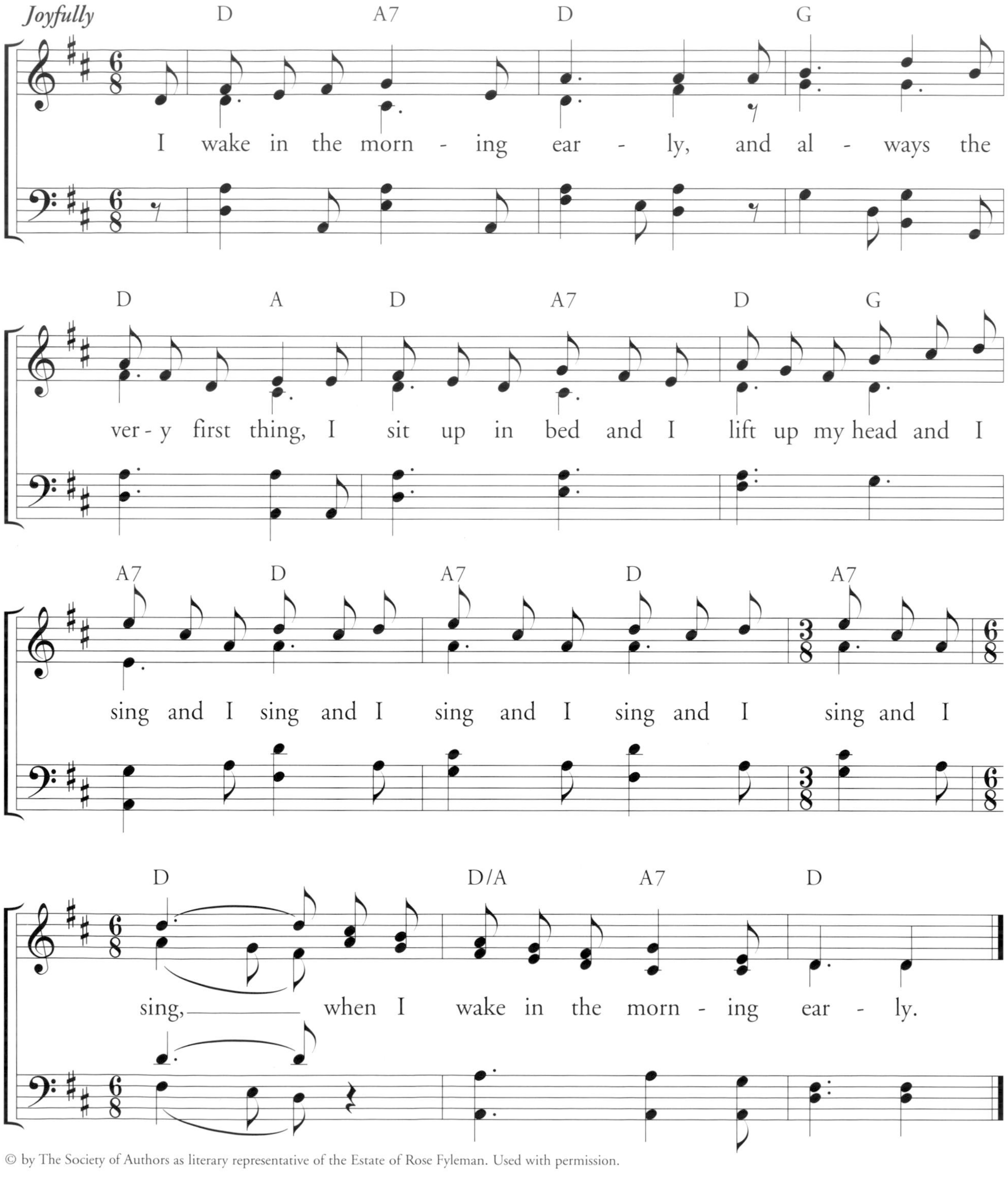

Joyfully

I wake in the morn - ing ear - ly, and al - ways the

ver - y first thing, I sit up in bed and I lift up my head and I

sing and I sing and I sing and I sing and I sing and I

sing,_____ when I wake in the morn - ing ear - ly.

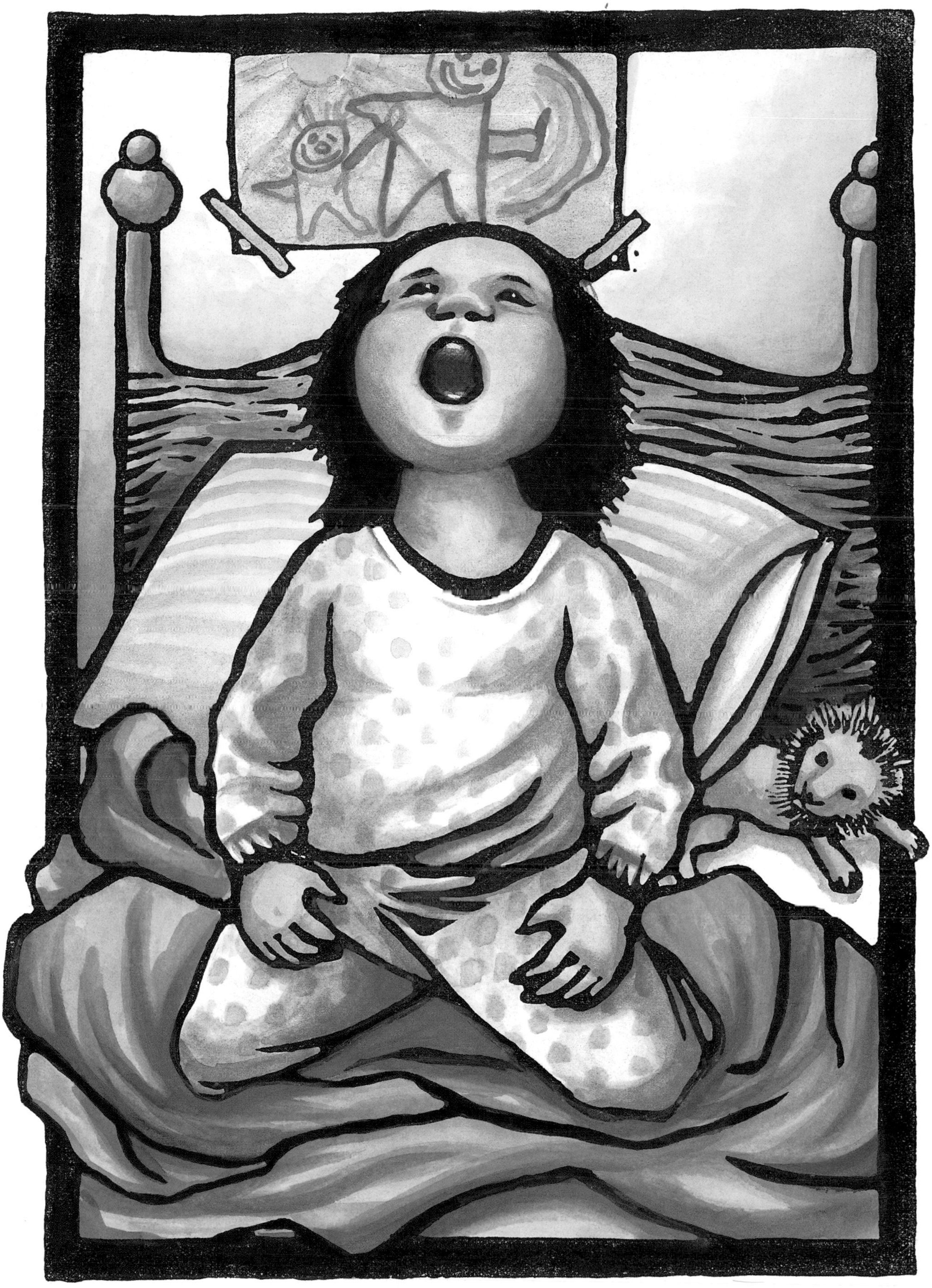

Dearest Sun

For a little fun, use a different percussion instrument to represent each family member.

Translated from the Swedish
by Maisie Radford

Words and Music
Alice Tegner

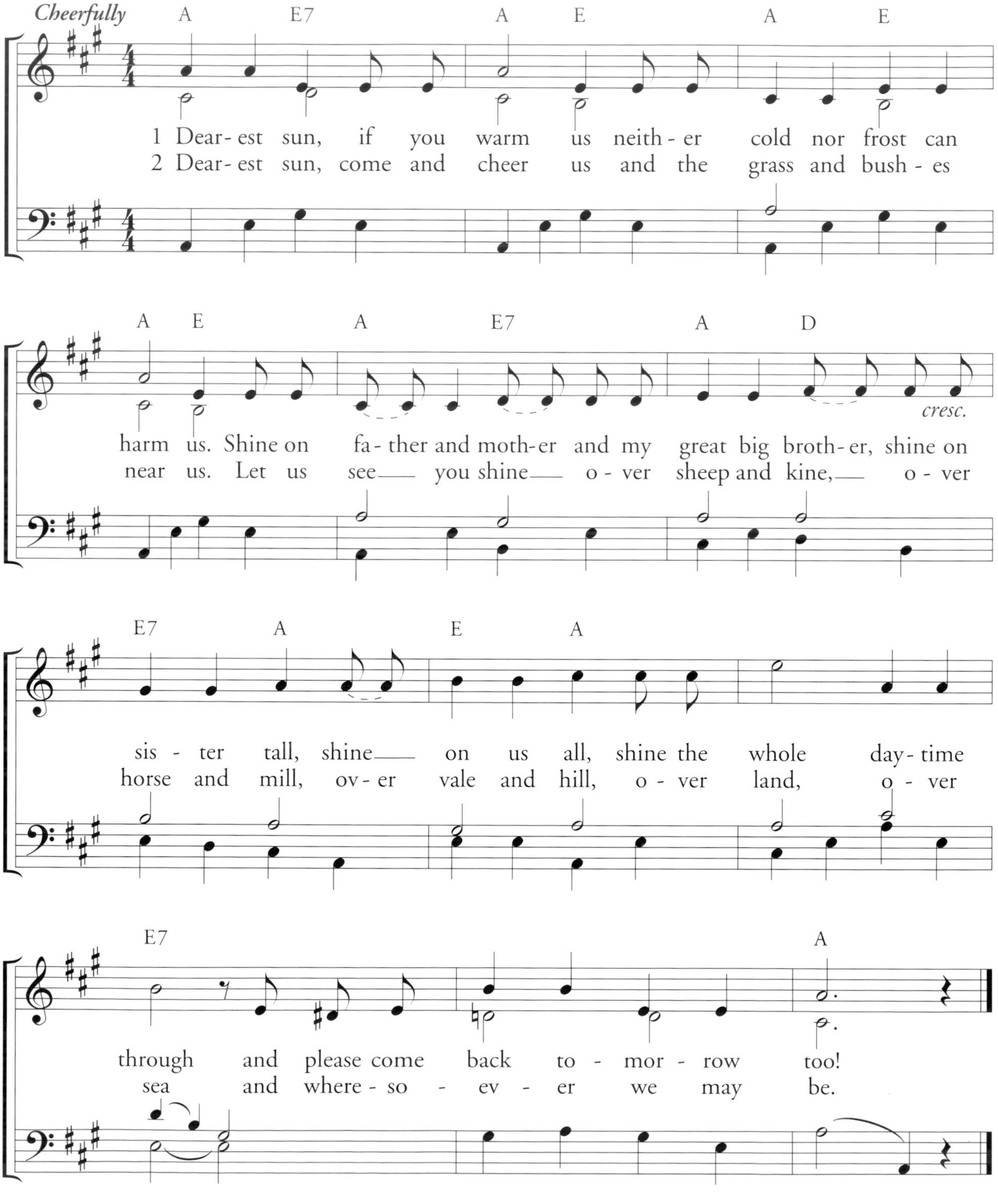

1 Dear-est sun, if you warm us neith-er cold nor frost can
2 Dear-est sun, come and cheer us and the grass and bush-es

harm us. Shine on fa-ther and moth-er and my great big broth-er, shine on
near us. Let us see you shine o-ver sheep and kine, o-ver

sis-ter tall, shine on us all, shine the whole day-time
horse and mill, ov-er vale and hill, o-ver land, o-ver

through and please come back to-mor-row too!
sea and where-so-ev-er we may be.

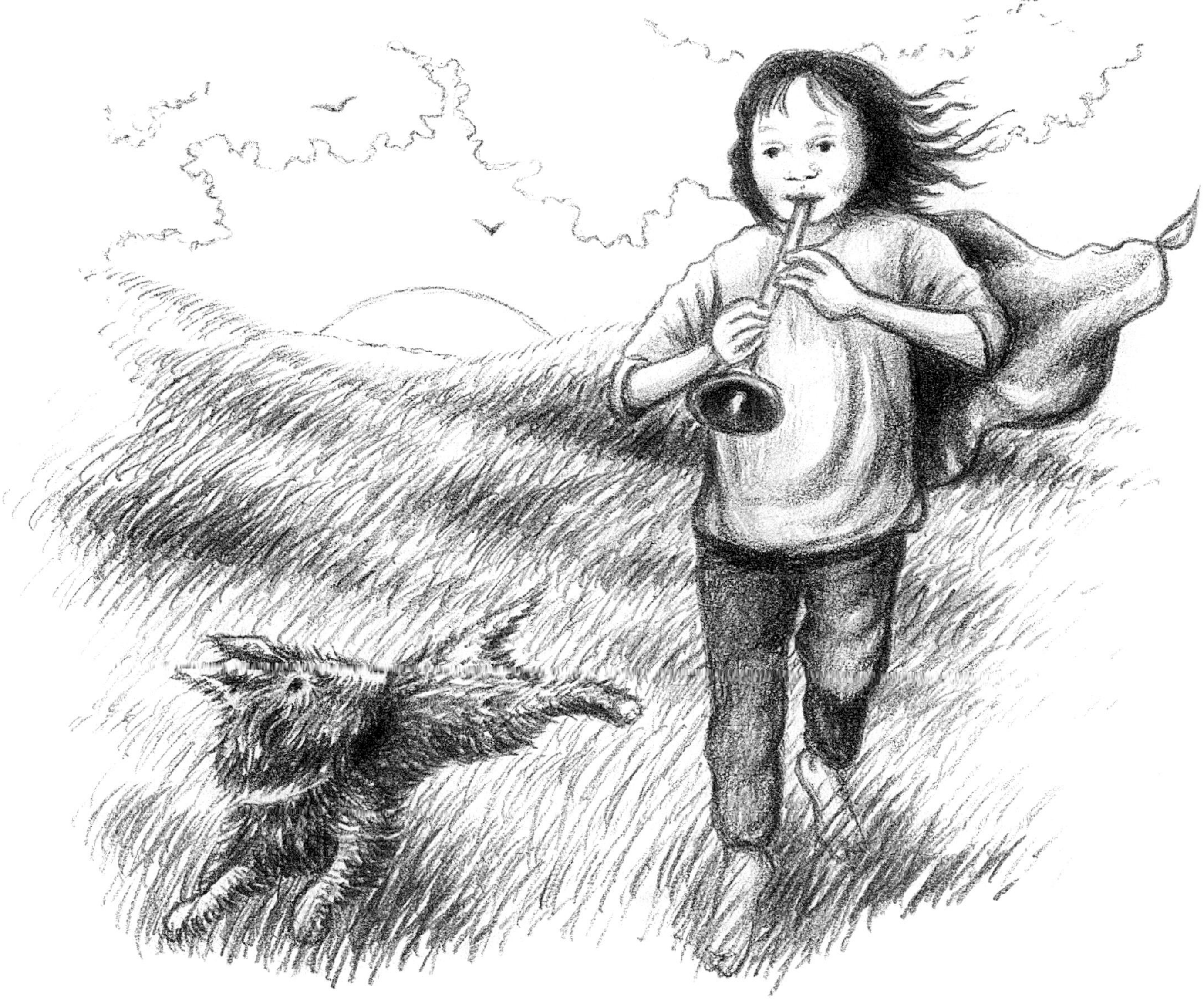

🎵 Merrily, Merrily, Greet the Morn

Children are fascinated by the interplay of rounds. This is an easy one, but start
with learning it well in unison. Then try it in two parts.

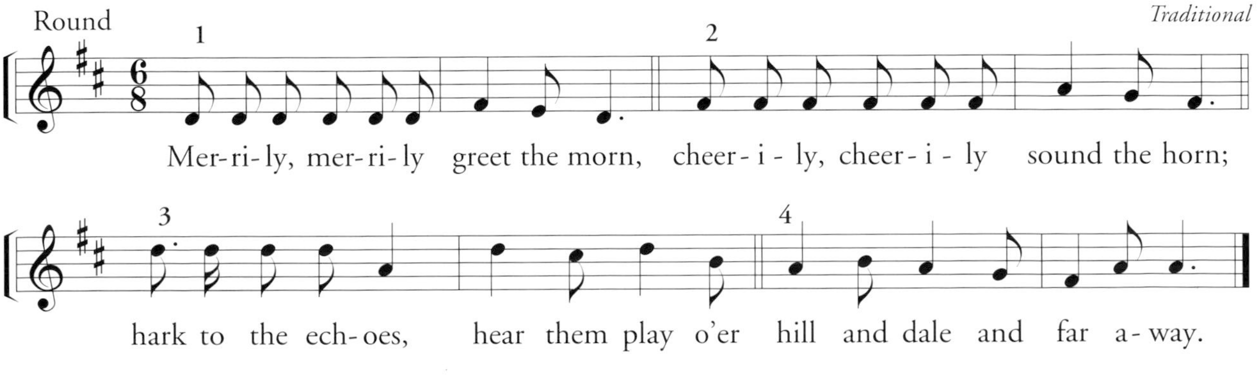

Round   *Traditional*

Mer-ri-ly, mer-ri-ly greet the morn, cheer-i-ly, cheer-i-ly sound the horn;

hark to the ech-oes, hear them play o'er hill and dale and far a-way.

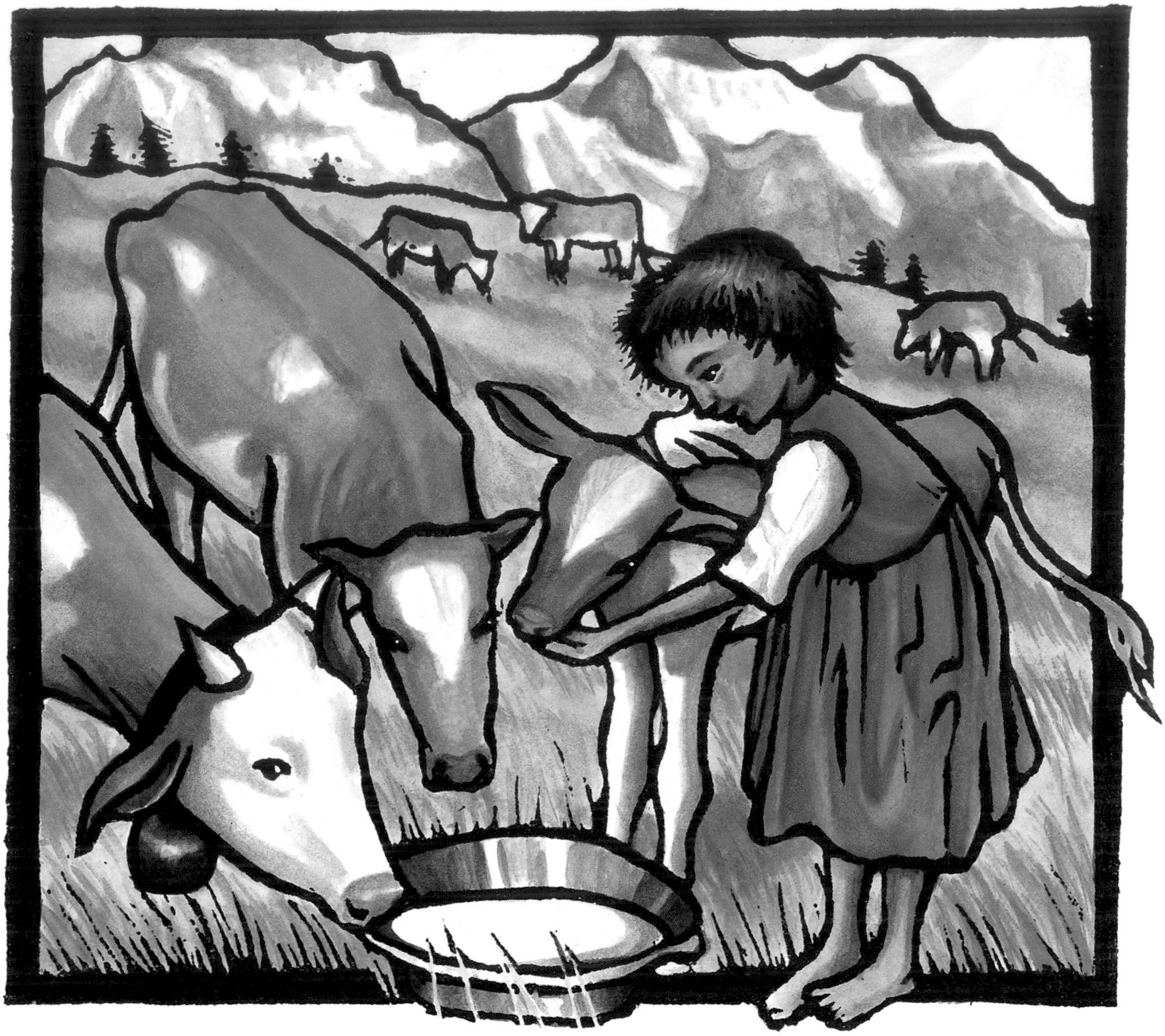

🔘 Alpine Song

For a cowbell, have a child play tone bells or xylophone on the verses.
Add rhythm instruments for the chorus.

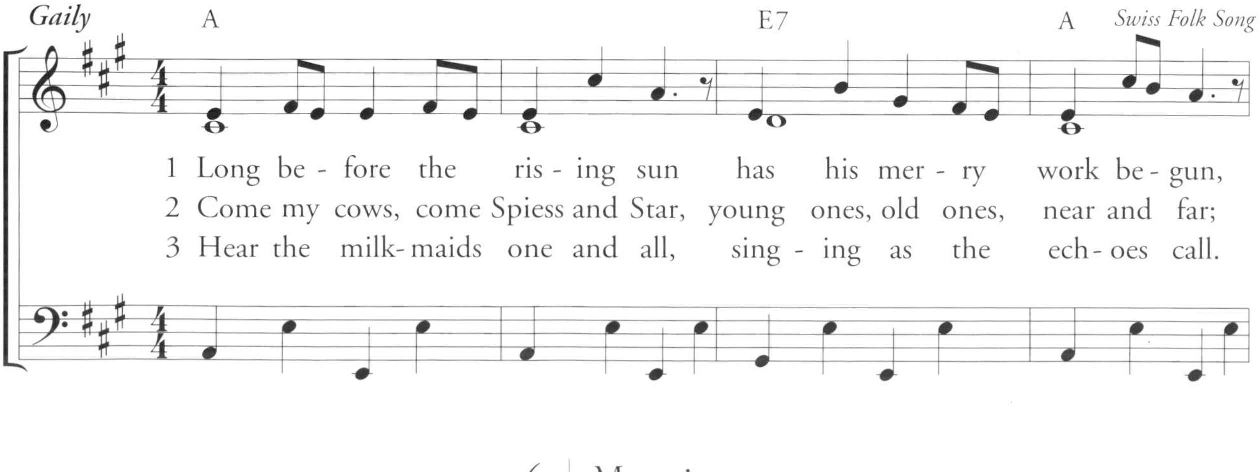

Gaily   A   E7   A   *Swiss Folk Song*

1 Long be - fore the ris - ing sun has his mer - ry work be - gun,
2 Come my cows, come Spiess and Star, young ones, old ones, near and far;
3 Hear the milk - maids one and all, sing - ing as the ech - oes call.

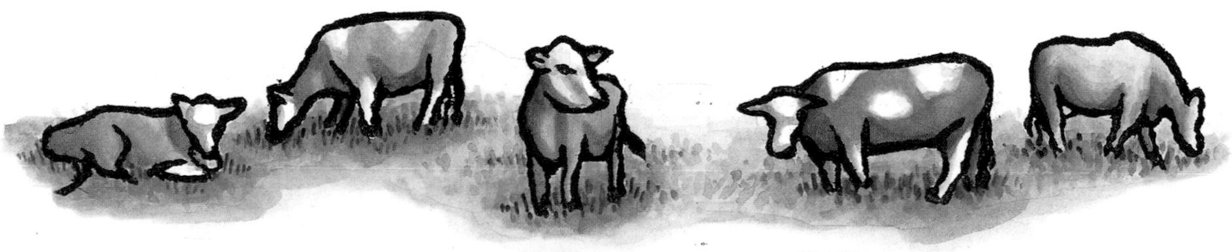

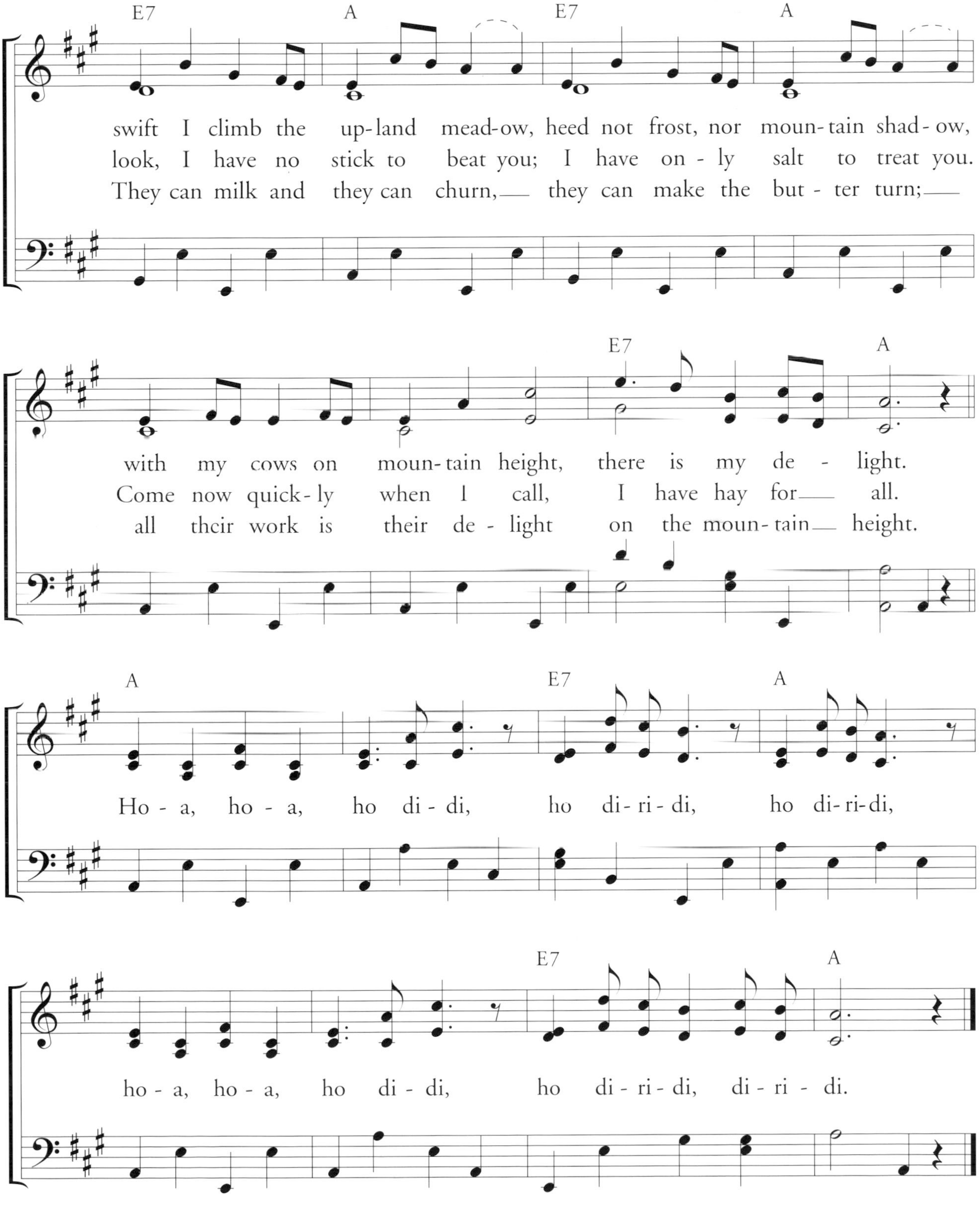

swift I climb the up-land mead-ow, heed not frost, nor moun-tain shad-ow,
look, I have no stick to beat you; I have on-ly salt to treat you.
They can milk and they can churn,— they can make the but-ter turn;—

with my cows on moun-tain height, there is my de-light.
Come now quick-ly when I call, I have hay for— all.
all their work is their de-light on the moun-tain— height.

Ho-a, ho-a, ho di-di, ho di-ri-di, ho di-ri-di,

ho-a, ho-a, ho di-di, ho di-ri-di, di-ri-di.

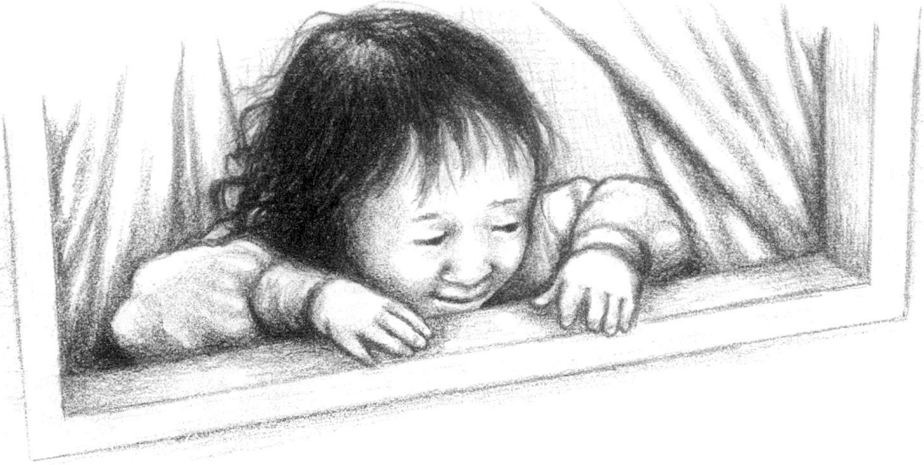

Morning Comes Early

Katherine Davis   Slovakian Melody

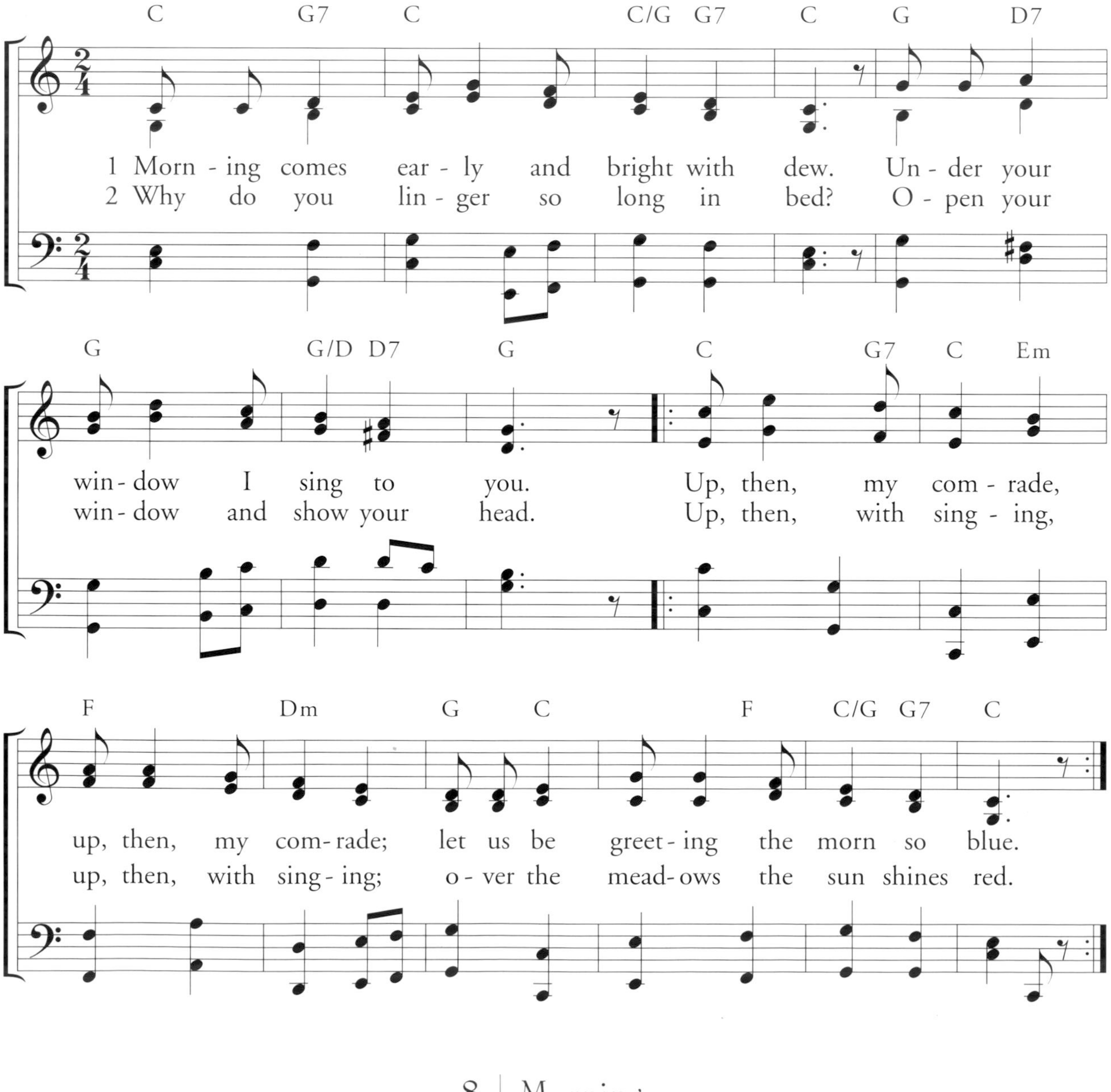

1 Morn - ing comes ear - ly and bright with dew. Un - der your
2 Why do you lin - ger so long in bed? O - pen your

win - dow I sing to you. Up, then, my com - rade,
win - dow and show your head. Up, then, with sing - ing,

up, then, my com - rade; let us be greet - ing the morn so blue.
up, then, with sing - ing; o - ver the mead - ows the sun shines red.

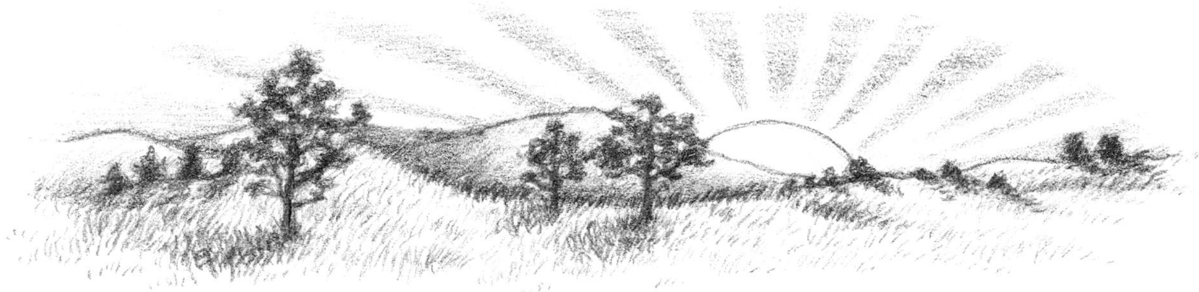

The Sweet Rosy Morning

Words and Music
Richard Leveridge

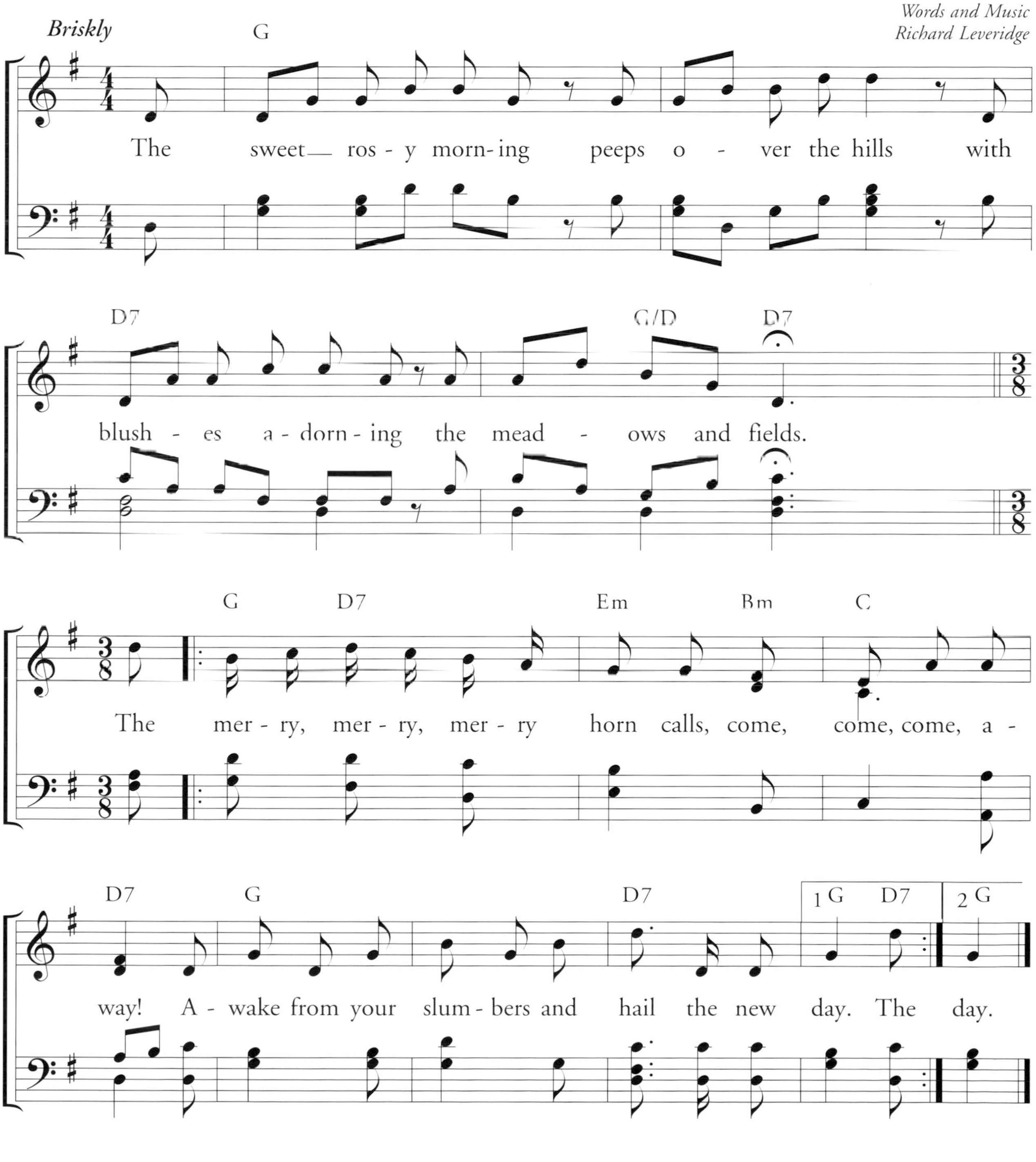

The sweet rosy morning peeps over the hills with
blushes adorning the meadows and fields.
The merry, merry, merry horn calls, come, come, come, away! Awake from your slumbers and hail the new day. The day.

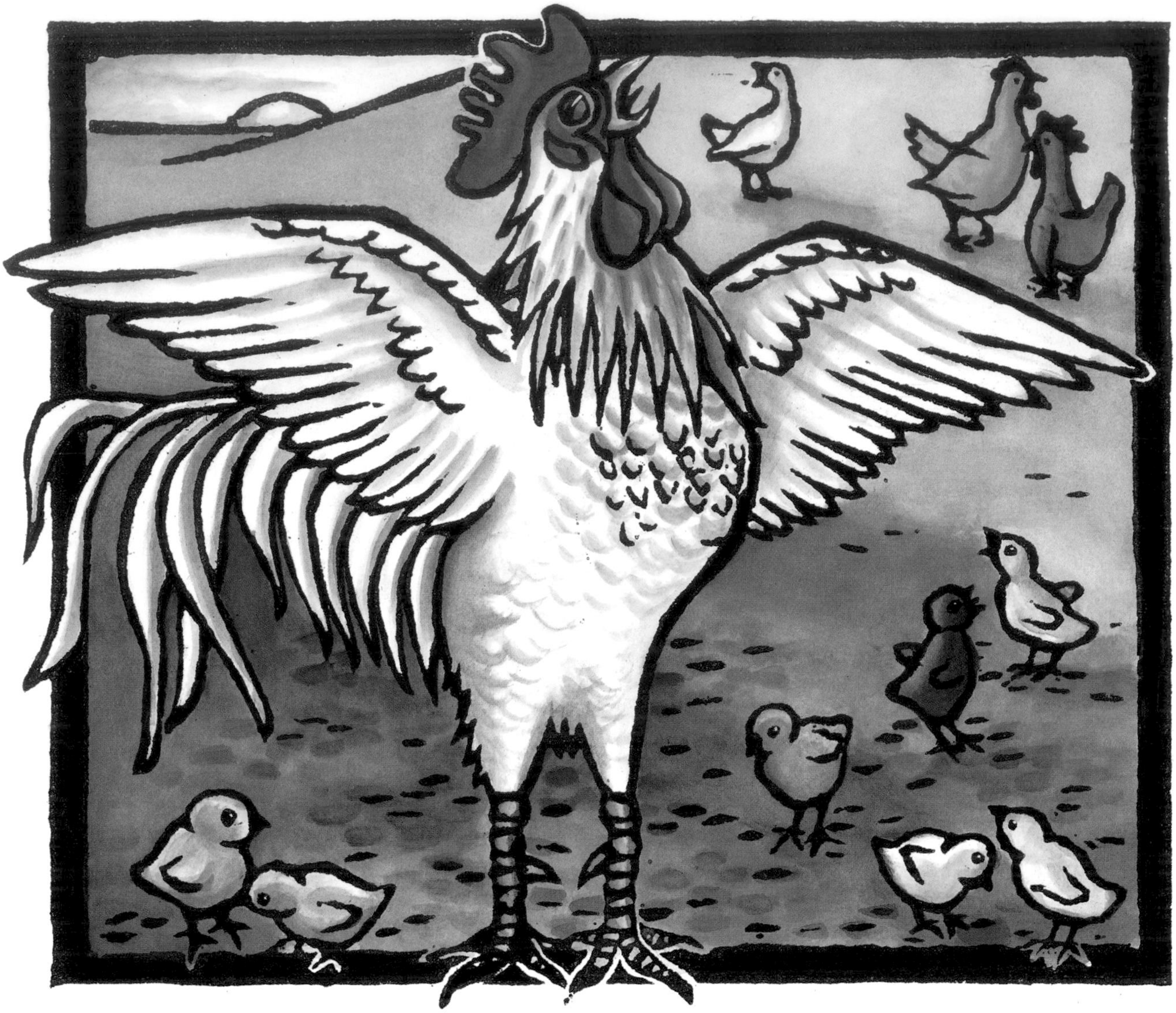

🎵 The Rooster's Our Watchman

Learn about the rooster and his barnyard companions, and sing about them. This song fits well with "Proud Missus Sheep" on page 40. Be sure to check your library for rooster books: Bill Peet's *Chanticleer,* and Barbara Cooney's *Chanticleer and the Fox* are two classics.

Thuringian Folk Song

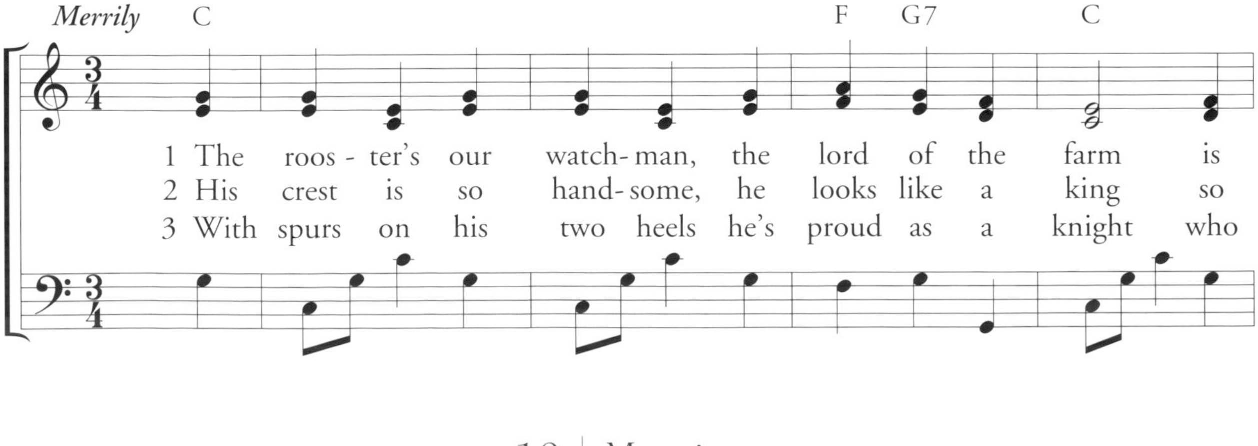

1 The roos-ter's our watch-man, the lord of the farm is
2 His crest is so hand-some, he looks like a king so
3 With spurs on his two heels he's proud as a knight who

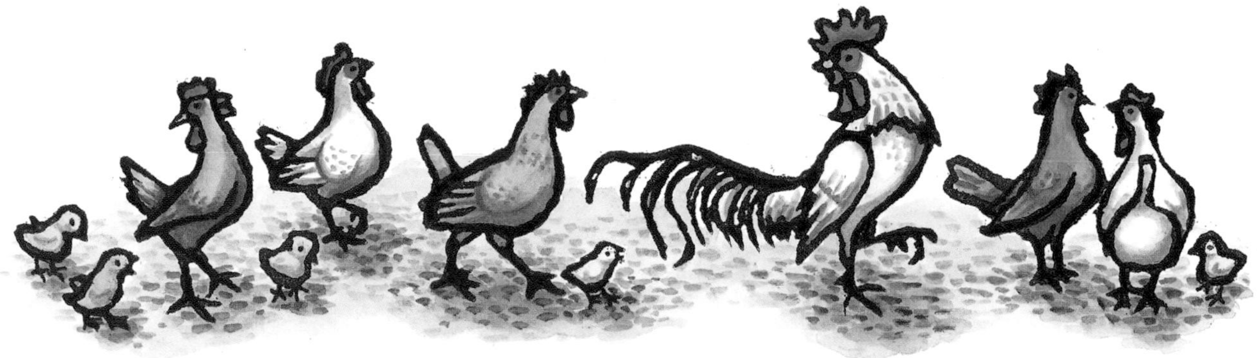

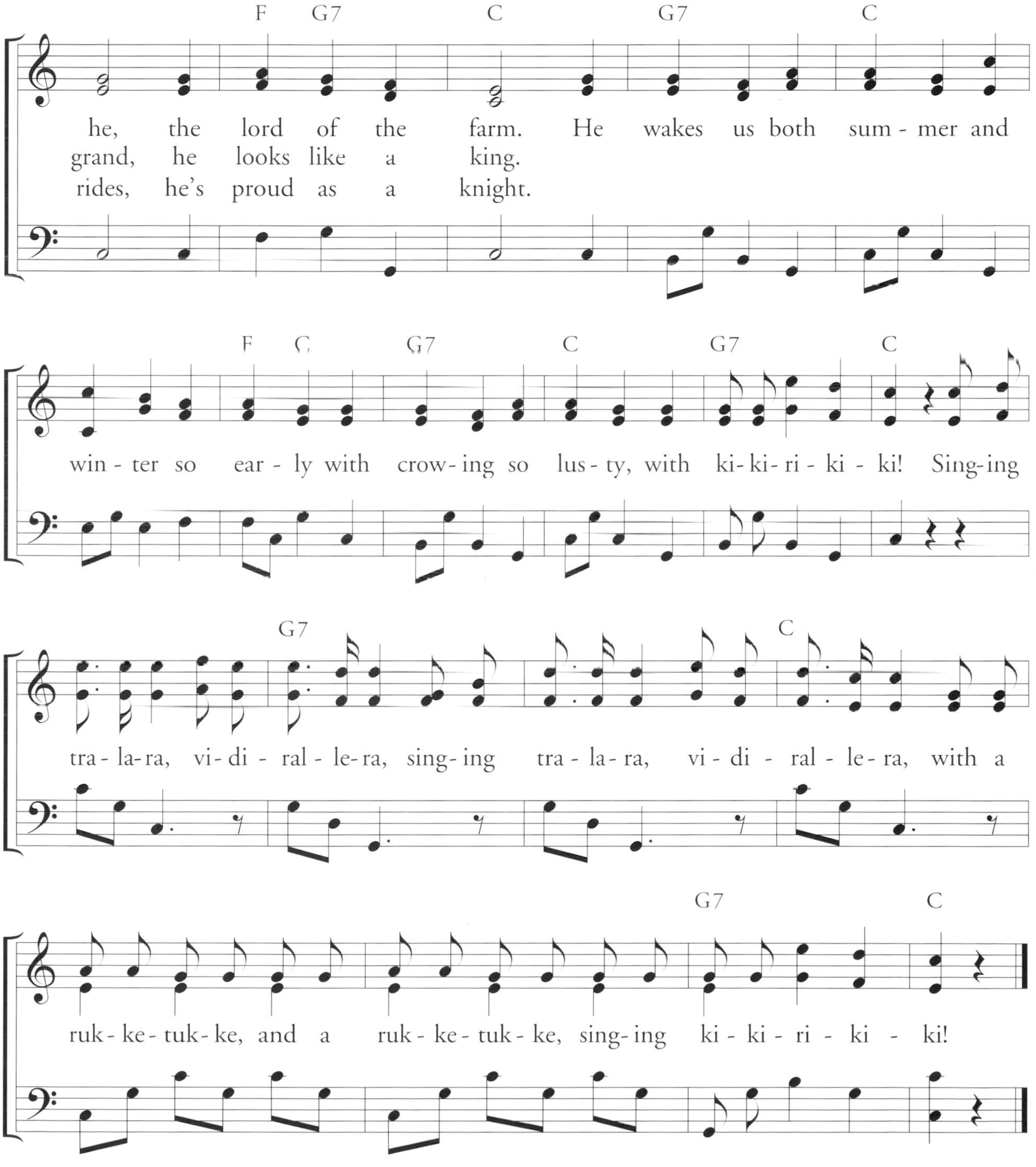

F G7 C G7 C
he, the lord of the farm. He wakes us both sum - mer and
grand, he looks like a king.
rides, he's proud as a knight.
F C G7 C G7 C
win - ter so ear - ly with crow - ing so lus - ty, with ki - ki - ri - ki - ki! Sing - ing
G7 C
tra - la - ra, vi - di - ral - le - ra, sing - ing tra - la - ra, vi - di - ral - le - ra, with a
G7 C
ruk - ke - tuk - ke, and a ruk - ke - tuk - ke, sing - ing ki - ki - ri - ki - ki!

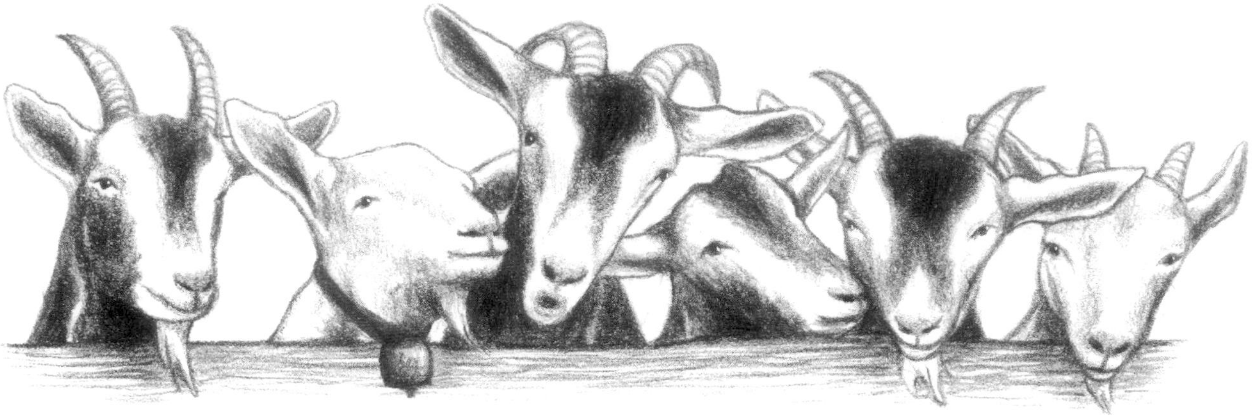

Come, Little Sennerin

Finnish Traditional

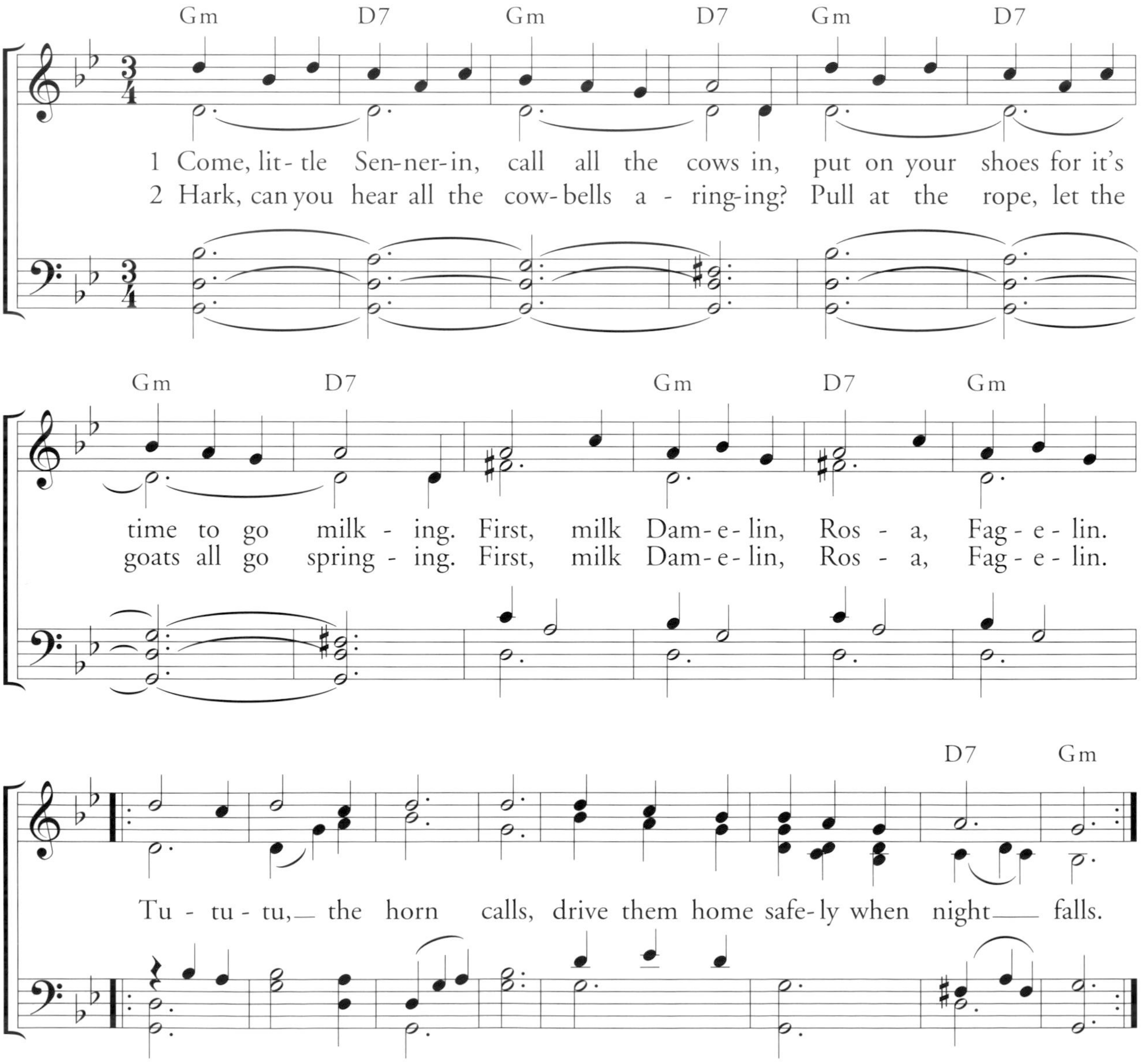

1 Come, lit-tle Sen-ner-in, call all the cows in, put on your shoes for it's
2 Hark, can you hear all the cow-bells a - ring-ing? Pull at the rope, let the

time to go milk - ing. First, milk Dam-e-lin, Ros - a, Fag - e - lin.
goats all go spring - ing. First, milk Dam-e-lin, Ros - a, Fag - e - lin.

Tu - tu - tu,— the horn calls, drive them home safe-ly when night—— falls.

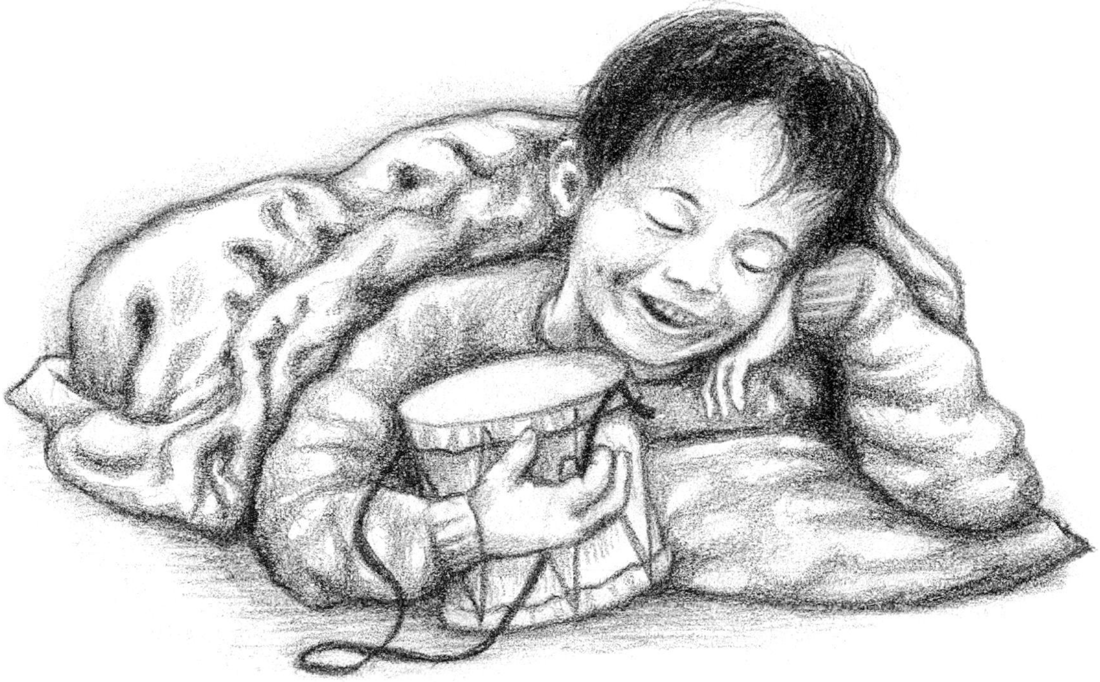

🎵 Up, Little Hans

Children love to dramatize this song. For each verse, choose a boy for lazy Hans, and a girl for his mother.

Danish Tune

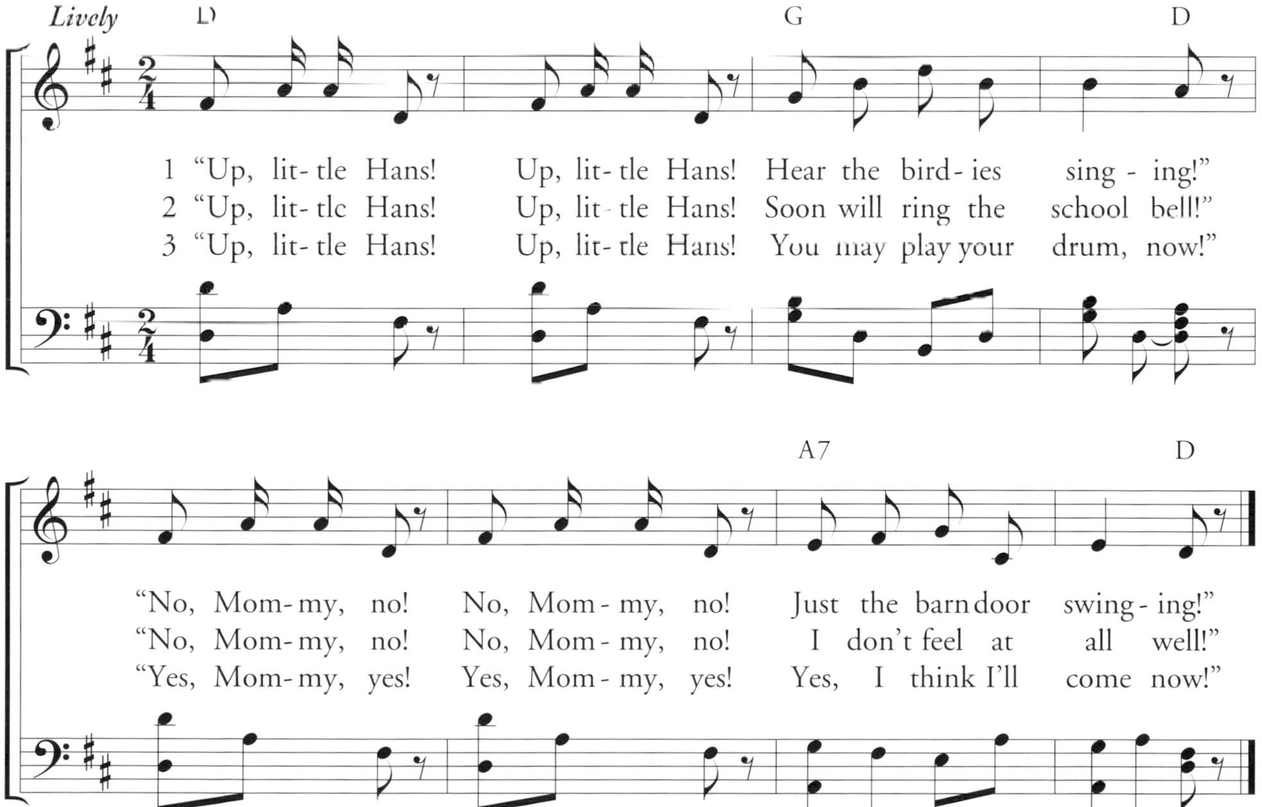

1 "Up, lit-tle Hans! Up, lit-tle Hans! Hear the bird-ies sing-ing!"
2 "Up, lit-tle Hans! Up, lit-tle Hans! Soon will ring the school bell!"
3 "Up, lit-tle Hans! Up, lit-tle Hans! You may play your drum, now!"

"No, Mom-my, no! No, Mom-my, no! Just the barn door swing-ing!"
"No, Mom-my, no! No, Mom-my, no! I don't feel at all well!"
"Yes, Mom-my, yes! Yes, Mom-my, yes! Yes, I think I'll come now!"

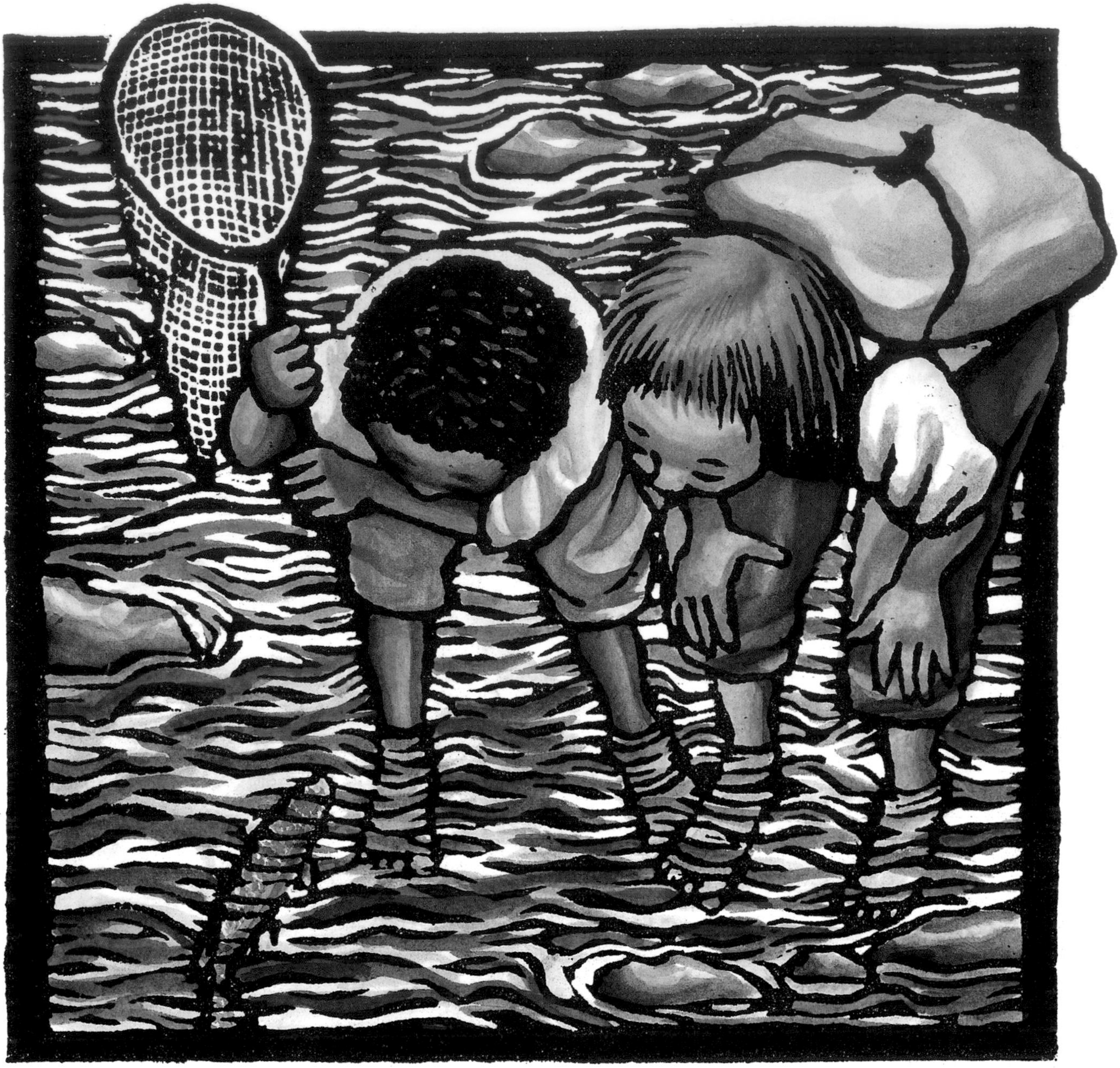

The Sun Is Rising Out of Bed

John Ferguson   *English Folk Tune*

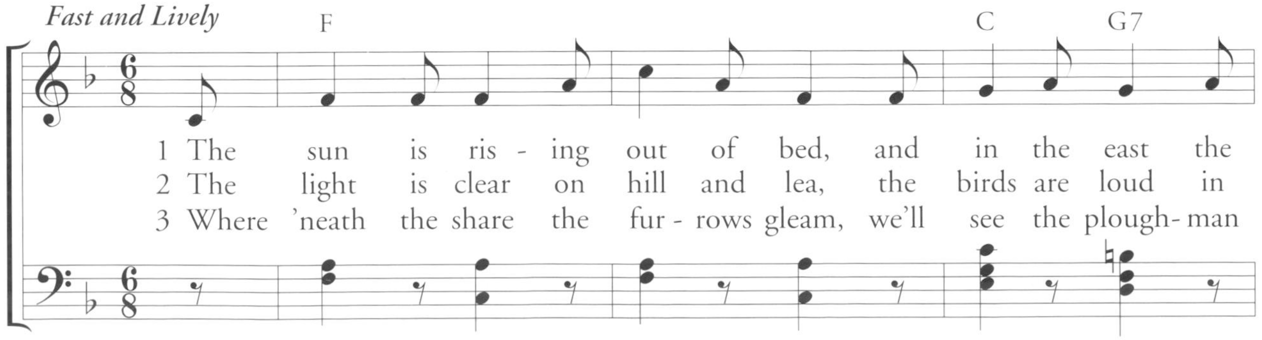

1 The sun is ris - ing out of bed, and in the east the
2 The light is clear on hill and lea, the birds are loud in
3 Where 'neath the share the fur - rows gleam, we'll see the plough-man

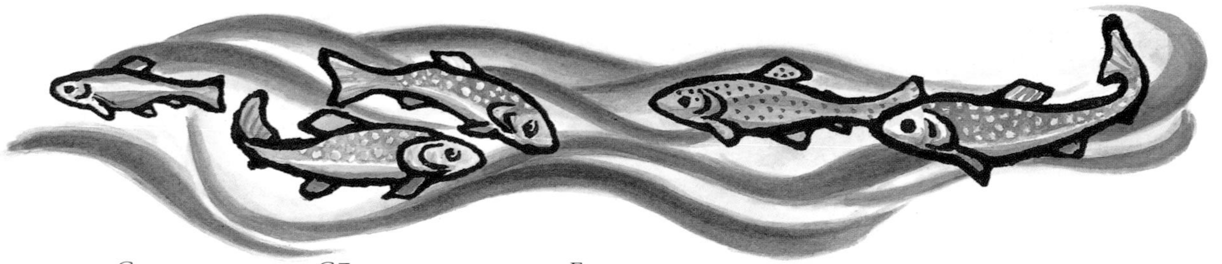

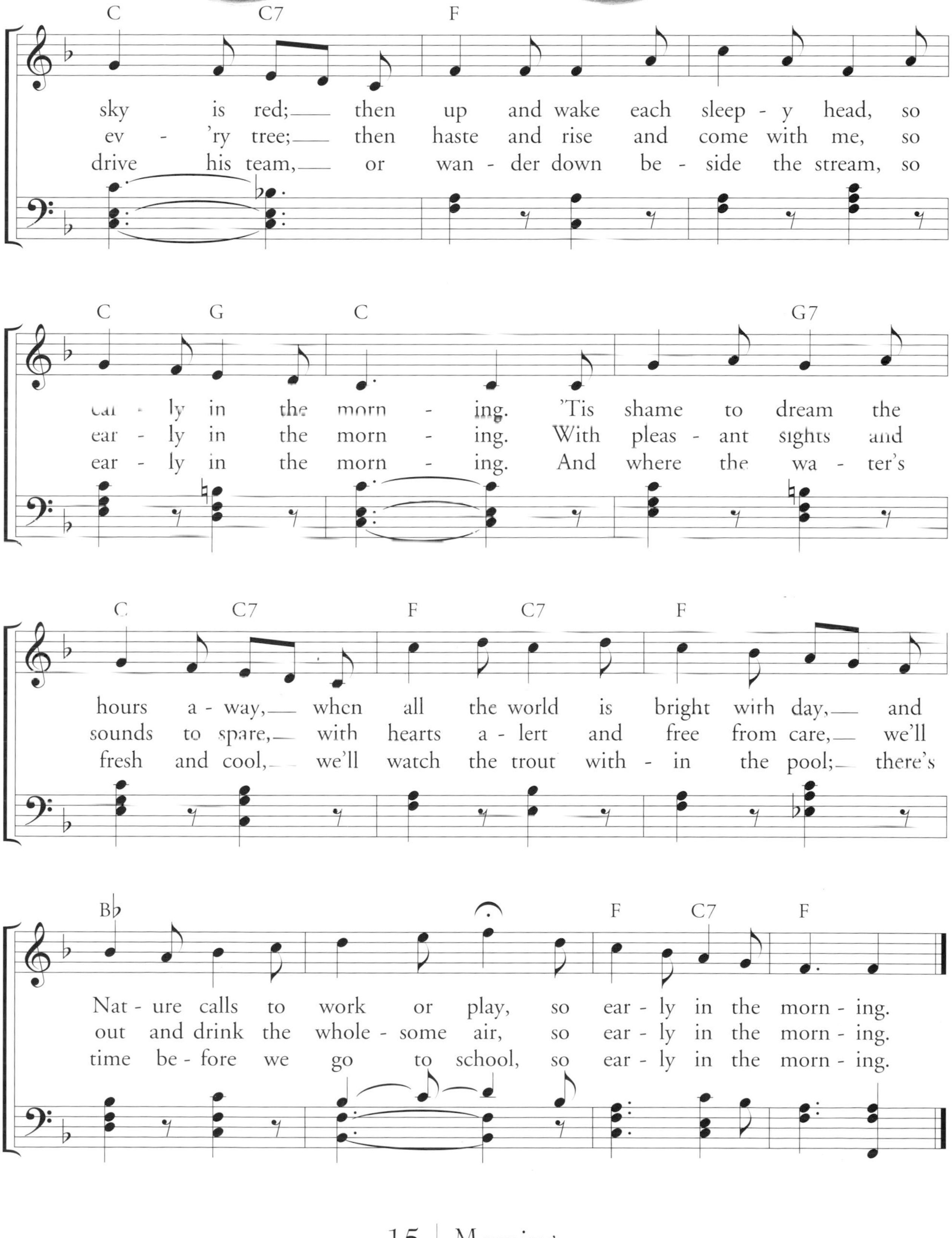

C C7 F
sky is red; then up and wake each sleep - y head, so
ev - 'ry tree; then haste and rise and come with me, so
drive his team, or wan - der down be - side the stream, so
C G C G7
ear - ly in the morn - ing. 'Tis shame to dream the
ear - ly in the morn - ing. With pleas - ant sights and
ear - ly in the morn - ing. And where the wa - ter's
C C7 F C7 F
hours a - way, when all the world is bright with day, and
sounds to spare, with hearts a - lert and free from care, we'll
fresh and cool, we'll watch the trout with - in the pool; there's
B♭ F C7 F
Nat - ure calls to work or play, so ear - ly in the morn - ing.
out and drink the whole - some air, so ear - ly in the morn - ing.
time be - fore we go to school, so ear - ly in the morn - ing.

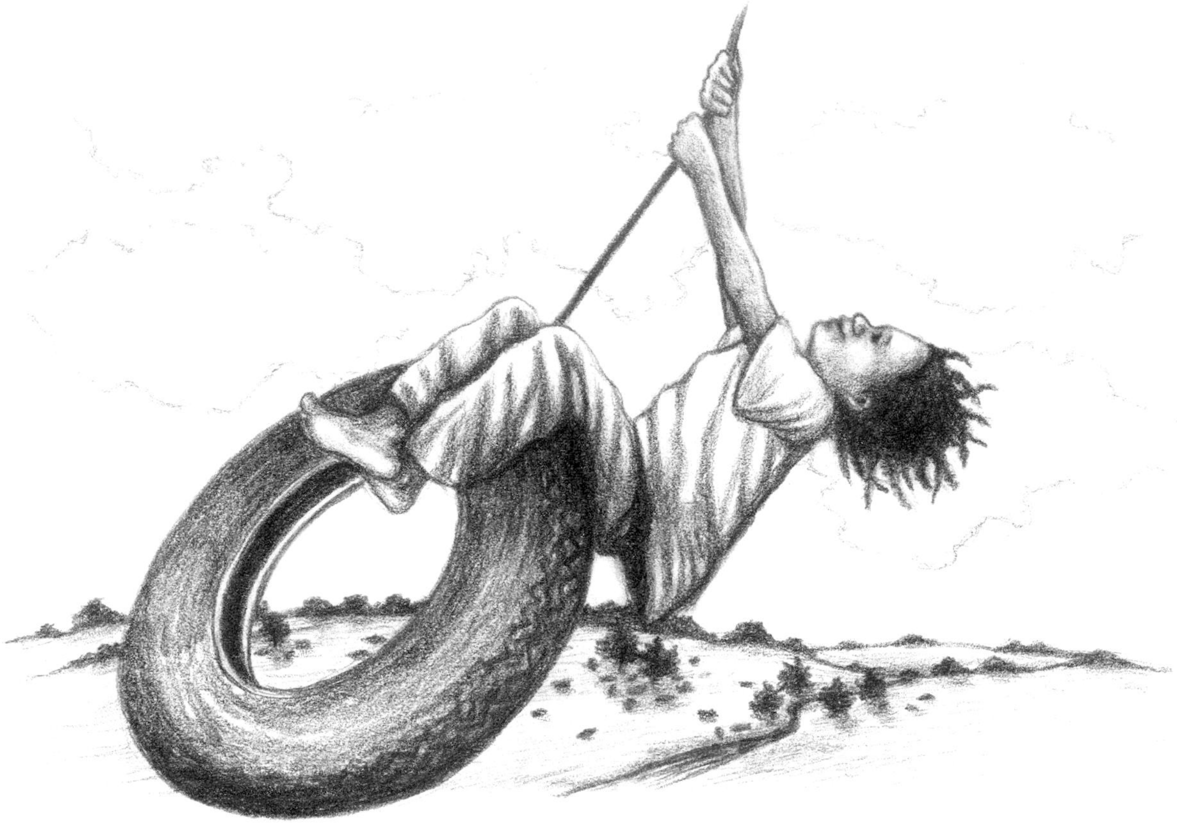

The Swing

Robert Louis Stevenson

Unknown

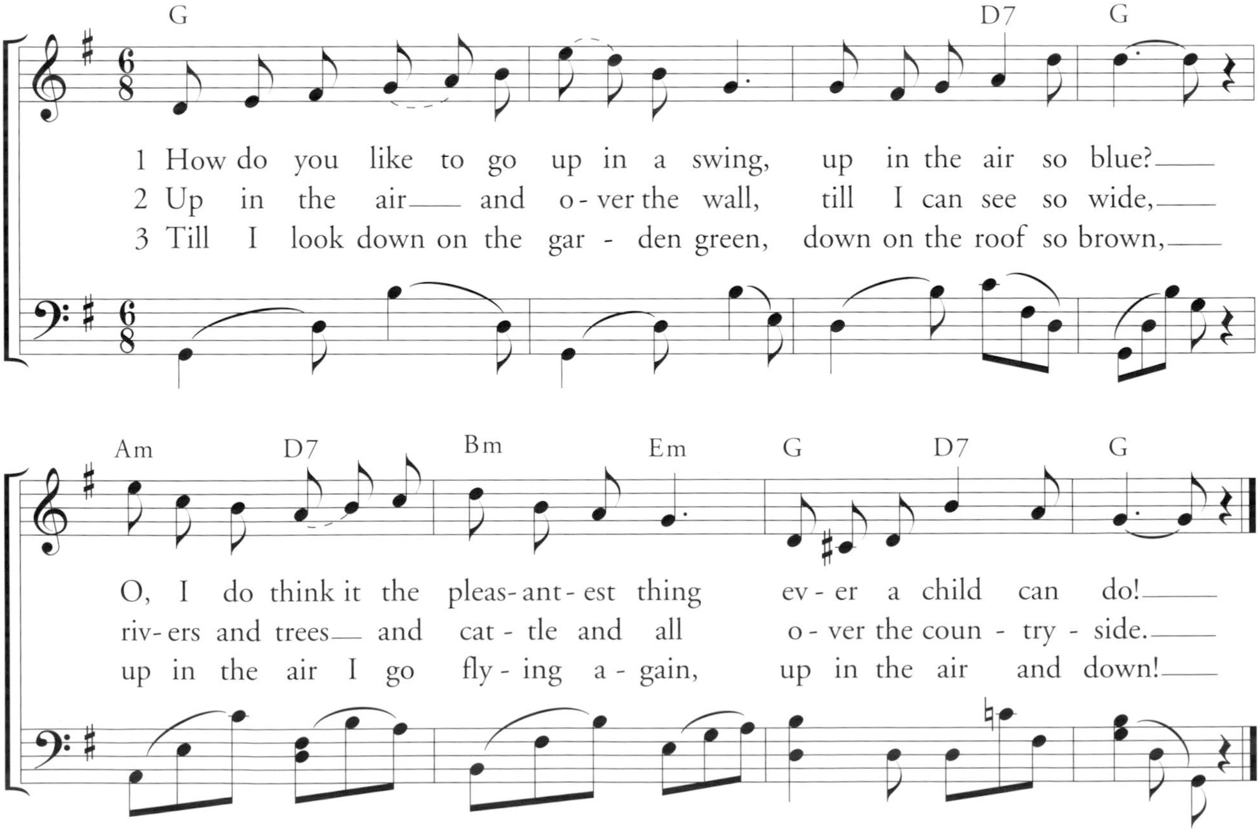

1 How do you like to go up in a swing, up in the air so blue?___
2 Up in the air___ and o - ver the wall, till I can see so wide,___
3 Till I look down on the gar - den green, down on the roof so brown,___

O, I do think it the pleas - ant - est thing ev - er a child can do!___
riv - ers and trees___ and cat - tle and all o - ver the coun - try - side.___
up in the air I go fly - ing a - gain, up in the air and down!___

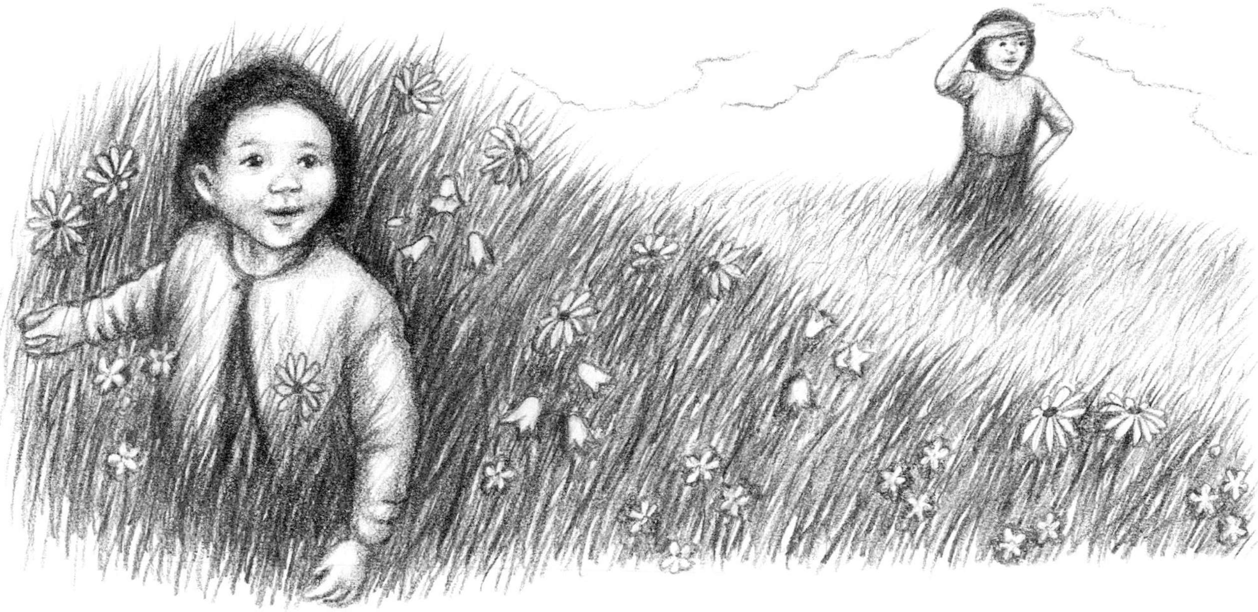

Marie in the Meadow

Choose a Marie and let her hide somewhere in the room or playground. During the first verses, have the other children shade their eyes with one hand and gaze around, anxiously searching for Marie. When you come to the last line, have Marie jump up and reveal her hiding place.

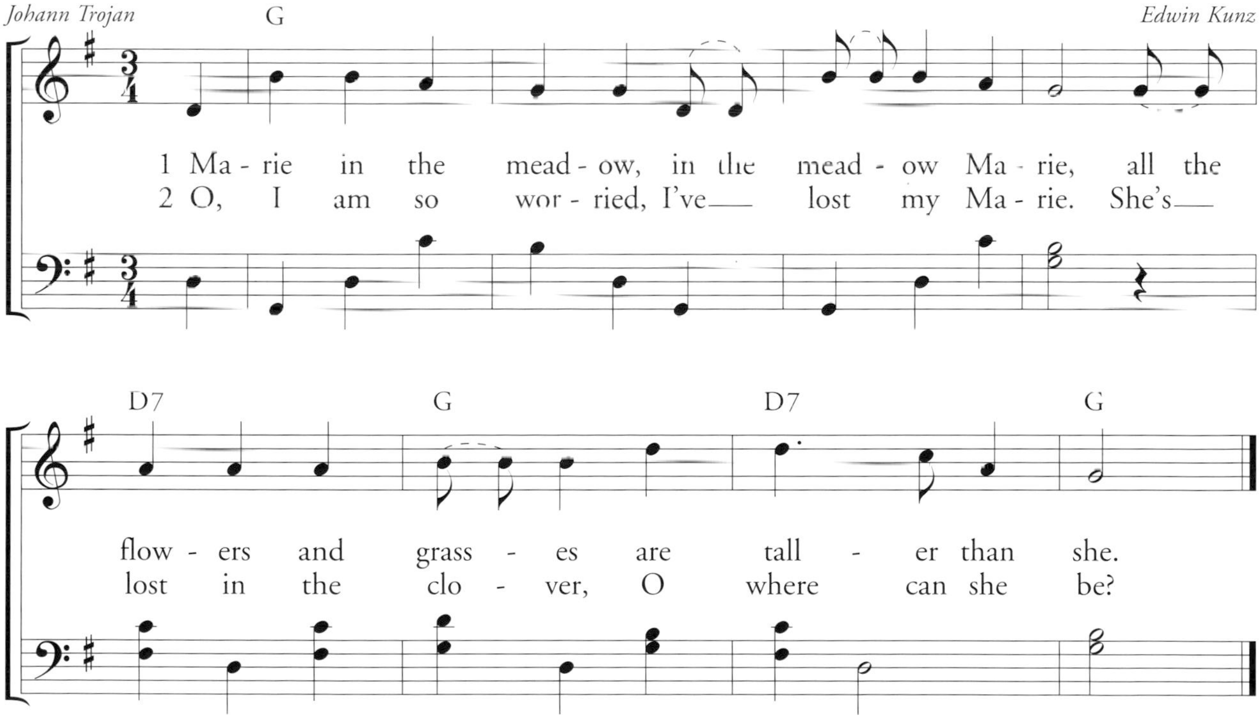

Johann Trojan   G   *Edwin Kunz*

1 Ma-rie in the mead-ow, in the mead-ow Ma-rie, all the
2 O, I am so wor-ried, I've— lost my Ma-rie. She's—

flow-ers and grass-es are tall-er than she.
lost in the clo-ver, O where can she be?

3. But who is it sitting
   'mid the flowers so bright,
   the harebells, the buttercups,
   the star daisies white?

4. This can't be a flower,
   a little head I see;
   I've found her, I've found
   her, I've found my Marie!

17 | Play

The Bicycle

Jane Tyson Clement

Marlys Swinger

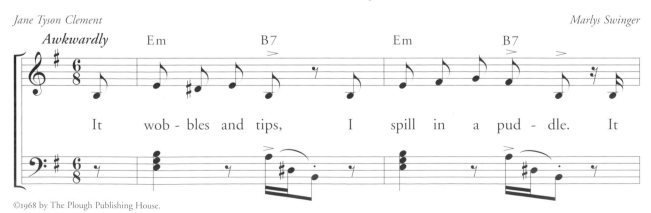

It wob-bles and tips, I spill in a pud-dle. It

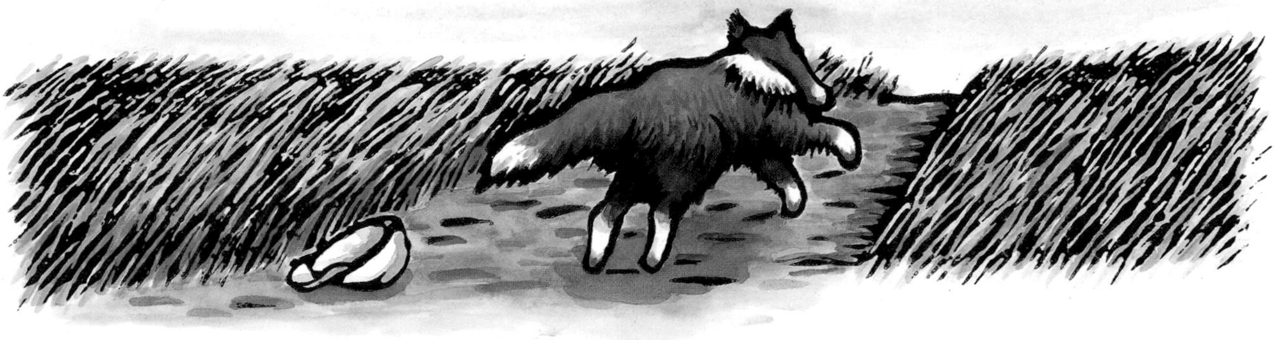

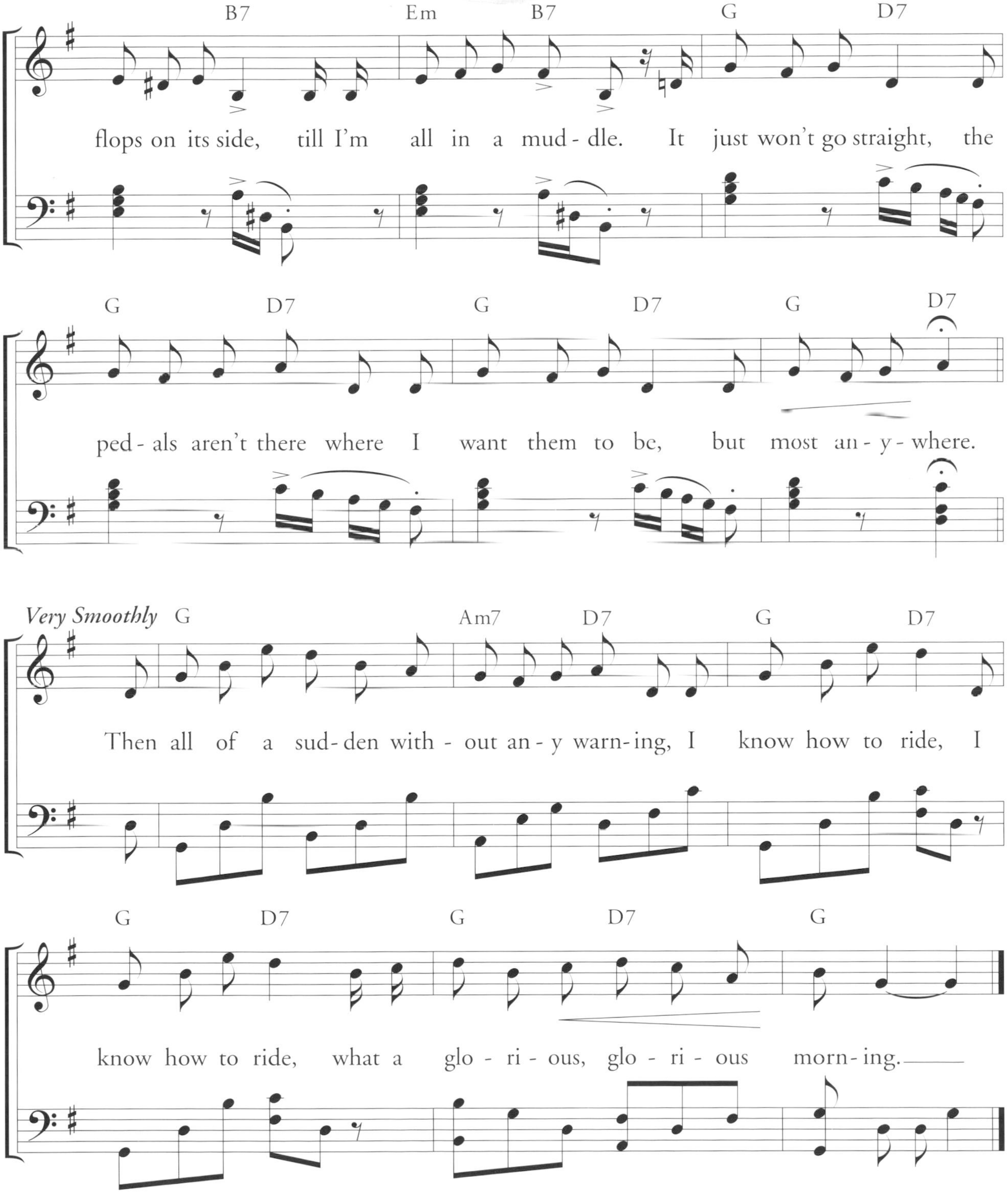

flops on its side, till I'm all in a mud - dle. It just won't go straight, the

ped - als aren't there where I want them to be, but most an - y - where.

Very Smoothly

Then all of a sud - den with - out an - y warn-ing, I know how to ride, I

know how to ride, what a glo - ri - ous, glo - ri - ous morn - ing.

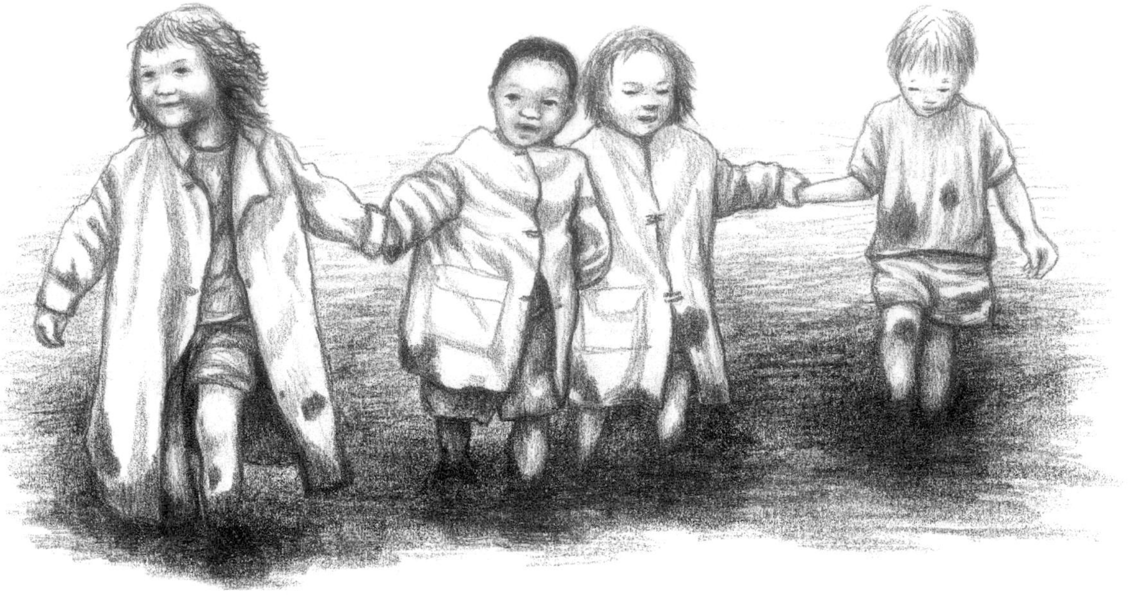

Mud!

Polly Chase Boyden

Marlys Swinger

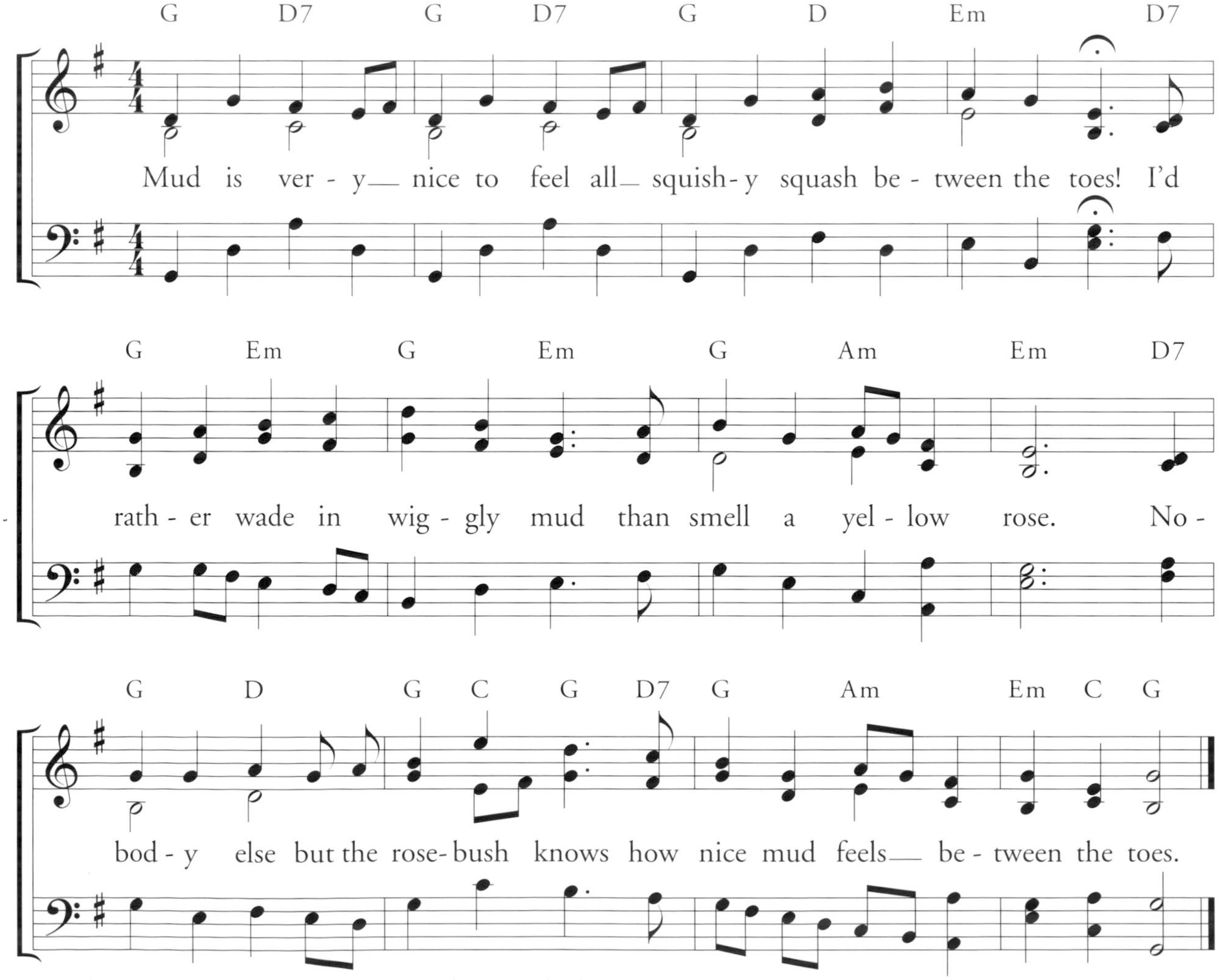

Mud is ver-y— nice to feel all— squish-y squash be-tween the toes! I'd
rath-er wade in wig-gly mud than smell a yel-low rose. No-
bod-y else but the rose-bush knows how nice mud feels— be-tween the toes.

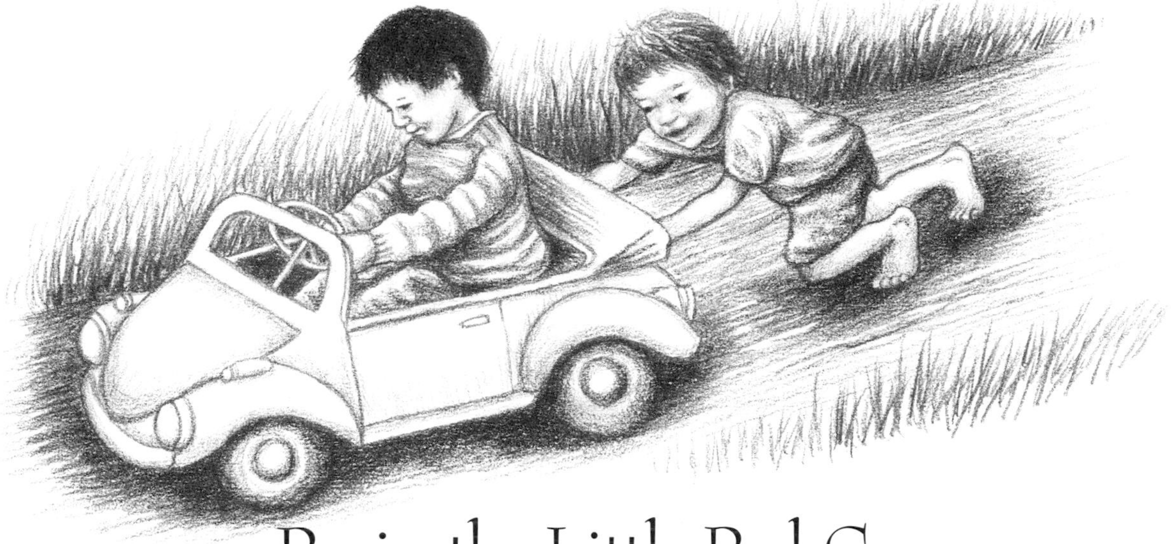

Rosie, the Little Red Car

Two- and three-year-olds love this one. Think up hand movements for each verse: turn an imaginary steering wheel, wave your arms back and forth for windshield wipers, and open and shut your fingers for blinking headlights.

Unknown

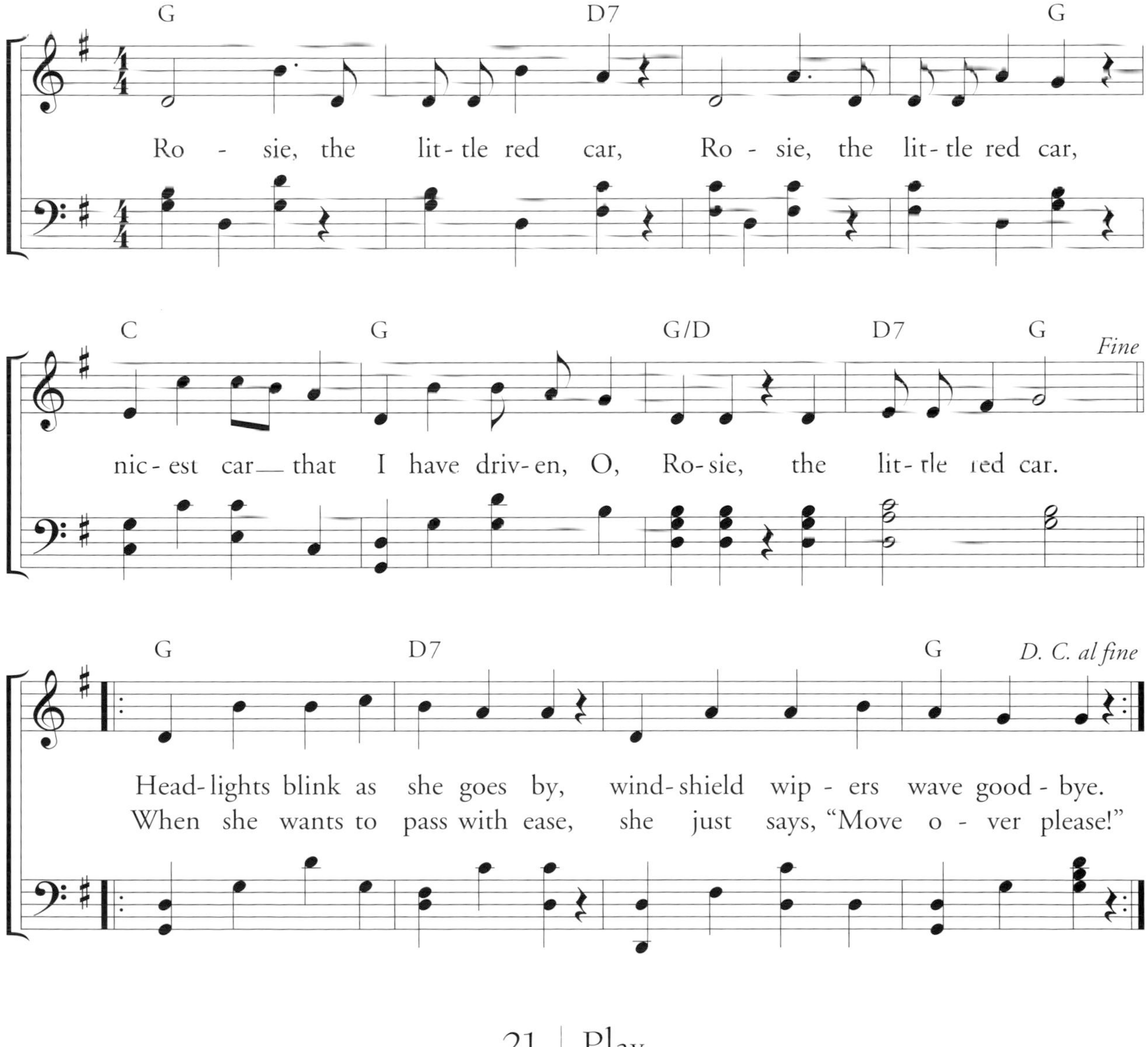

Ro - sie, the lit - tle red car, Ro - sie, the lit - tle red car,

nic - est car—that I have driv - en, O, Ro - sie, the lit - tle red car.

Head - lights blink as she goes by, wind - shield wip - ers wave good - bye.
When she wants to pass with ease, she just says, "Move o - ver please!"

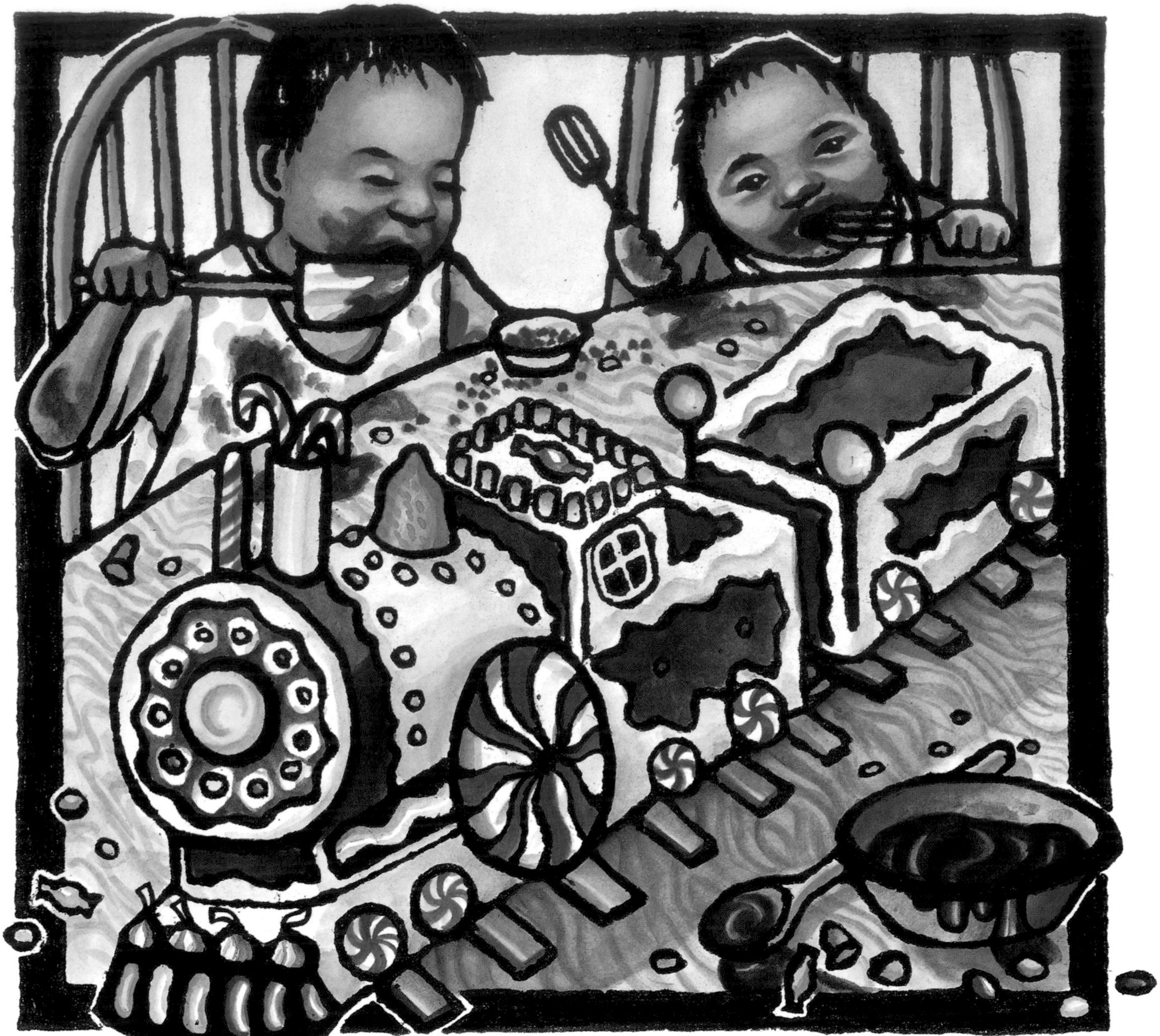

🎵 The Chocolate Train

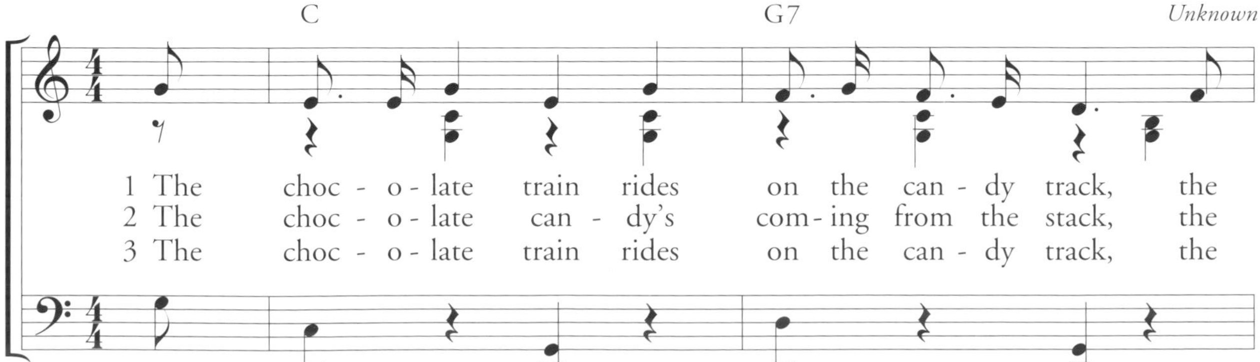

C   G7   *Unknown*

1 The   choc - o - late   train   rides   on   the   can - dy   track,   the
2 The   choc - o - late   can - dy's   com - ing   from   the   stack,   the
3 The   choc - o - late   train   rides   on   the   can - dy   track,   the

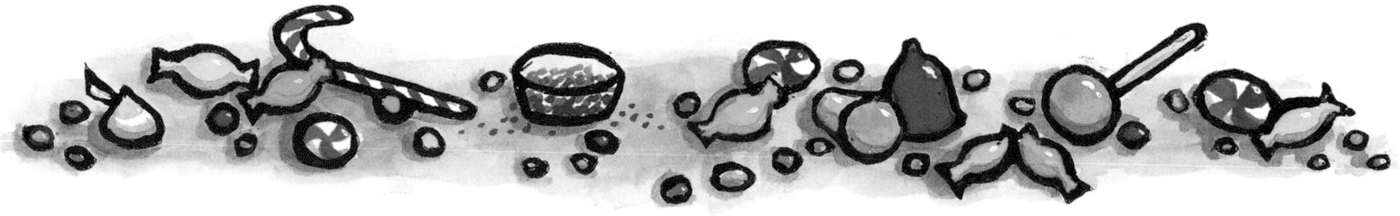

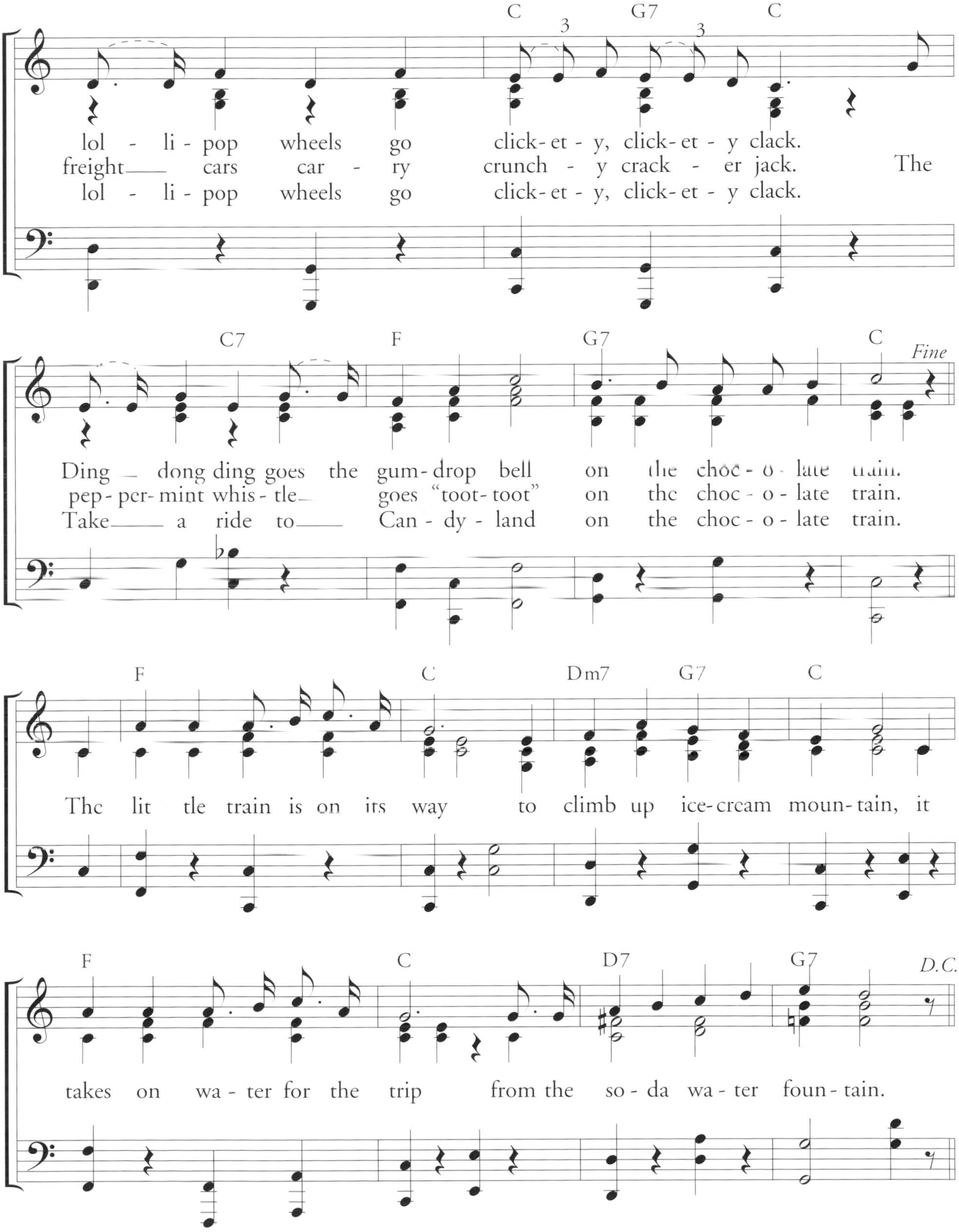

lol - li - pop wheels go click-et - y, click-et - y clack.
freight___ cars car - ry crunch - y crack - er jack. The
lol - li - pop wheels go click-et - y, click-et - y clack.

Ding ___ dong ding goes the gum-drop bell on the choc - o - late train.
pep - per - mint whis - tle___ goes "toot - toot" on the choc - o - late train.
Take___ a ride to___ Can - dy - land on the choc - o - late train.

The lit - tle train is on its way to climb up ice-cream moun - tain, it

takes on wa - ter for the trip from the so - da wa - ter foun - tain.

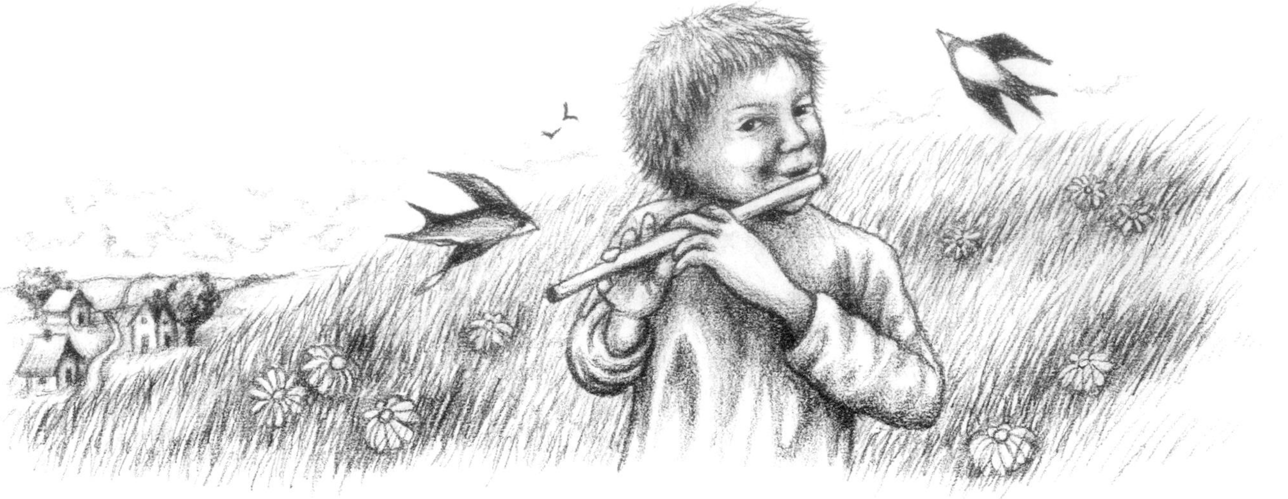

The Fairy Flute

Rose Fyleman

Wolfgang Loewenthal

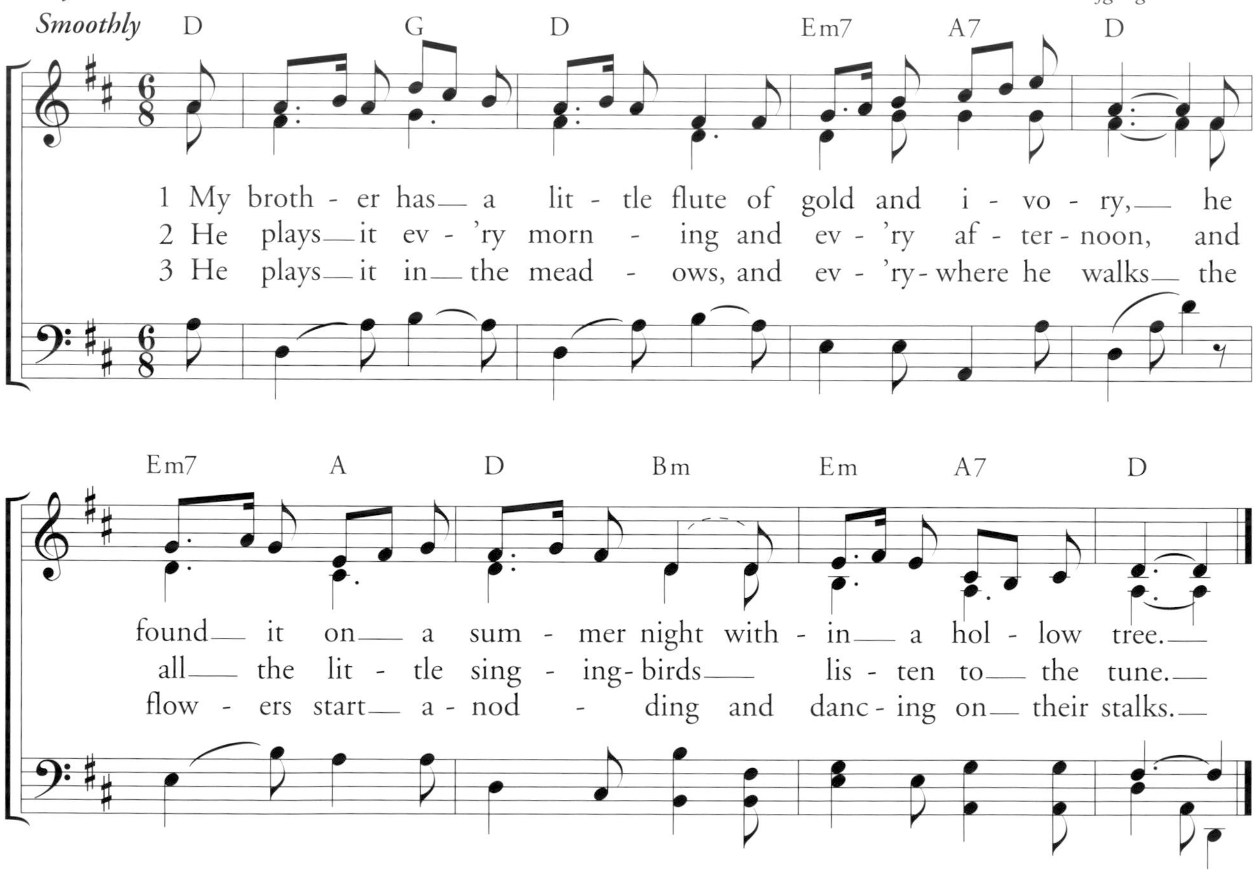

Smoothly

1 My broth-er has a lit-tle flute of gold and i-vo-ry, he
2 He plays it ev-'ry morn-ing and ev-'ry af-ter-noon, and
3 He plays it in the mead-ows, and ev-'ry-where he walks the

found it on a sum-mer night with-in a hol-low tree.
all the lit-tle sing-ing-birds lis-ten to the tune.
flow-ers start a-nod-ding and danc-ing on their stalks.

4. He plays it in the village,
   and all along the street
   the people stop to listen,
   the music is so sweet.

5. And none but he can play it
   and none can understand,
   because it is a fairy flute
   and comes from Fairyland.

My Magic Pony

Few children can afford a pet horse, but every child loves to imagine riding his or her very
own magic pony. Use claves or woodblocks for rhythmic hoofbeats.

Robert A. Coan

G. Meyerbeer

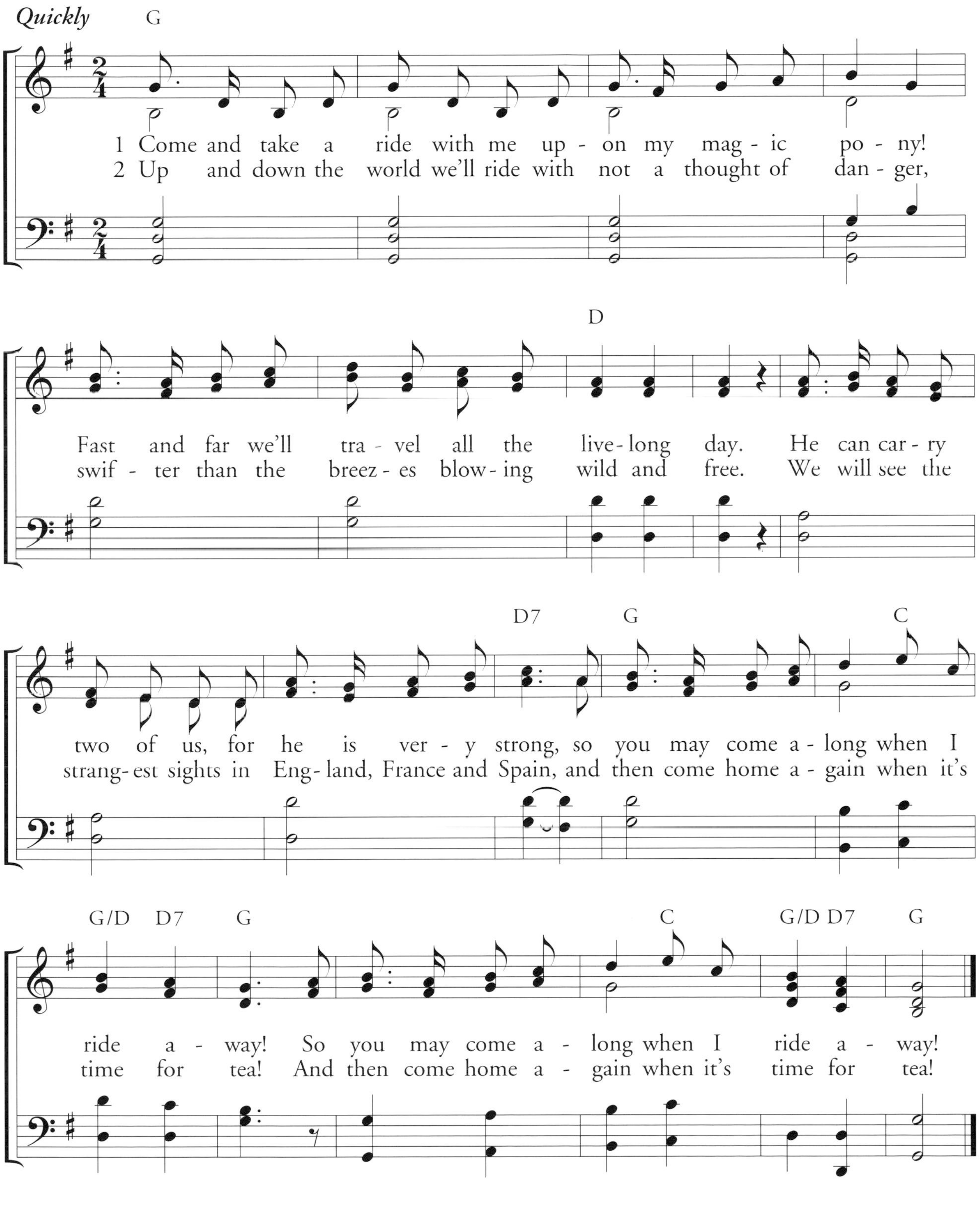

1 Come and take a ride with me up - on my mag - ic po - ny!
2 Up and down the world we'll ride with not a thought of dan - ger,

Fast and far we'll tra - vel all the live - long day. He can car - ry
swif - ter than the breez - es blow - ing wild and free. We will see the

two of us, for he is ver - y strong, so you may come a - long when I
strang - est sights in Eng - land, France and Spain, and then come home a - gain when it's

ride a - way! So you may come a - long when I ride a - way!
time for tea! And then come home a - gain when it's time for tea!

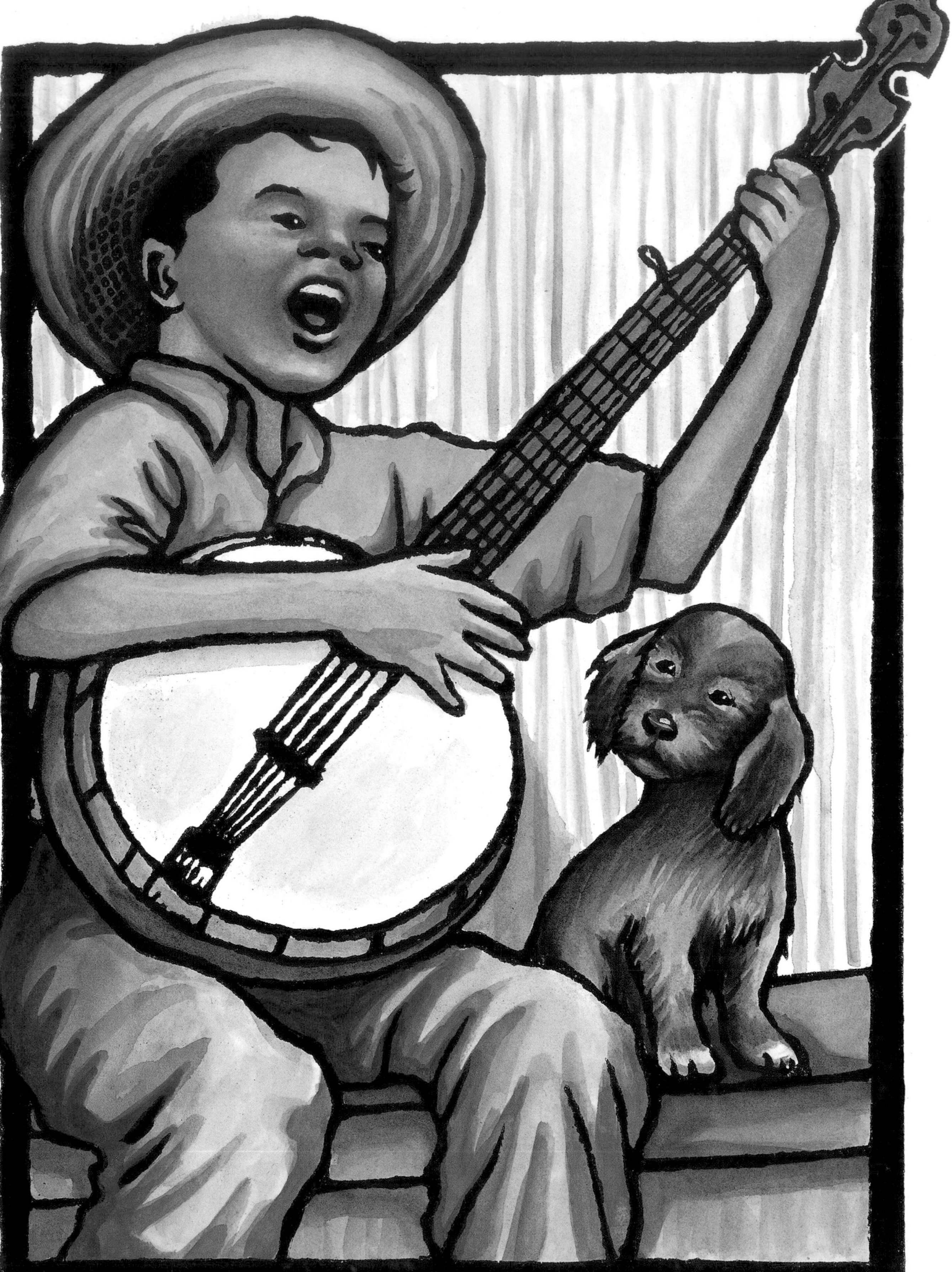

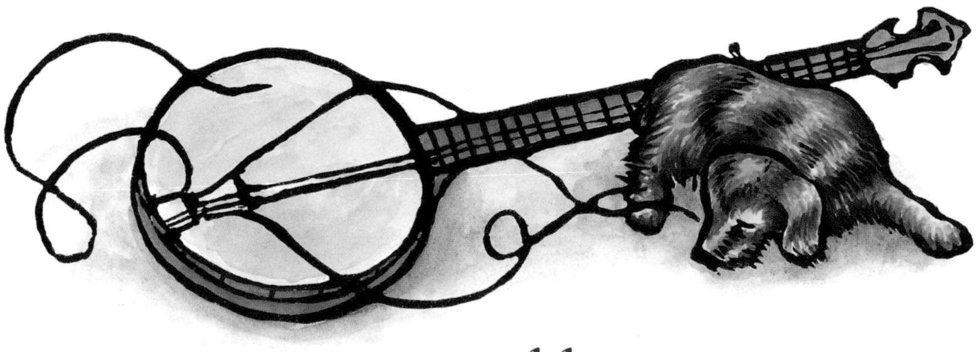

⊗ My Old Banjo

Traditional

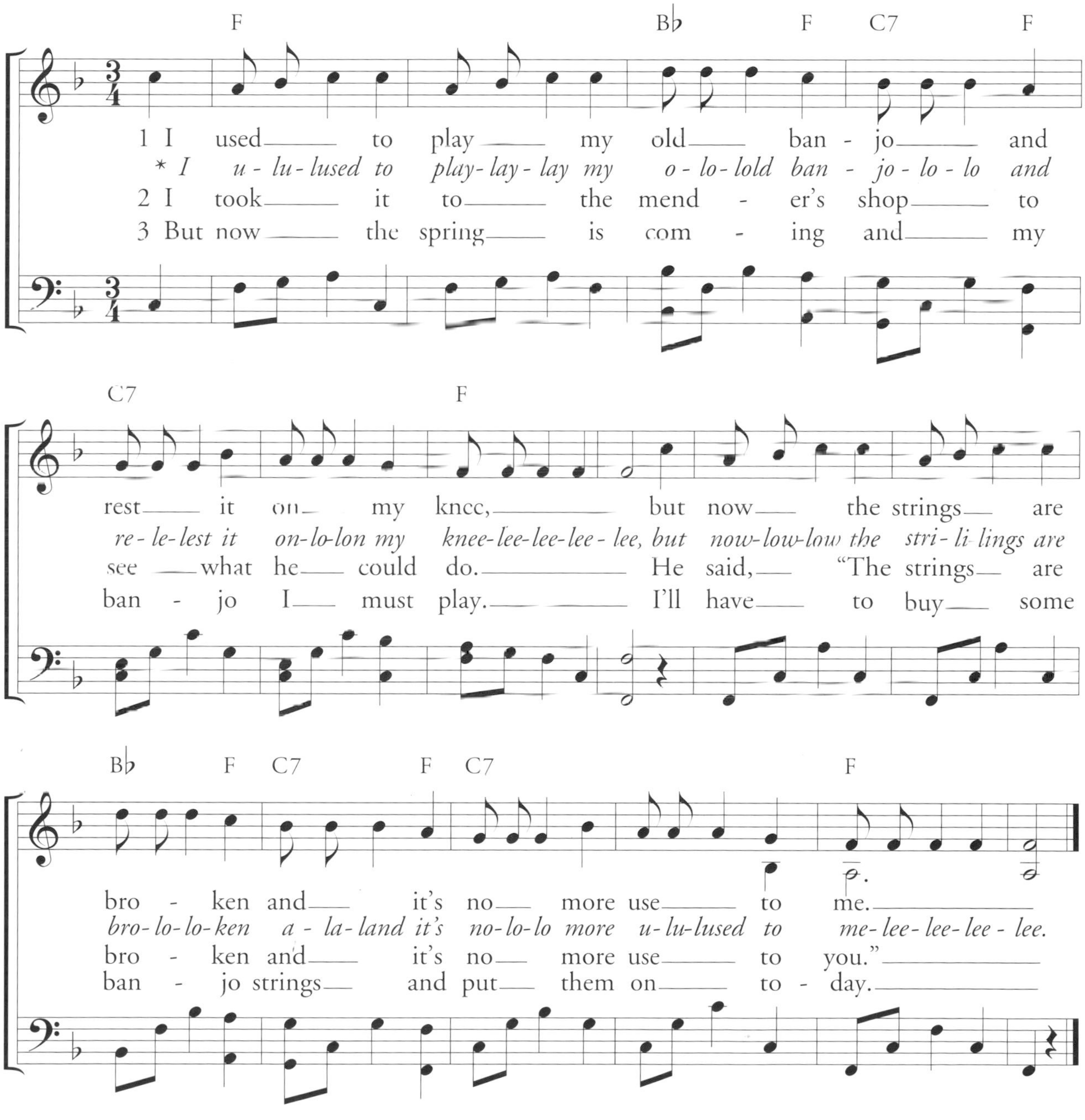

1 I used to play my old banjo and
I u-lu-lused to play-lay-lay my o-lo-lold ban-jo-lo-lo and
2 I took it to the mend-er's shop to
3 But now the spring is com-ing and my

rest it on my knee, but now the strings are
re-le-lest it on-lo-lon my knee-lee-lee-lee-lee, but now-low-low the stri-li lings are
see what he could do. He said, "The strings are
ban-jo I must play. I'll have to buy some

bro-ken and it's no more use to me.
bro-lo-lo-ken a-la-land it's no-lo-lo more u-lu-lused to me-lee-lee-lee-lee.
bro-ken and it's no more use to you."
ban-jo strings and put them on to-day.

*The entire song should be sung like the first verse, inserting the "l" sound as shown in the italicized version.

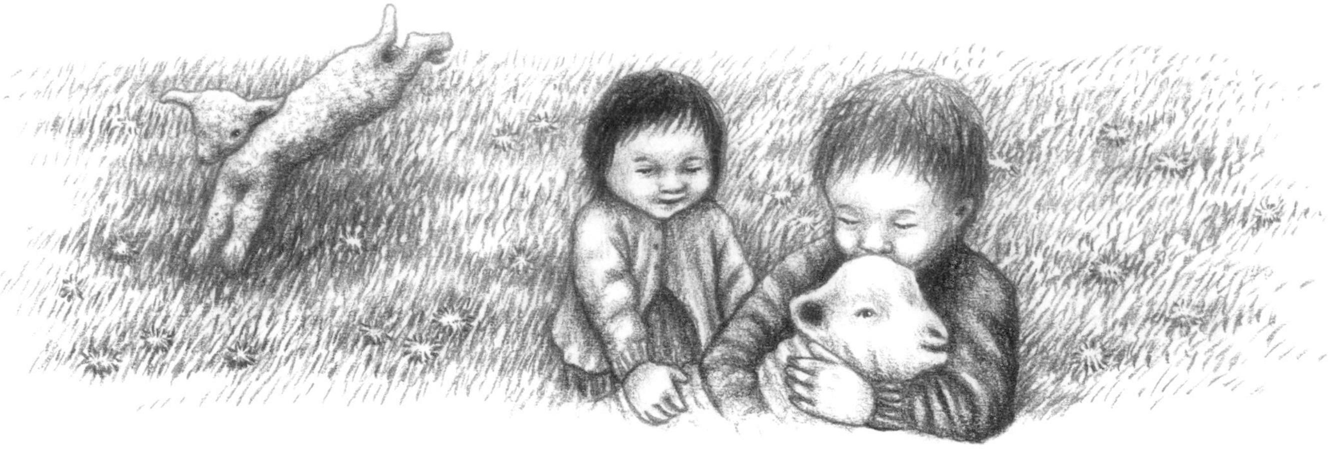

🎵 Spring

William Blake   *Russian Tune*

Delicately

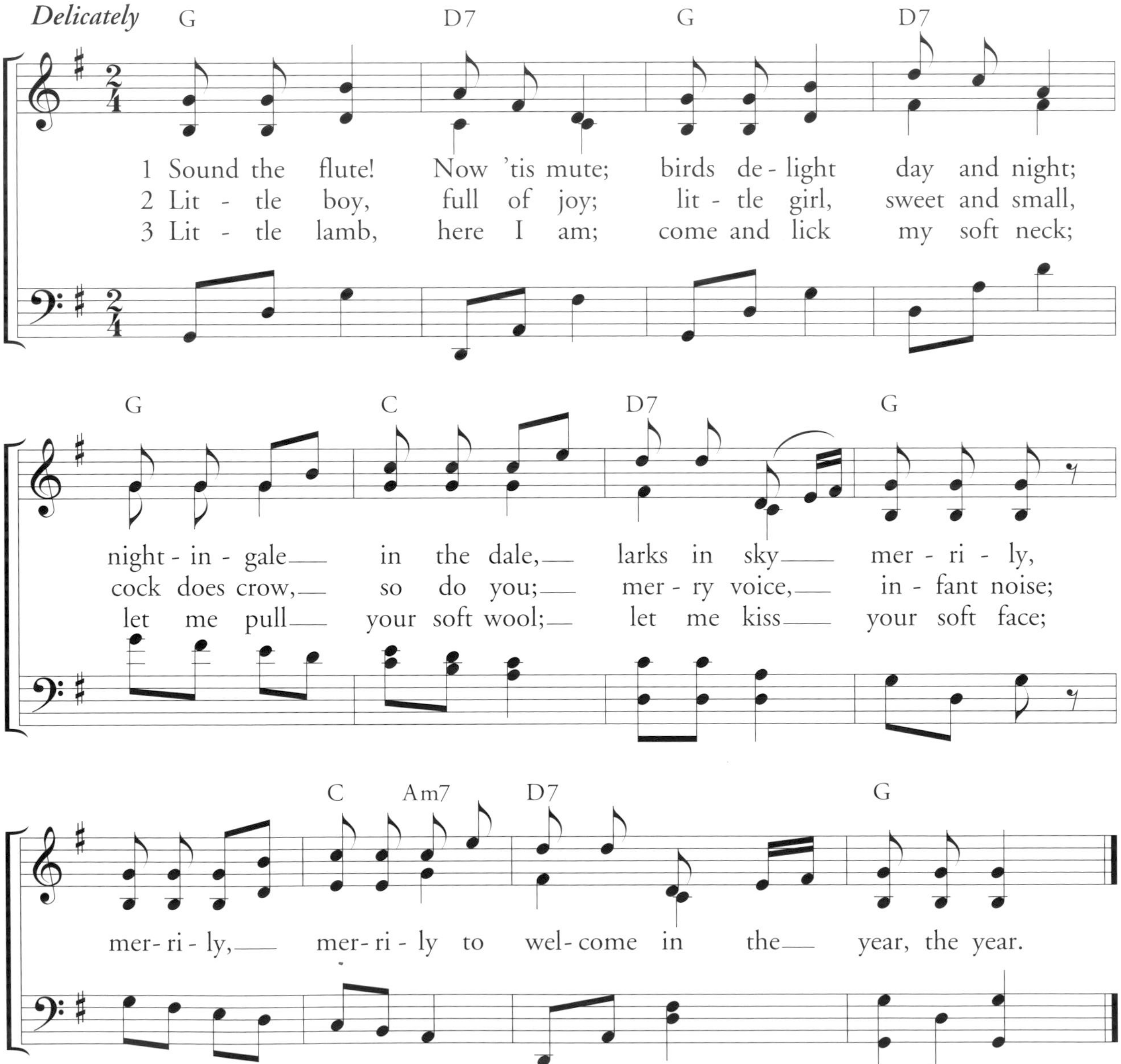

1 Sound the flute! Now 'tis mute; birds de-light day and night;
2 Lit-tle boy, full of joy; lit-tle girl, sweet and small,
3 Lit-tle lamb, here I am; come and lick my soft neck;

night-in-gale in the dale, larks in sky mer-ri-ly,
cock does crow, so do you; mer-ry voice, in-fant noise;
let me pull your soft wool; let me kiss your soft face;

mer-ri-ly, mer-ri-ly to wel-come in the year, the year.

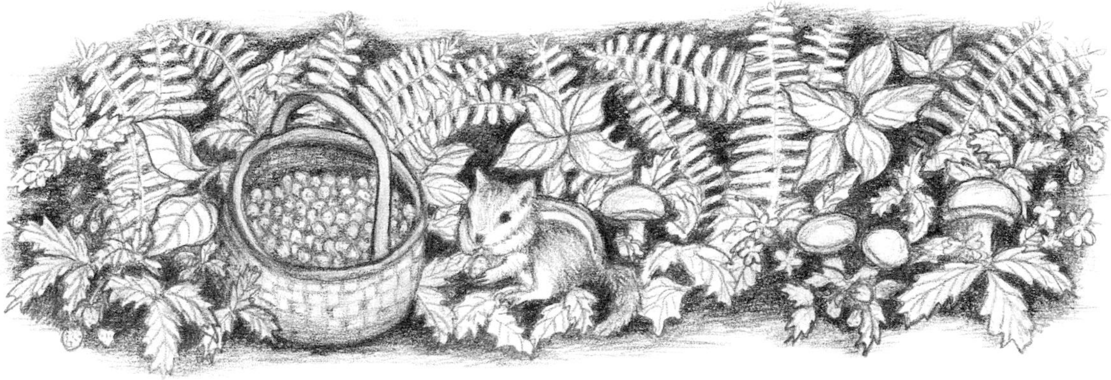

Let's Hike to the Woodlands Today

Berry picking is an unfamiliar pleasure for most kids. Discuss the different types of berries: strawberries, raspberries, blackberries, blueberries, and how they grow wild in fields and woods.

Thuringian Folk Song

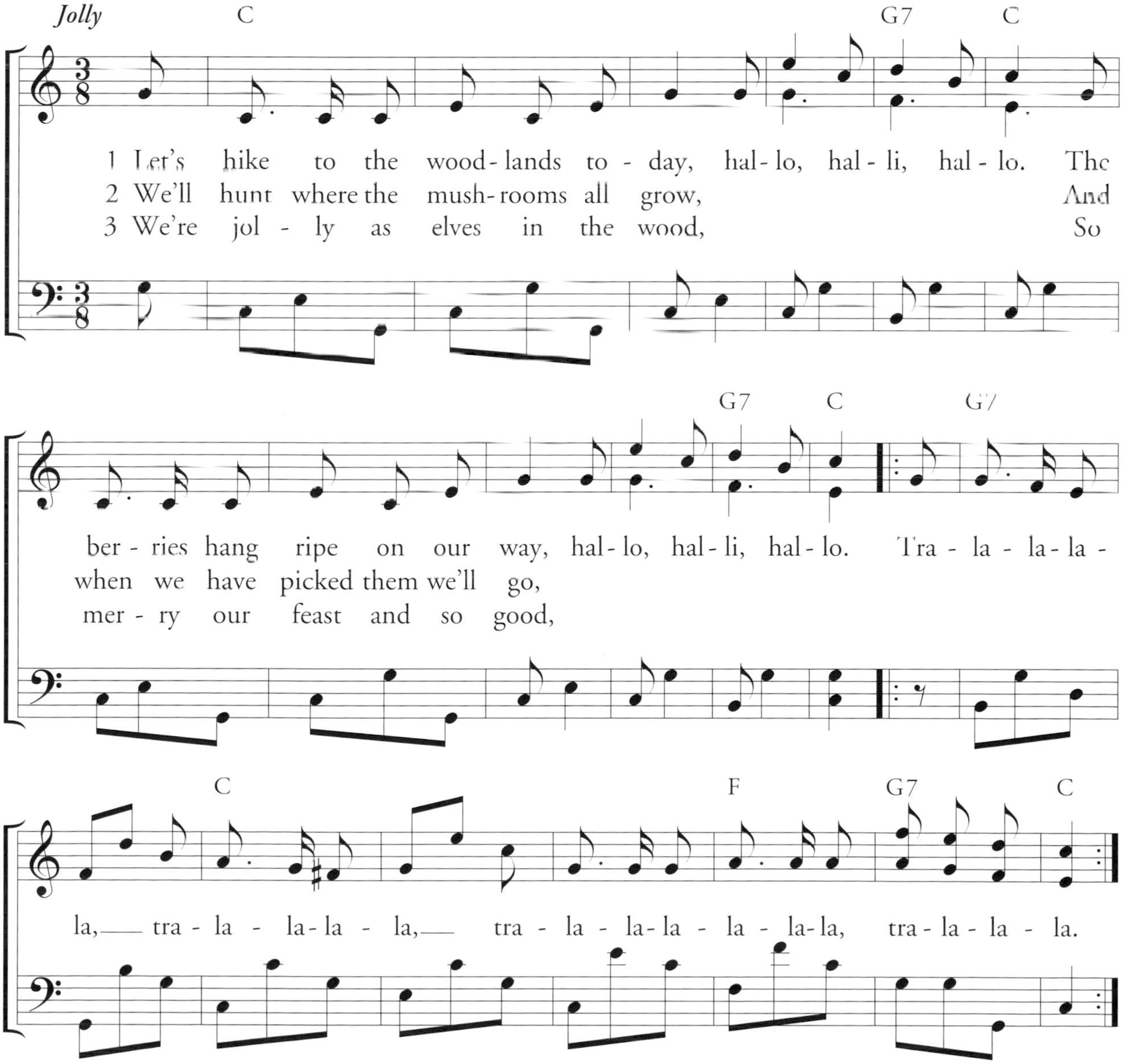

1 Let's hike to the wood-lands to-day, hal-lo, hal-li, hal-lo. The
2 We'll hunt where the mush-rooms all grow, And
3 We're jol-ly as elves in the wood, So

ber-ries hang ripe on our way, hal-lo, hal-li, hal-lo. Tra-la-la-la-
when we have picked them we'll go,
mer-ry our feast and so good,

la,___ tra-la-la-la-la,___ tra-la-la-la-la-la, tra-la-la-la.

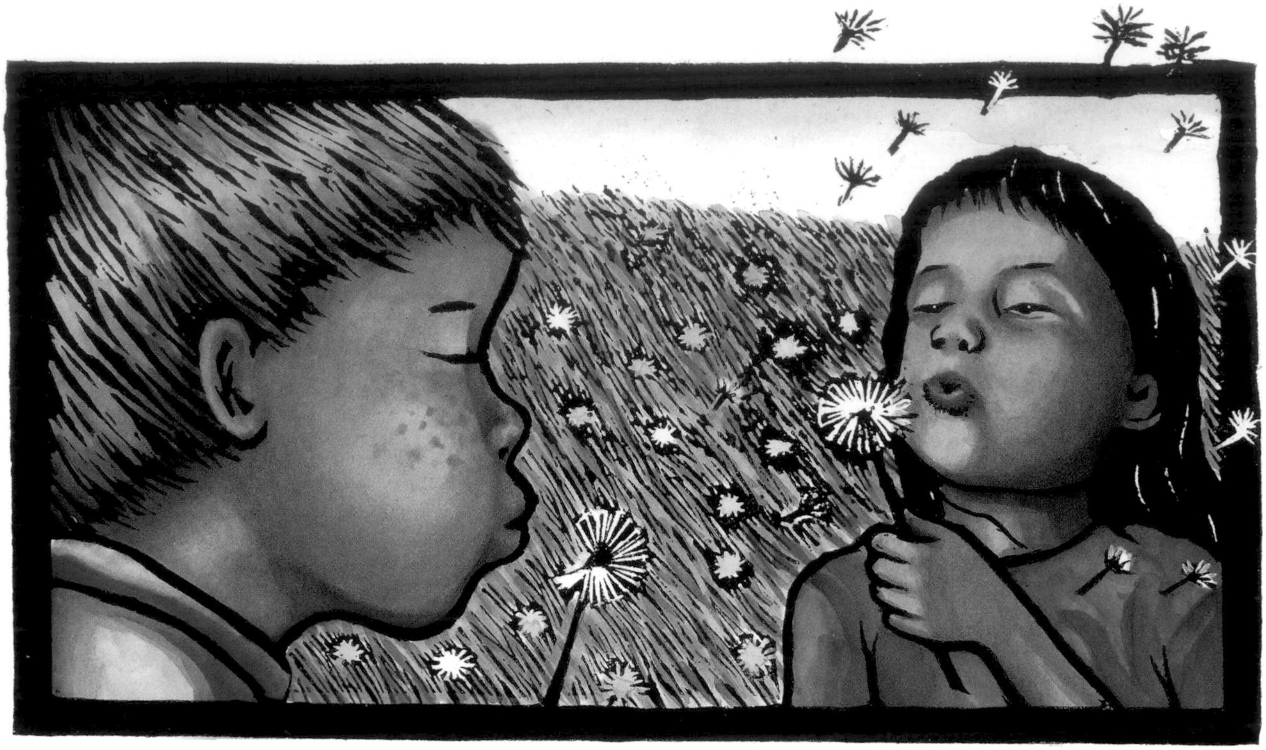

⊚ Dandelion, Yellow as Gold

This is a good question-and-answer song. Half the children can ask the questions; the other half can answer them.
Or, take children to a playground to gather dandelions that have gone to seed. The number of times
you have to blow before all the seeds are gone determines the time on your "clock."

Words and Music
Noreen Bath

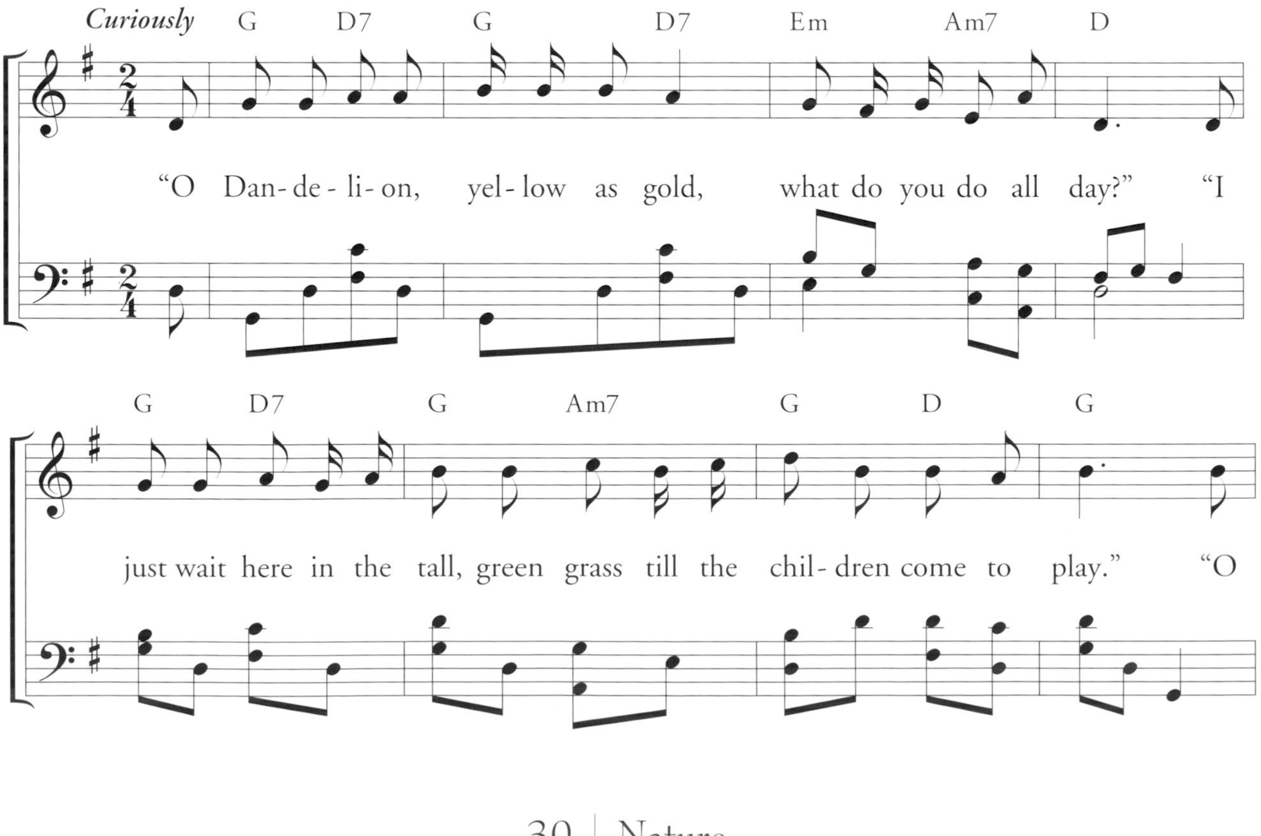

"O Dan-de-li-on, yel-low as gold, what do you do all day?" "I

just wait here in the tall, green grass till the chil-dren come to play." "O

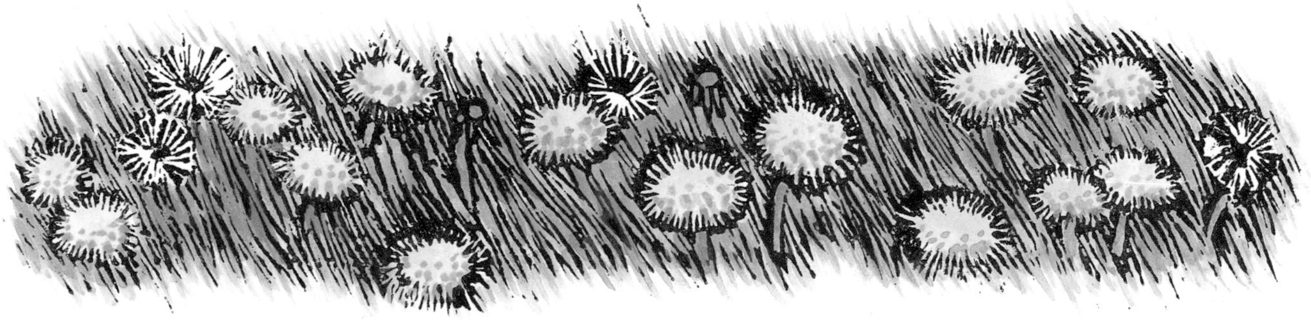

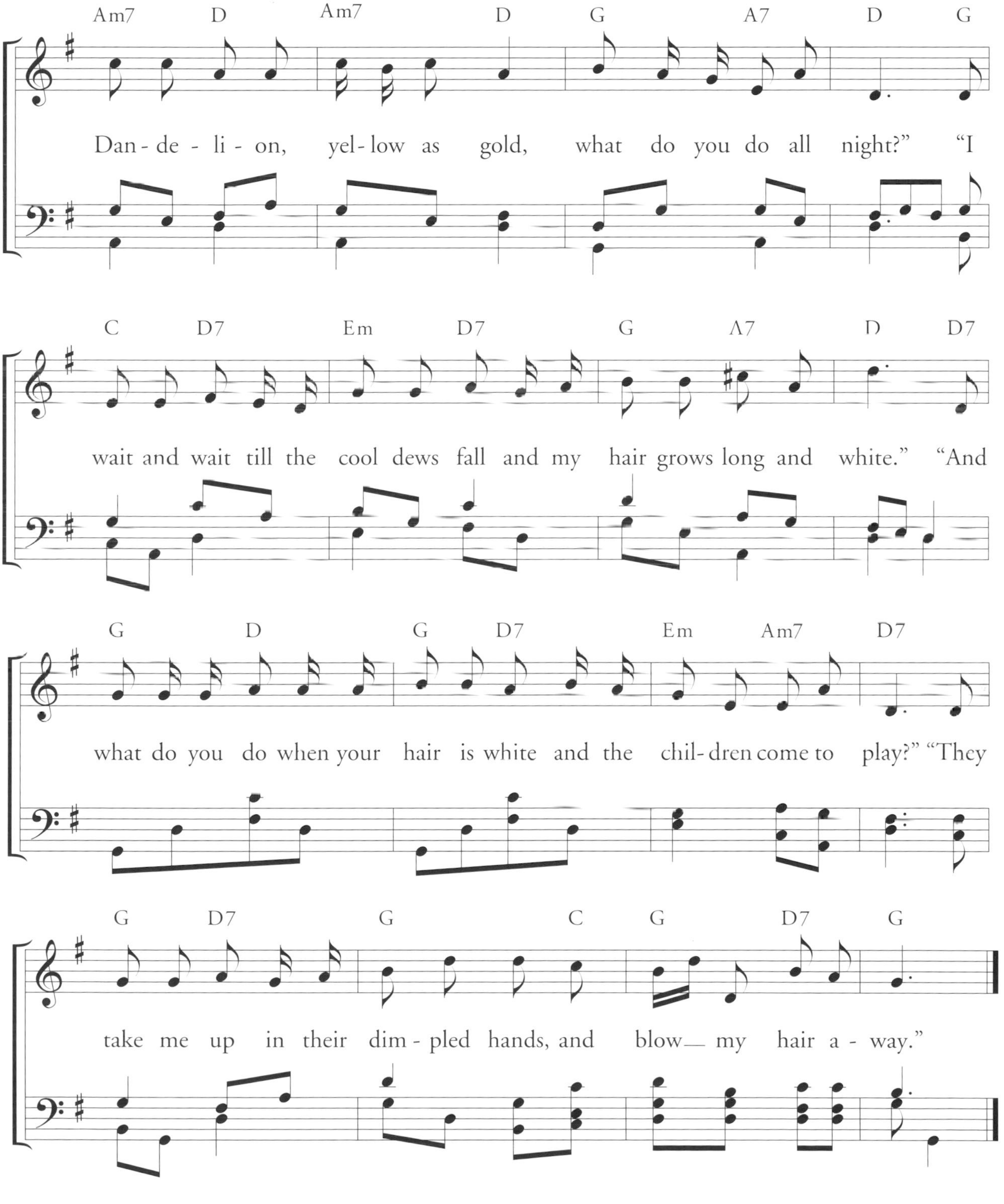

Am7 D Am7 D G A7 D G
Dan-de-li-on, yel-low as gold, what do you do all night?" "I
C D7 Em D7 G A7 D D7
wait and wait till the cool dews fall and my hair grows long and white." "And
G D G D7 Em Am7 D7
what do you do when your hair is white and the chil-dren come to play?" "They
G D7 G C G D7 G
take me up in their dim-pled hands, and blow— my hair a-way."

God Made the Shy, the Wild Ones

This is a great song to supplement a nature unit. Make a bulletin board
showing wild animals and their homes.

Elizabeth Gould

Hugh S. Roberton

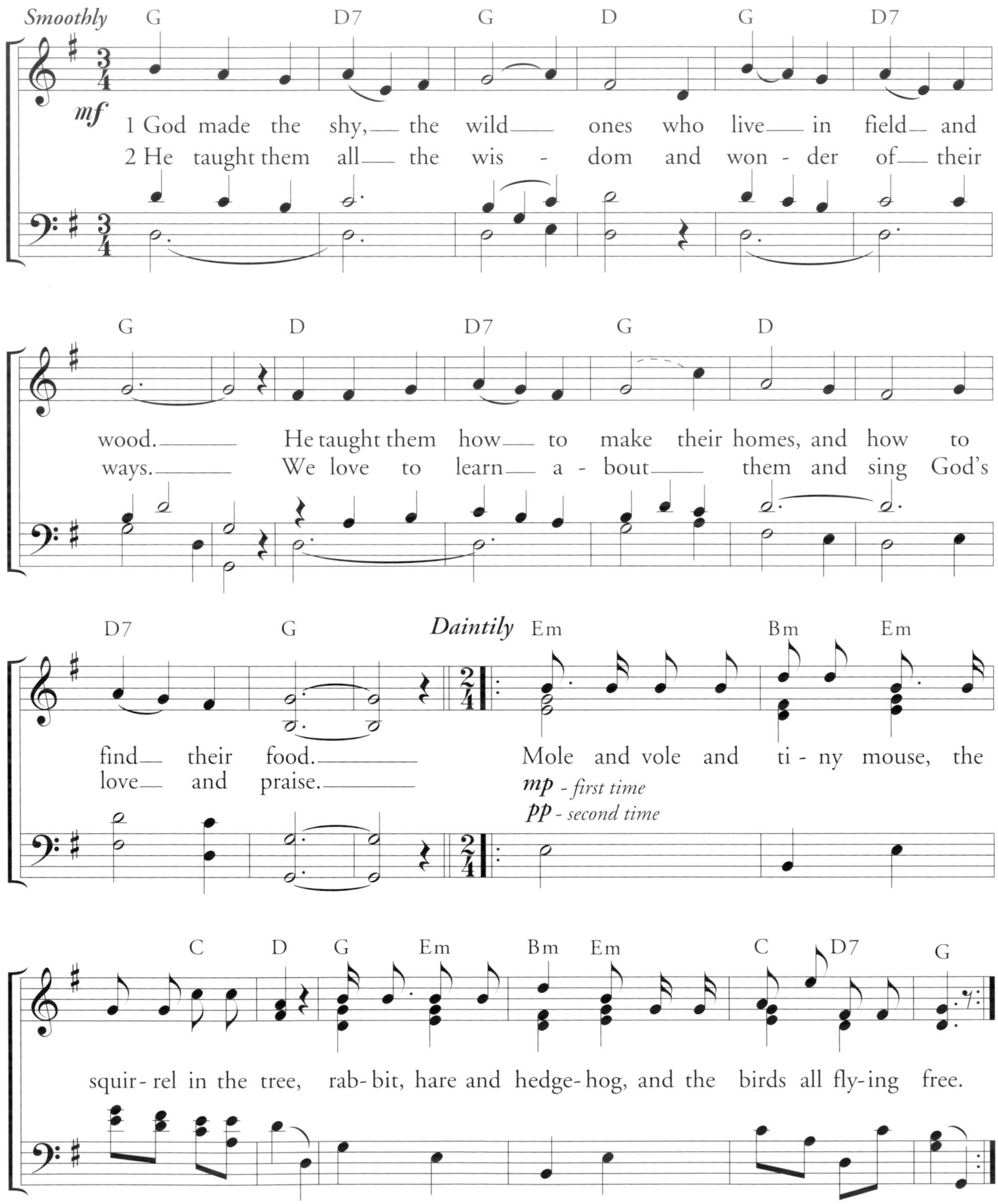

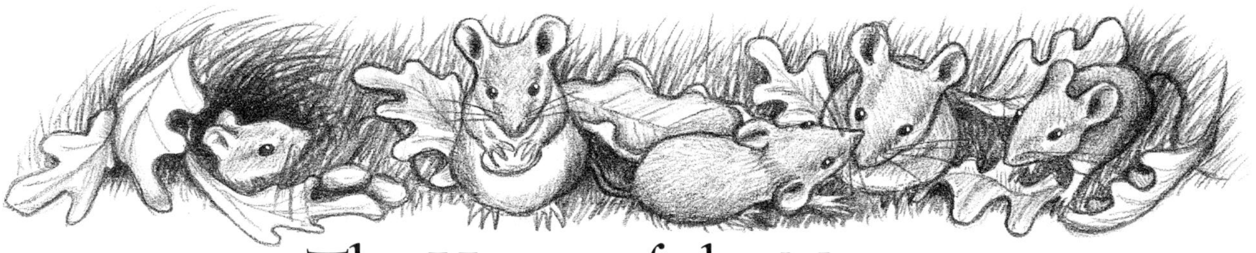

The House of the Mouse

Lucy Sprague Mitchell   *Marlys Swinger*

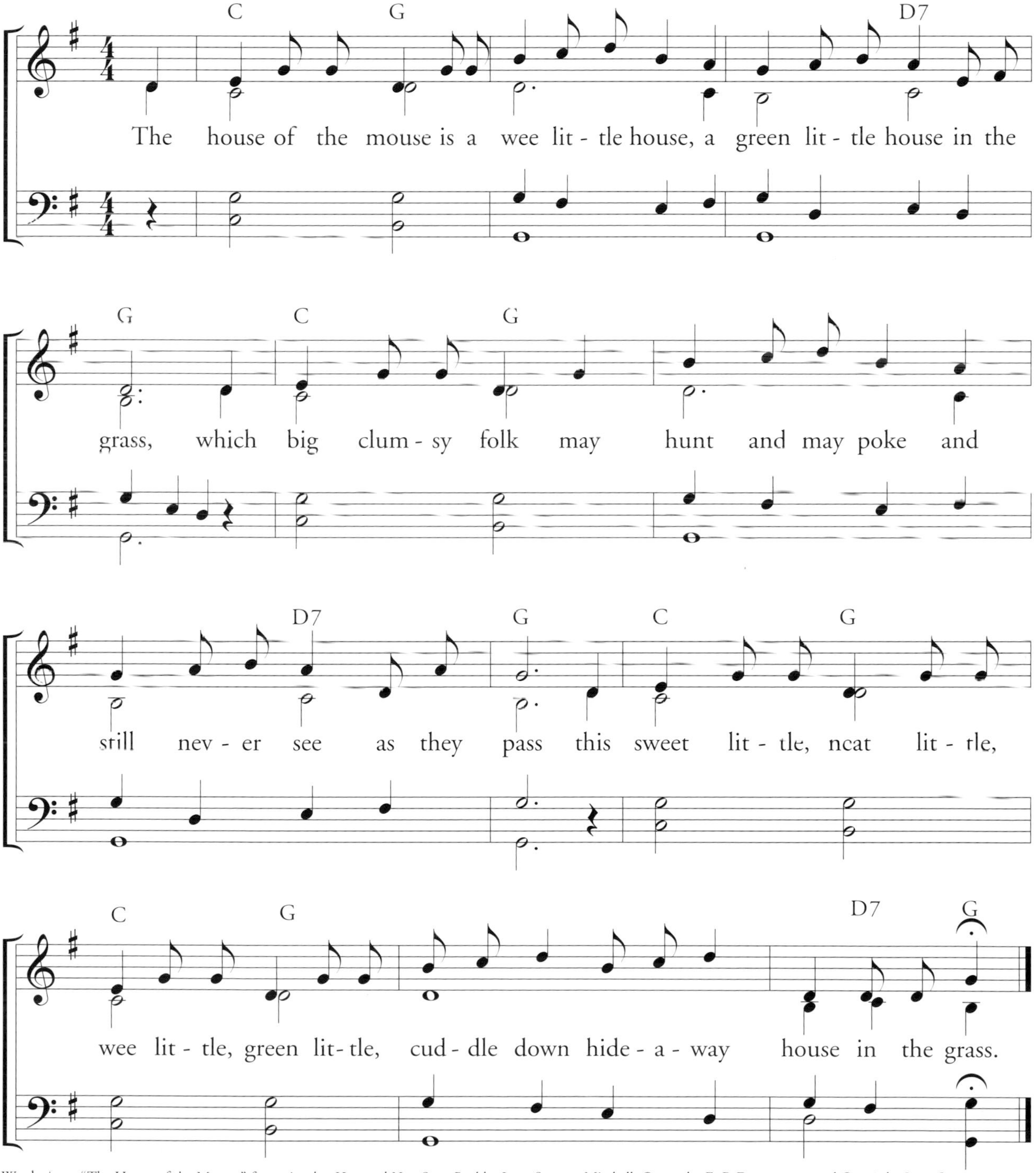

The house of the mouse is a wee lit-tle house, a green lit-tle house in the

grass, which big clum-sy folk may hunt and may poke and

still nev-er see as they pass this sweet lit-tle, neat lit-tle,

wee lit-tle, green lit-tle, cud-dle down hide-a-way house in the grass.

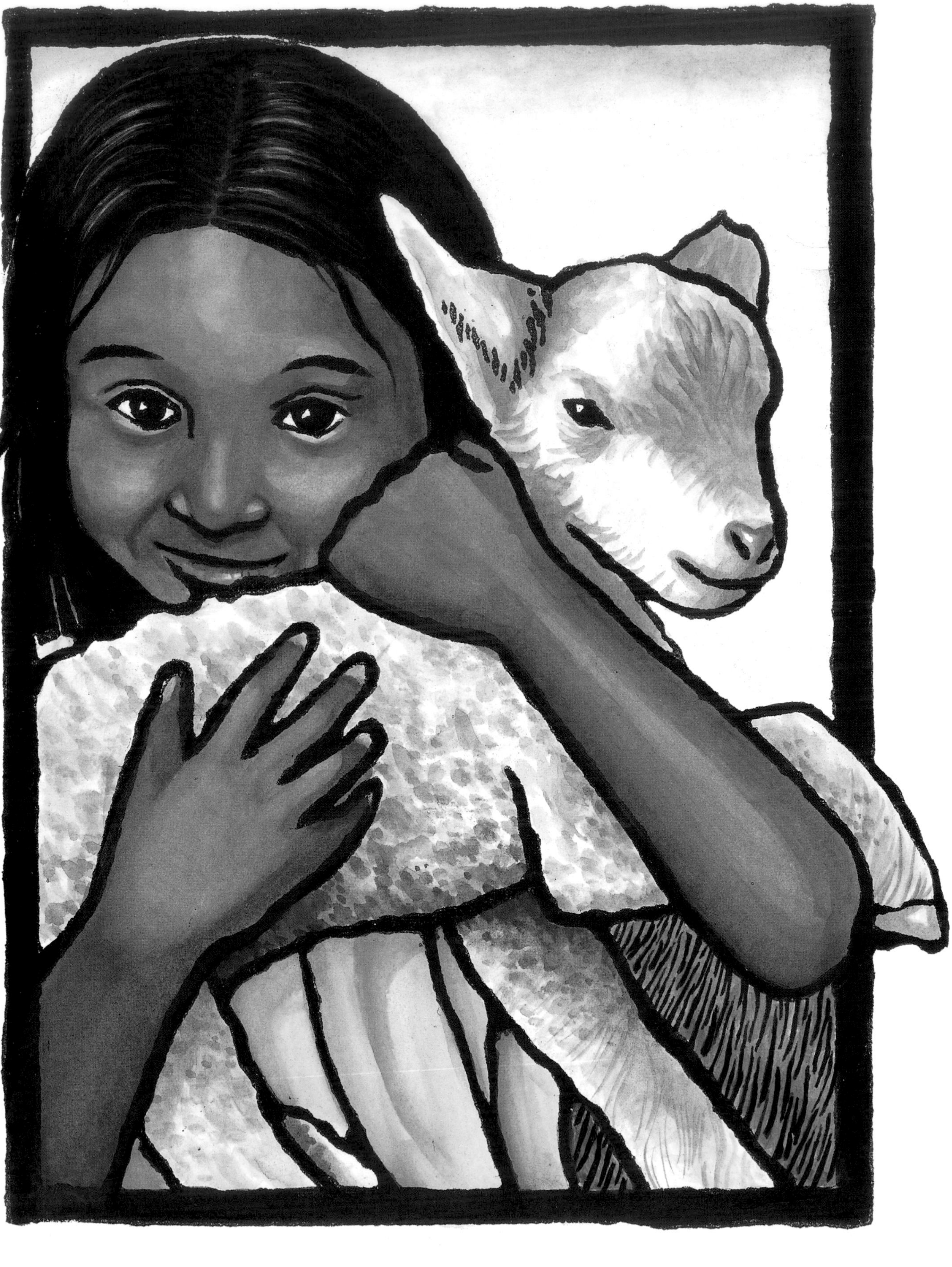

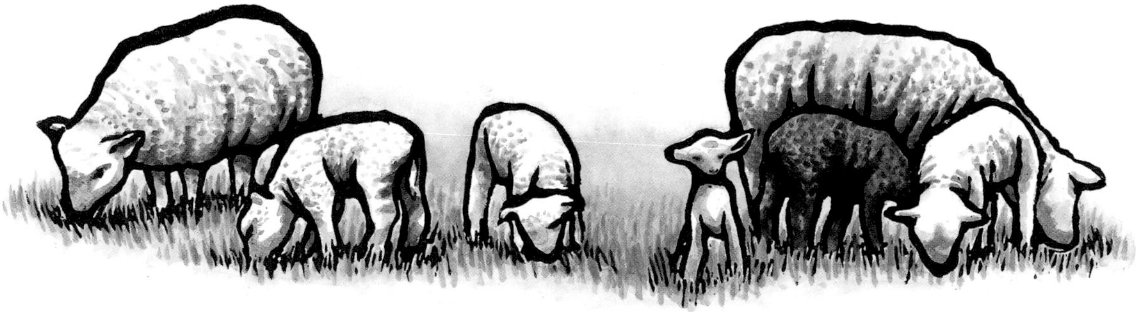

I Held a Lamb

Kim Worthington   Marlys Swinger

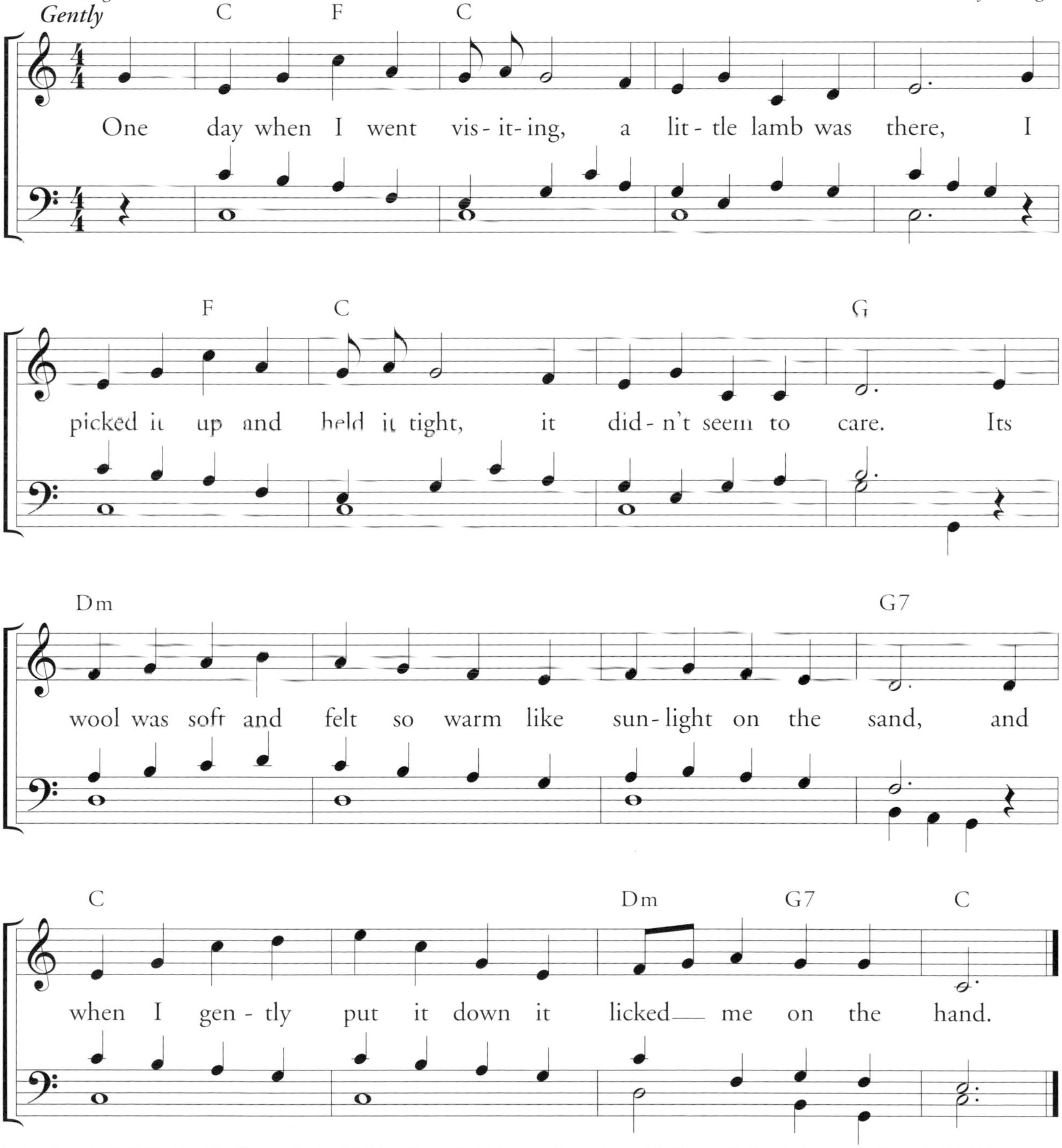

One day when I went vis-it-ing, a lit-tle lamb was there, I picked it up and held it tight, it did-n't seem to care. Its wool was soft and felt so warm like sun-light on the sand, and when I gen-tly put it down it licked___ me on the hand.

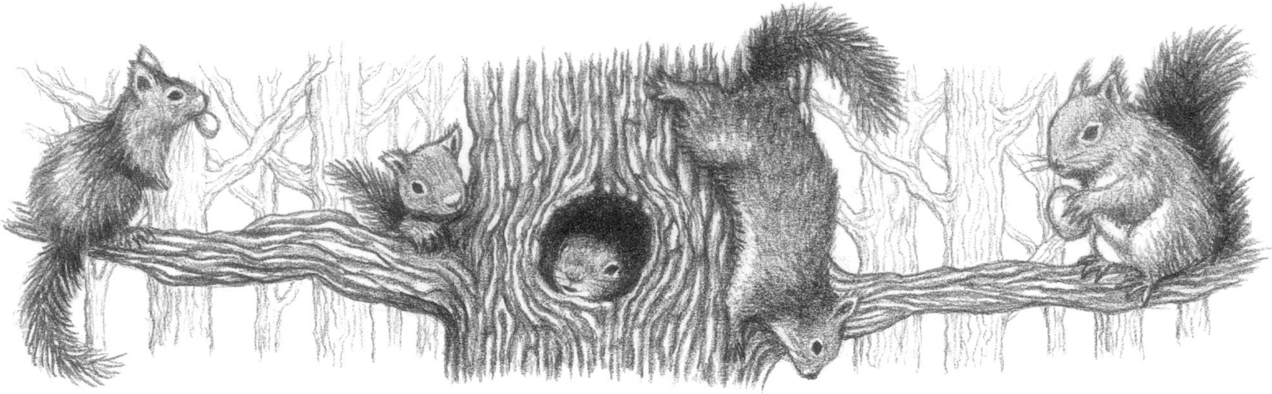

Squirrel Nutkin

Frances B. Wood

Spanish Folk Tune

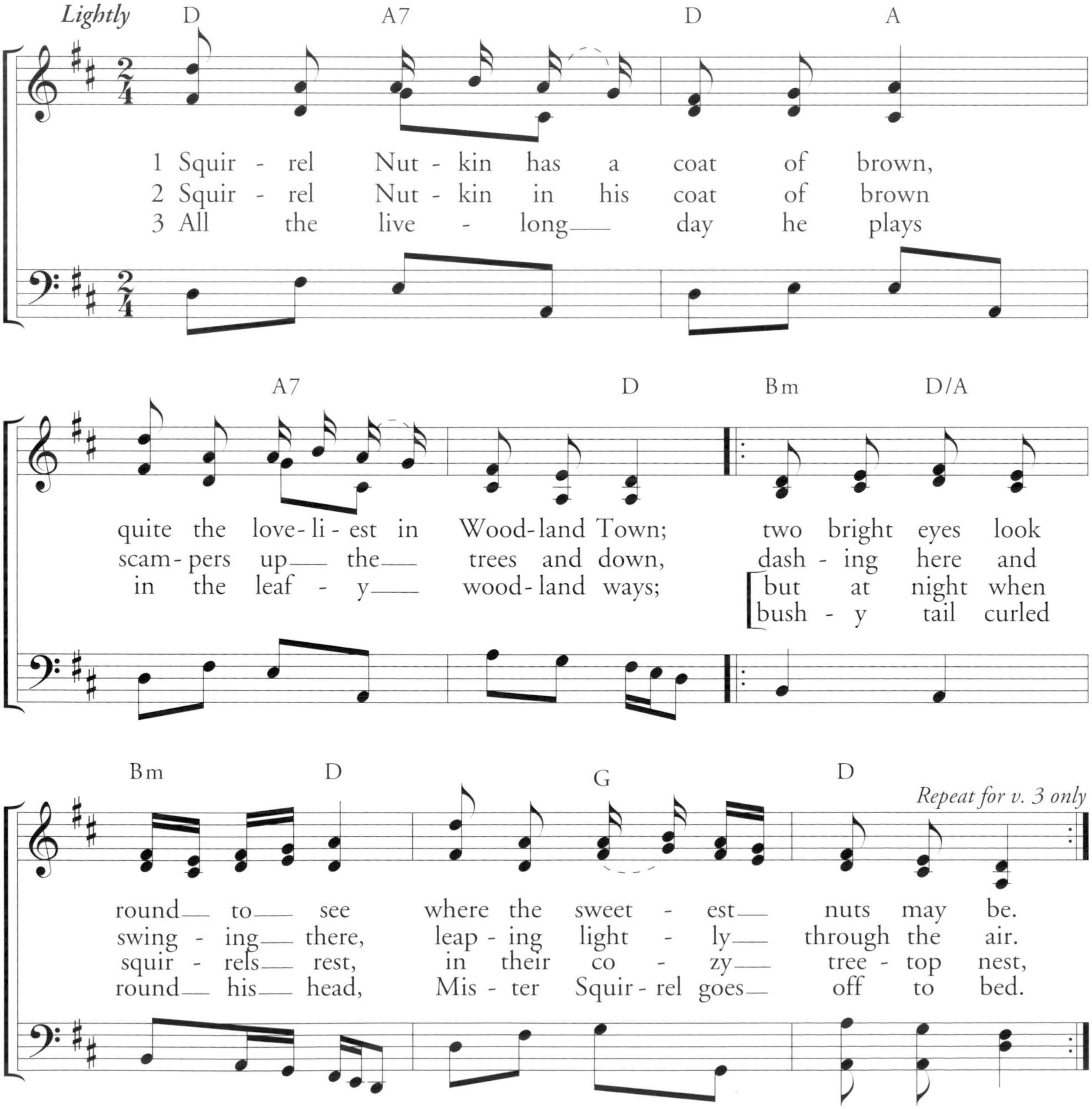

1 Squir - rel Nut - kin has a coat of brown,
2 Squir - rel Nut - kin in his coat of brown
3 All the live - long____ day he plays

quite the love - li - est in Wood - land Town;
scam - pers up____ the____ trees and down,
in the leaf - y____ wood - land ways;

two bright eyes look
dash - ing here and
[but at night when
[bush - y tail curled

round____ to____ see where the sweet - est____ nuts may be.
swing - ing____ there, leap - ing light - ly____ through the air.
squir - rels____ rest, in their co - zy____ tree - top nest,
round____ his____ head, Mis - ter Squir - rel goes____ off to bed.

Repeat for v. 3 only

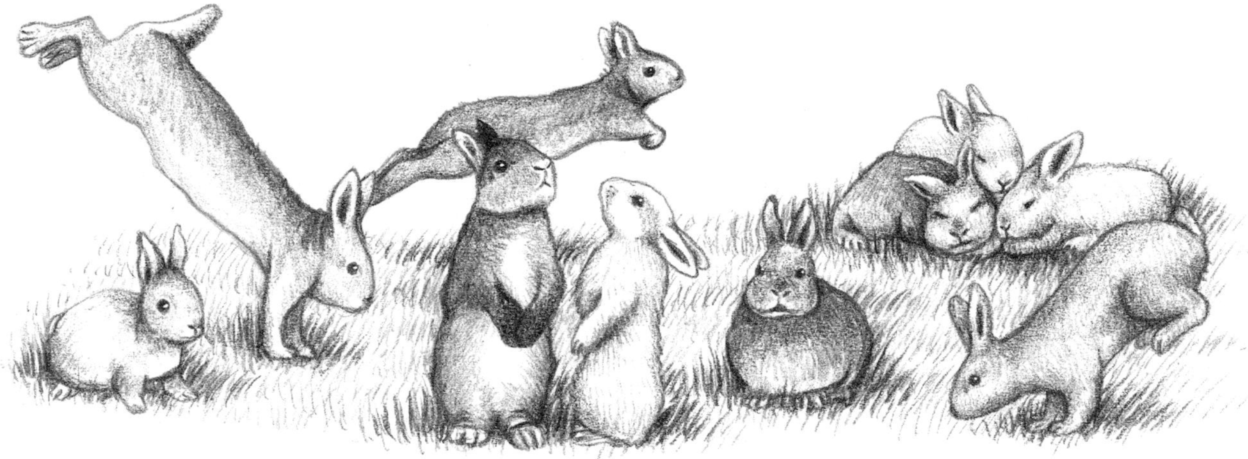

🎵 Song of the Bunnies

Even if children grow up never having held a real rabbit, they can learn this song. Look for the book,
Home for a Bunny, a classic by Margaret Wise Brown that every child should know.

Margaret Wise Brown   *Marlys Swinger*

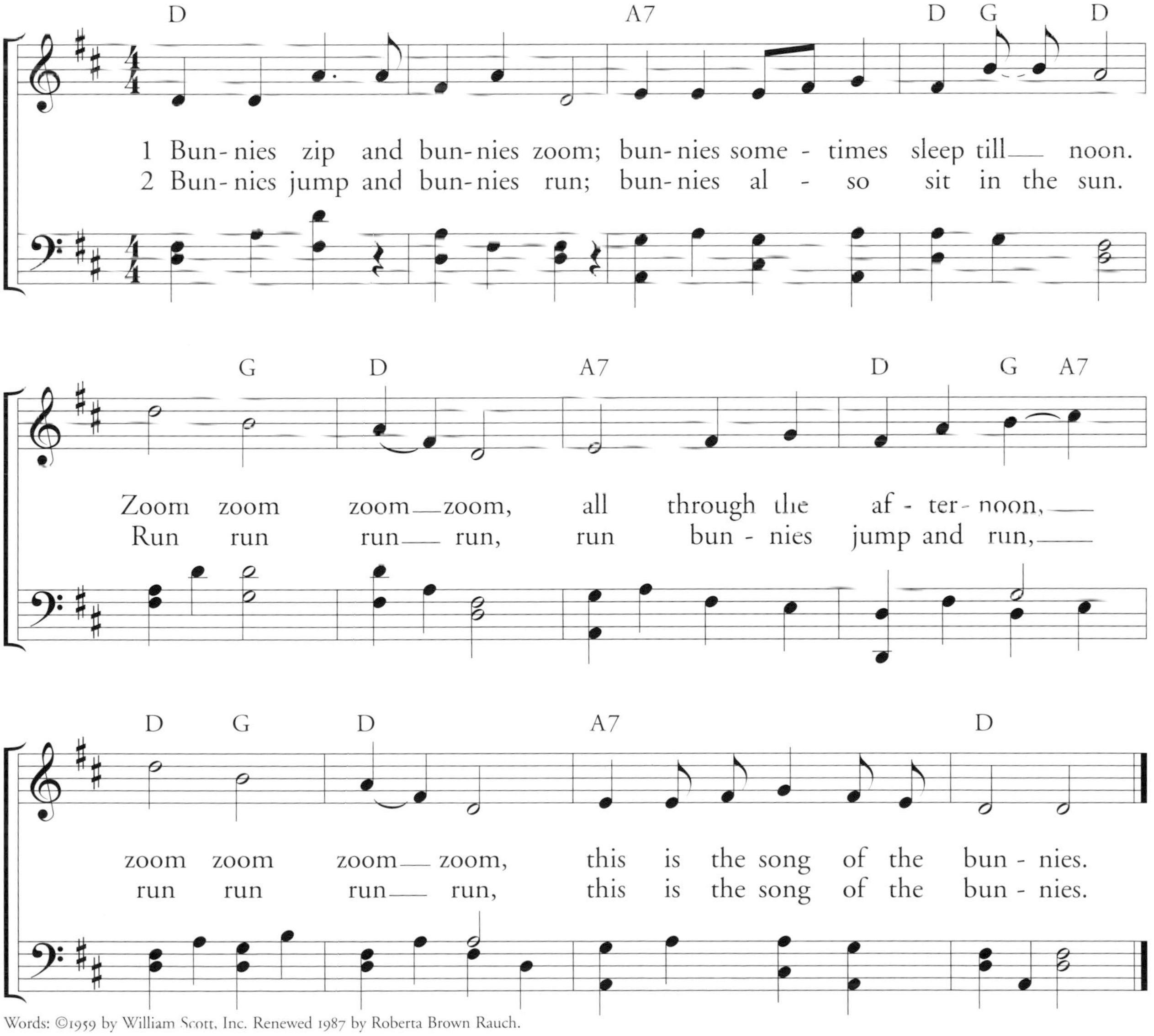

1 Bun - nies zip and bun - nies zoom; bun - nies some - times sleep till— noon.
2 Bun - nies jump and bun - nies run; bun - nies al - so sit in the sun.

Zoom zoom zoom— zoom, all through the af - ter - noon, —
Run run run— run, run bun - nies jump and run, —

zoom zoom zoom— zoom, this is the song of the bun - nies.
run run run— run, this is the song of the bun - nies.

Stefan Is a Stable Lad

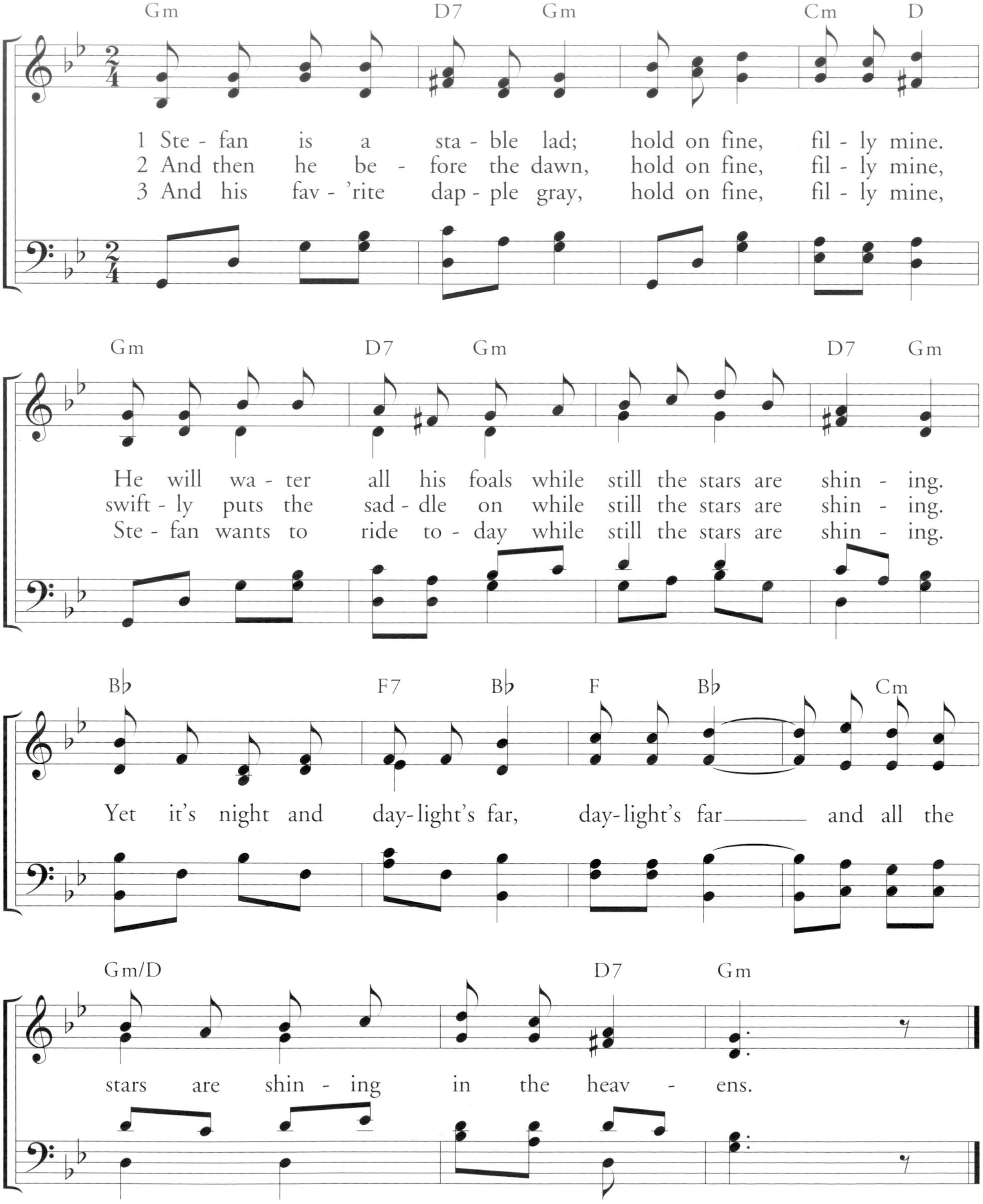

Traditional Swedish

1 Ste - fan is a sta - ble lad; hold on fine, fil - ly mine.
2 And then he be - fore the dawn, hold on fine, fil - ly mine,
3 And his fav - 'rite dap - ple gray, hold on fine, fil - ly mine,

He will wa - ter all his foals while still the stars are shin - ing.
swift - ly puts the sad - dle on while still the stars are shin - ing.
Ste - fan wants to ride to - day while still the stars are shin - ing.

Yet it's night and day-light's far, day-light's far_____ and all the

stars are shin - ing in the heav - ens.

4. Old black bear in forest deep…
   Can no longer rest or sleep…

5. On each hearth the fire burns bright…
   Gather joyfully in its light…

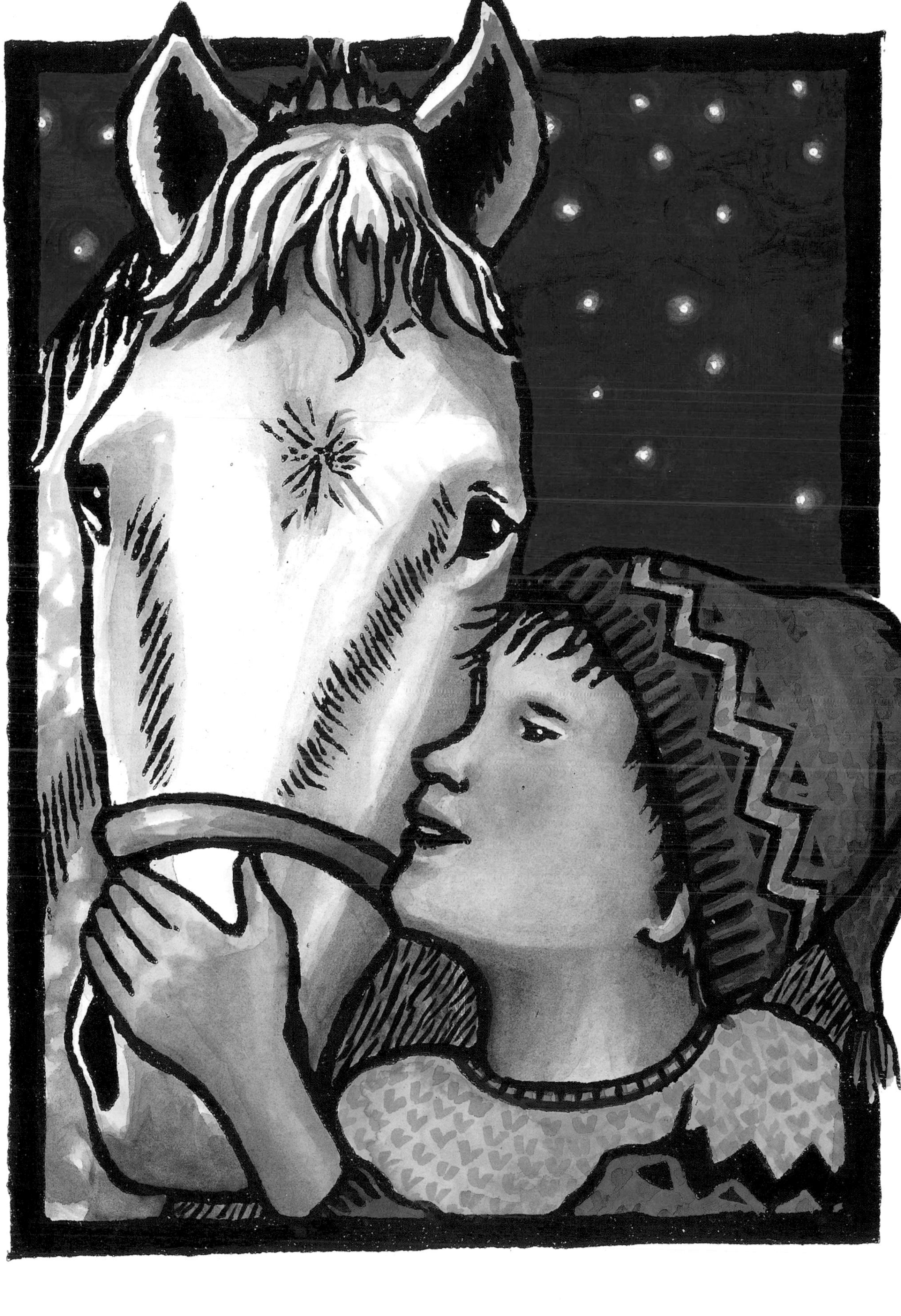

Proud Missus Sheep

Children love to imitate animal noises. After letting everyone experiment, choose a child or children for each verse. By all means add your own verses and expand the menagerie.

Unknown

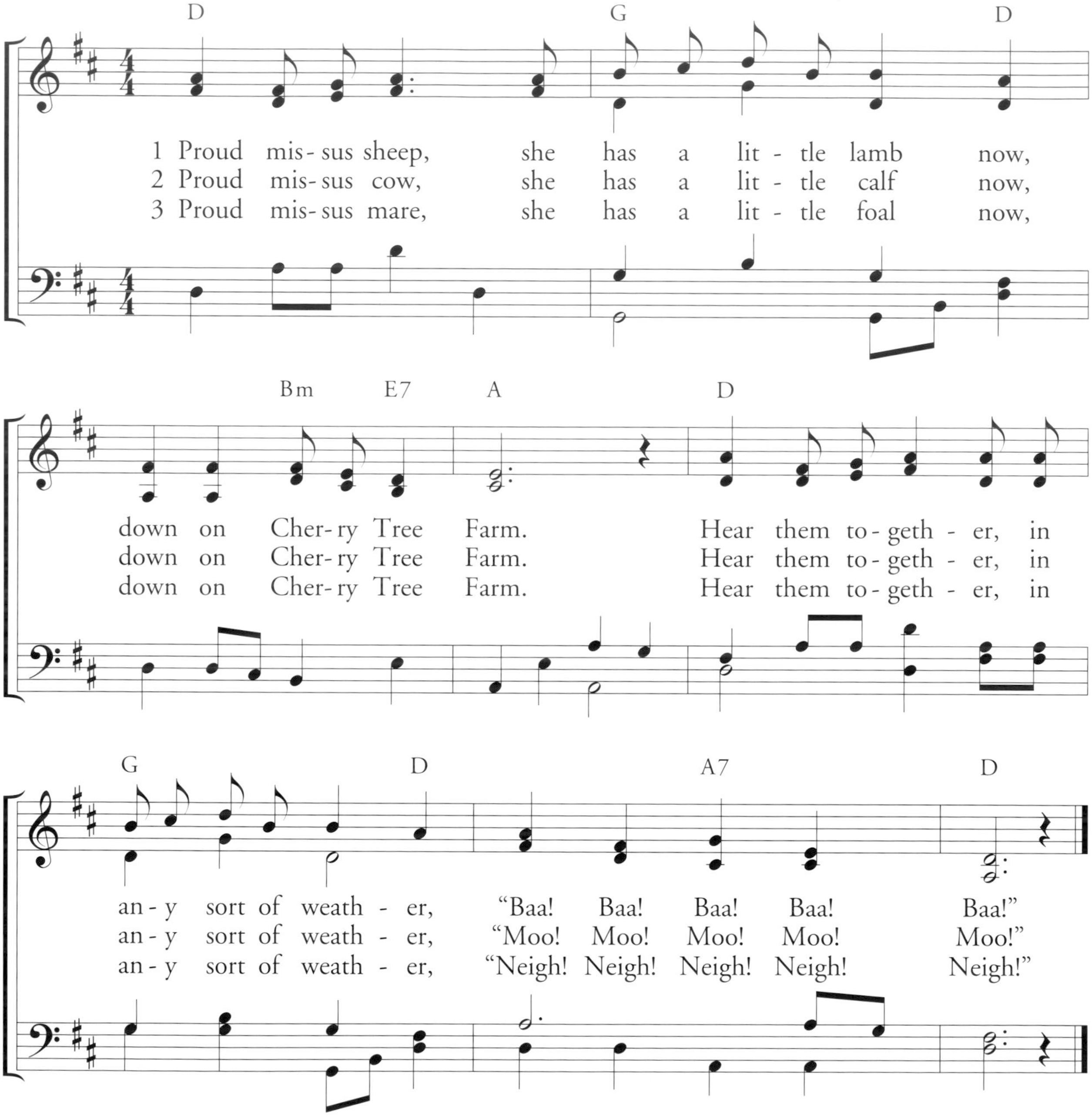

1 Proud mis-sus sheep, she has a lit-tle lamb now,
2 Proud mis-sus cow, she has a lit-tle calf now,
3 Proud mis-sus mare, she has a lit-tle foal now,

down on Cher-ry Tree Farm. Hear them to-geth-er, in
down on Cher-ry Tree Farm. Hear them to-geth-er, in
down on Cher-ry Tree Farm. Hear them to-geth-er, in

an-y sort of weath-er, "Baa! Baa! Baa! Baa! Baa!"
an-y sort of weath-er, "Moo! Moo! Moo! Moo! Moo!"
an-y sort of weath-er, "Neigh! Neigh! Neigh! Neigh! Neigh!"

4. Cat – kittens – meow   7. Rabbit – bunnies – munch

5. Duck – ducklings – quack   8. Pig – piglets – grunt

6. Hen – chicks – cluck   9. Dog – puppies – bow-wow

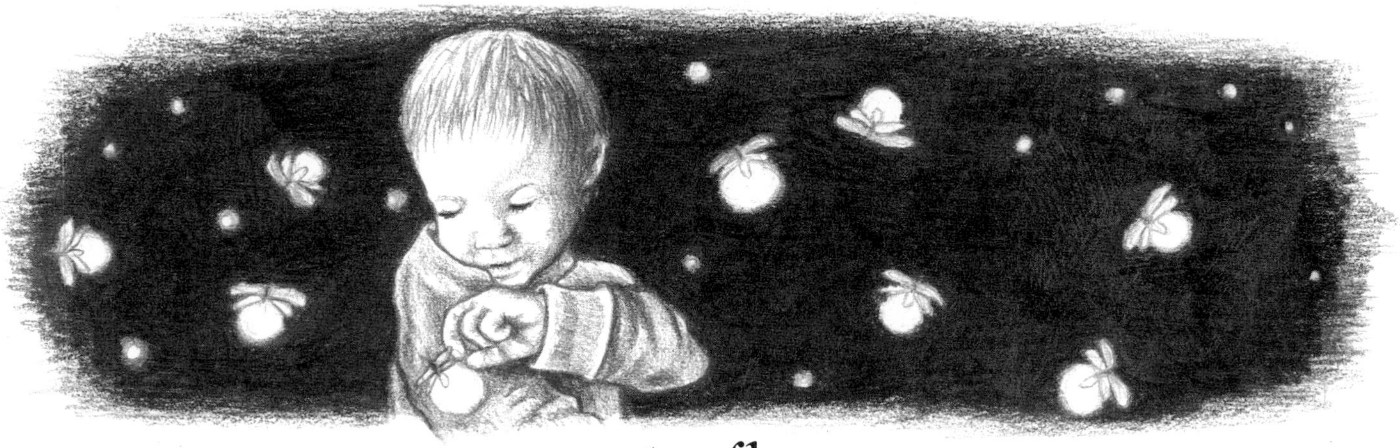

ⓧ Firefly

By adding simple steps and motions, this lovely little song can become a dance as well. Once you've taught the words, divide the class in two groups and take turns: one part twirling and skipping, the other singing.

Elizabeth Madox Roberts   *Croatian Air*

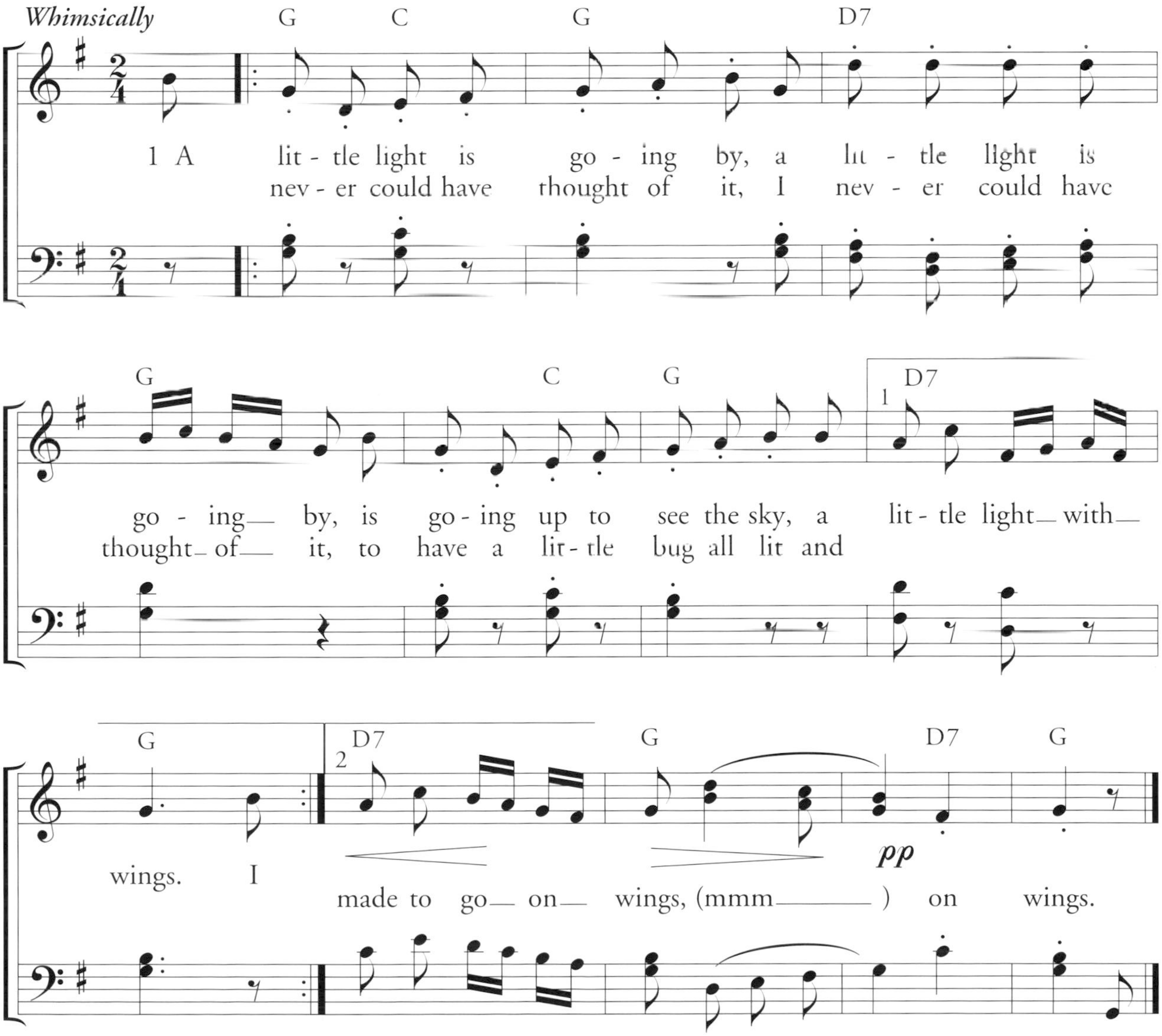

1 A lit-tle light is go-ing by, a lit-tle light is
nev-er could have thought of it, I nev-er could have

go-ing— by, is go-ing up to see the sky, a lit-tle light— with—
thought— of— it, to have a lit-tle bug all lit and

wings.   I
made to go—on— wings, (mmm_____) on wings.

From *The Whole World Singing,* compiled by Edith Lovell Thomas, ©1950 Friendship Press. Used by permission. Words: from *Under the Tree* by Elizabeth Madox Roberts. ©1922 by B. W. Huebsch, Inc., renewed 1950 by Ivor S. Roberts. ©1930 by Viking Penguin, Inc., renewed ©1958 by Ivor S. Roberts. Used by permission of Viking Penguin, a division of Penguin Putnam, Inc.

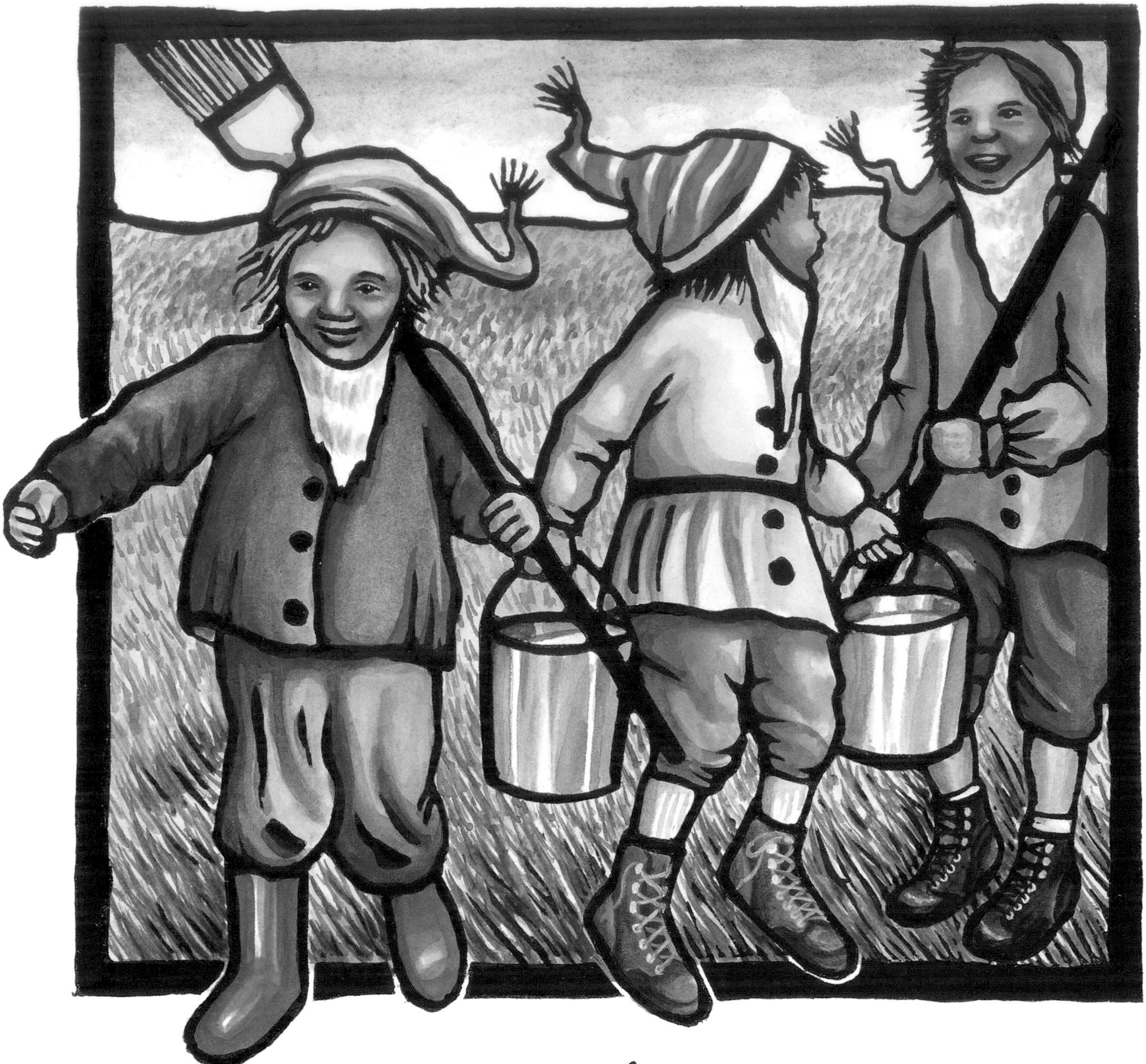

🎵 Dwarf Song

Here's a good one to complement a reading of *Snow White*. Let your dwarves act out the
different verses (they'll surely think up something for "nix nax nox").

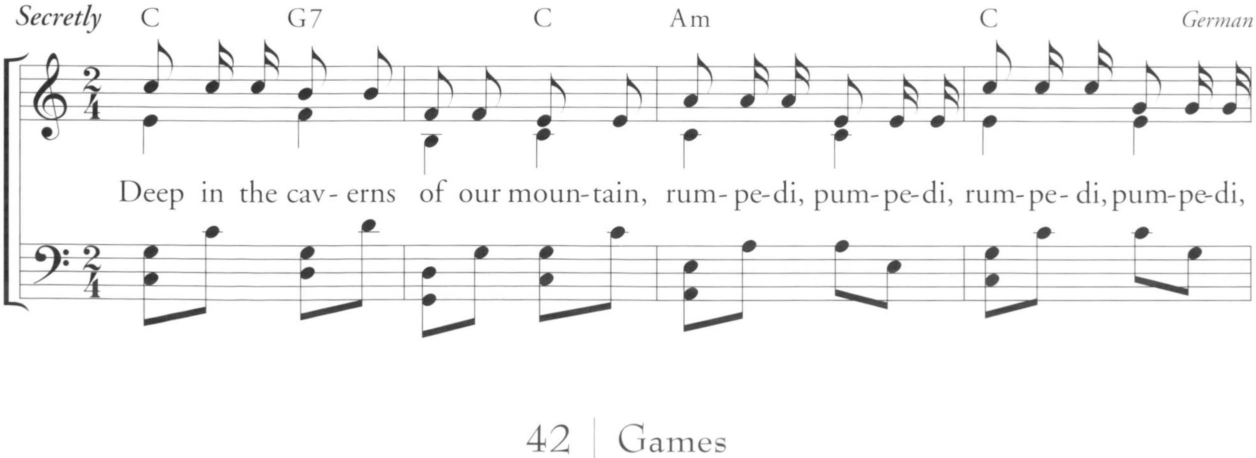

Secretly

Deep in the cav-erns of our moun-tain, rum-pe-di, pum-pe-di, rum-pe-di, pum-pe-di,

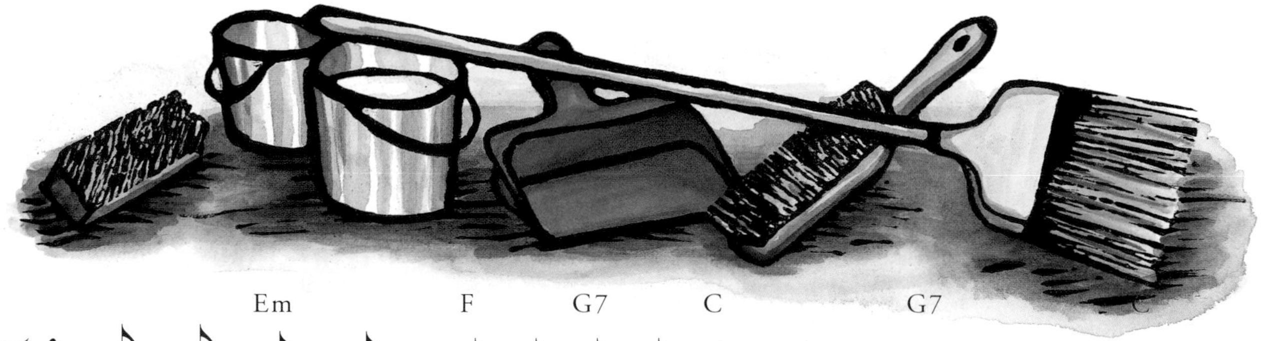

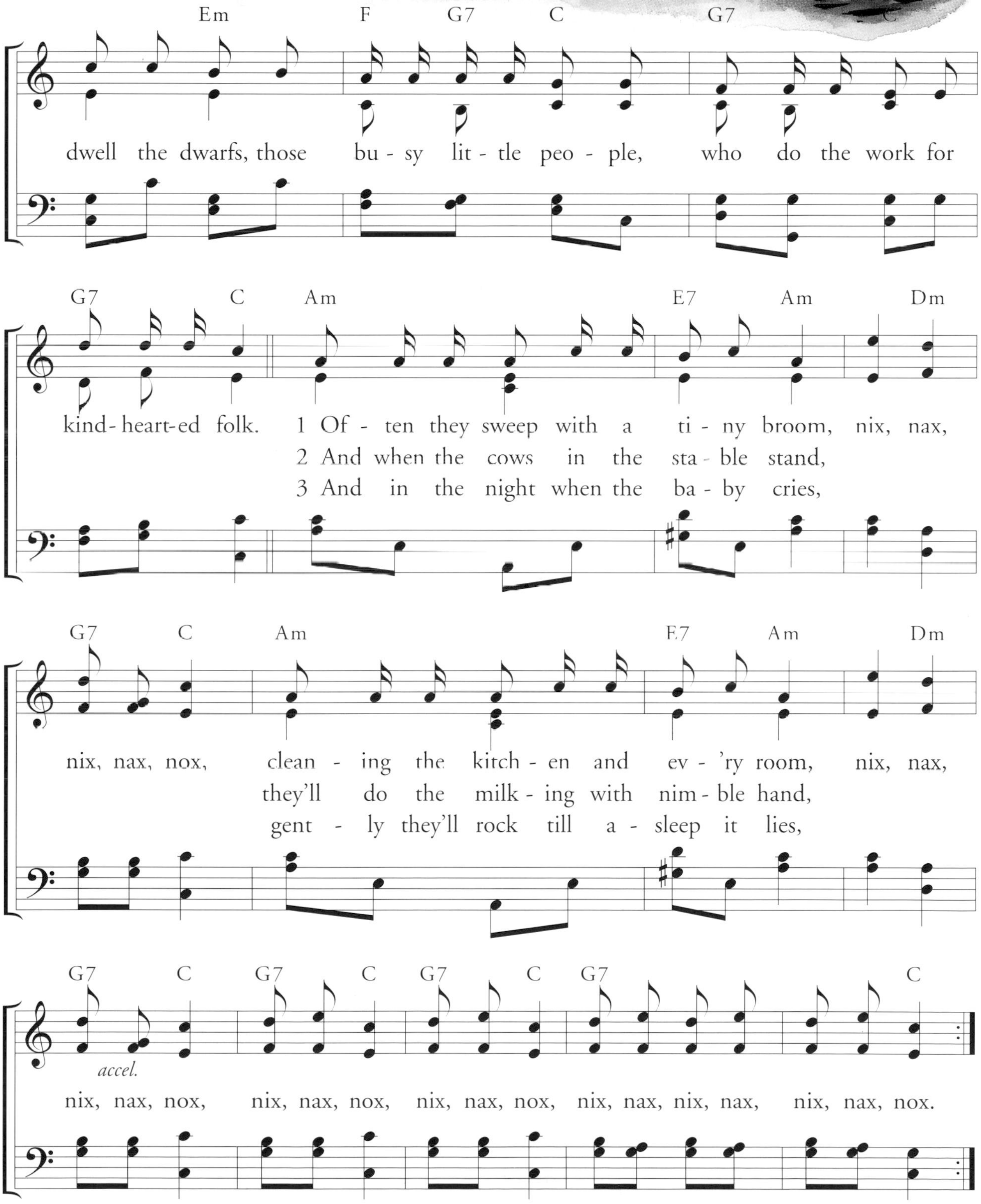

dwell the dwarfs, those bu-sy lit-tle peo-ple, who do the work for

kind-heart-ed folk.
1 Of – ten they sweep with a ti – ny broom, nix, nax,
2 And when the cows in the sta – ble stand,
3 And in the night when the ba – by cries,

nix, nax, nox, clean – ing the kitch – en and ev – 'ry room, nix, nax,
they'll do the milk – ing with nim – ble hand,
gent – ly they'll rock till a – sleep it lies,

accel.

nix, nax, nox, nix, nax, nox, nix, nax, nox, nix, nax, nix, nax, nix, nax, nox.

Oh, We Are Two Musicians

G   D7   G   German

Oh, we are two mu - si - cians, we come from Mu - sic - land. Oh, we are two mu -

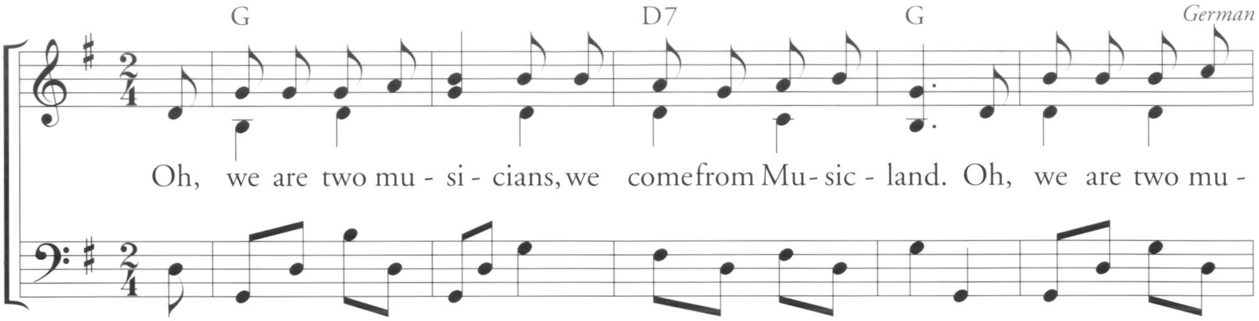

The circle dances left as couple A (holding hands) goes around the inside to the right.

D7   G   D7   G

si - cians, we come from Mu - sic - land. We can play the vi - o, vi - o, vi - o - lin,

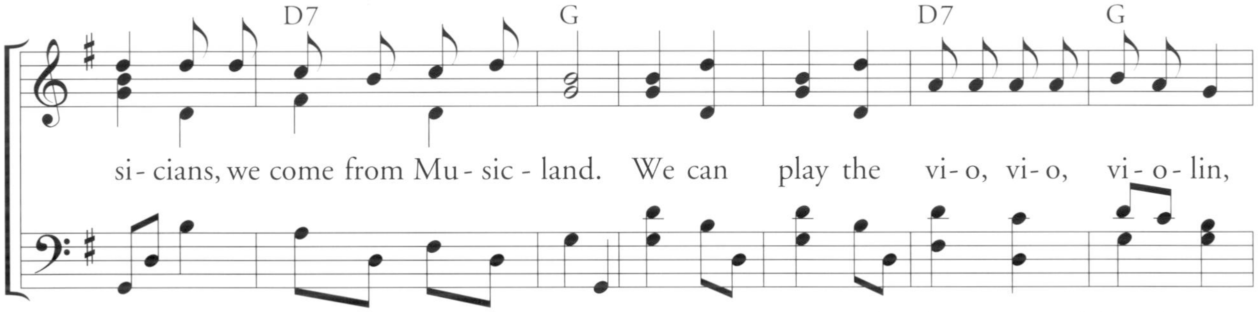

Everyone stops and couple A faces two more children (couple B).
All four imitate playing a violin, cello, and a flute.

D7   G

we can play the cel - lo and the flute. And we can dance and sing fa - la - la,

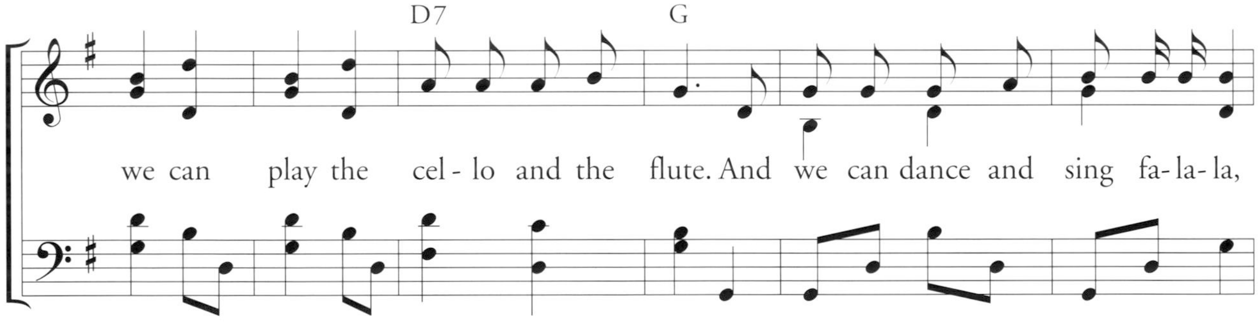

Couples A and B skip around holding hands while
those in the circle clap.

D7   G   D7   G

sing fa - la la, sing fa - la la, and we can dance and sing fa - la - la, fa - la - la.

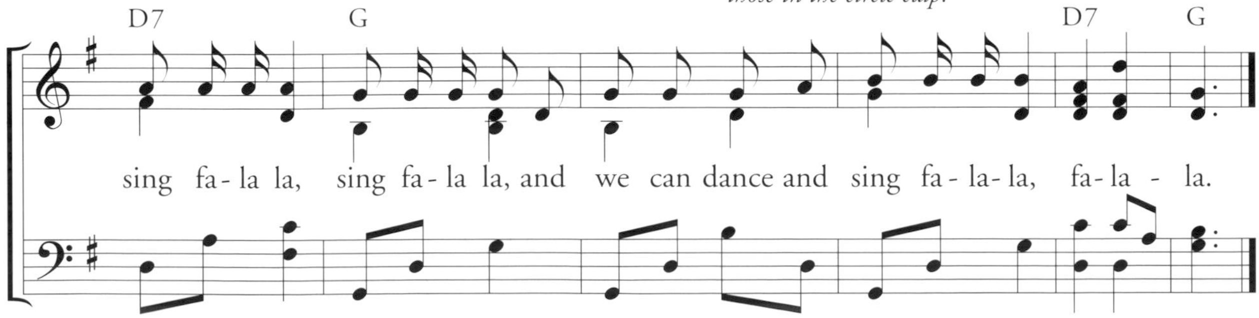

For repeat of dance, couple A returns to circle and is replaced by couple B.

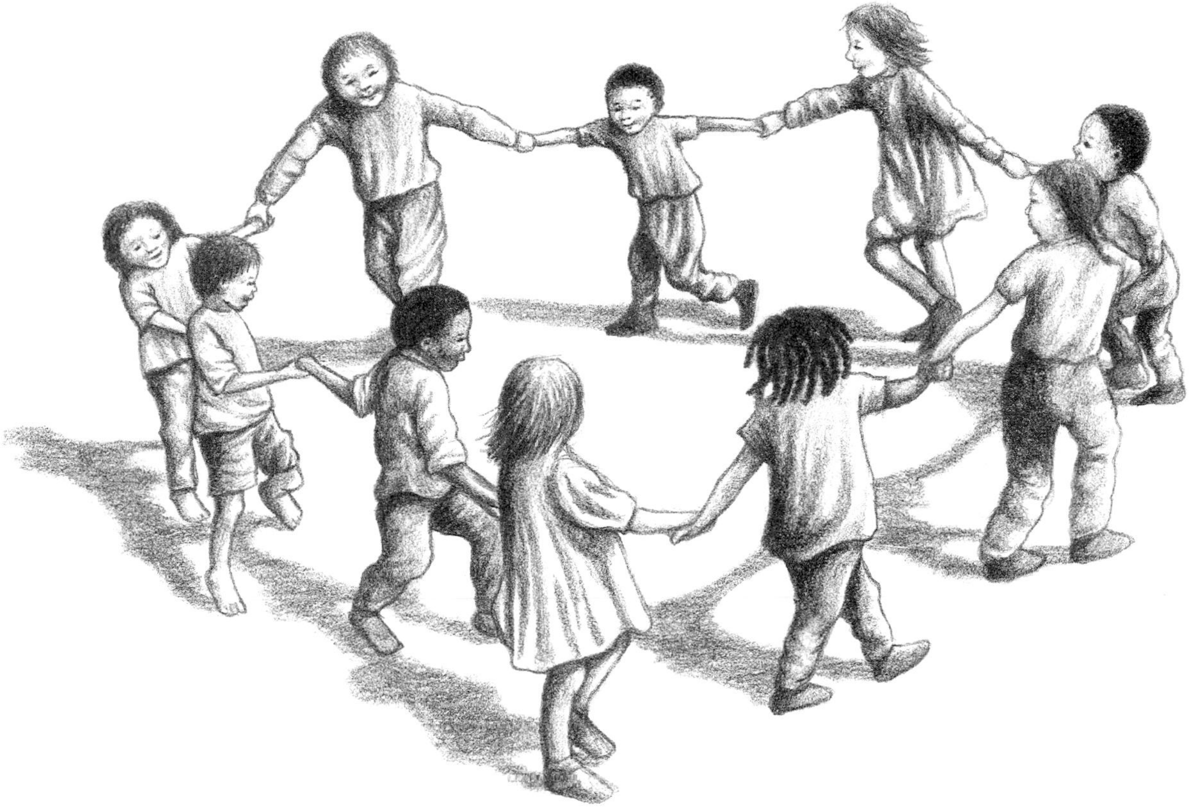

Wind the Bobbin

Danish

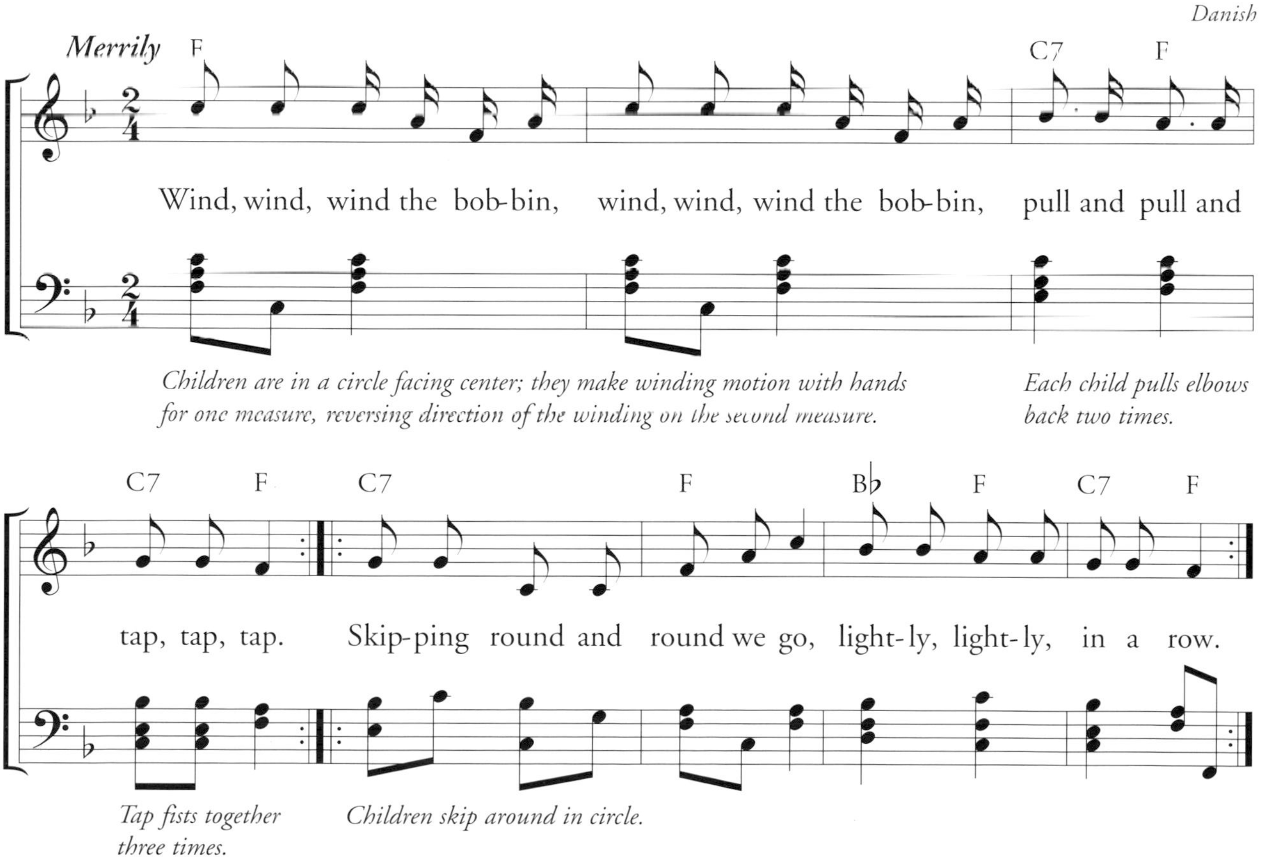

Merrily

Wind, wind, wind the bob-bin, wind, wind, wind the bob-bin, pull and pull and

Children are in a circle facing center; they make winding motion with hands for one measure, reversing direction of the winding on the second measure.

Each child pulls elbows back two times.

tap, tap, tap. Skip-ping round and round we go, light-ly, light-ly, in a row.

Tap fists together three times.

Children skip around in circle.

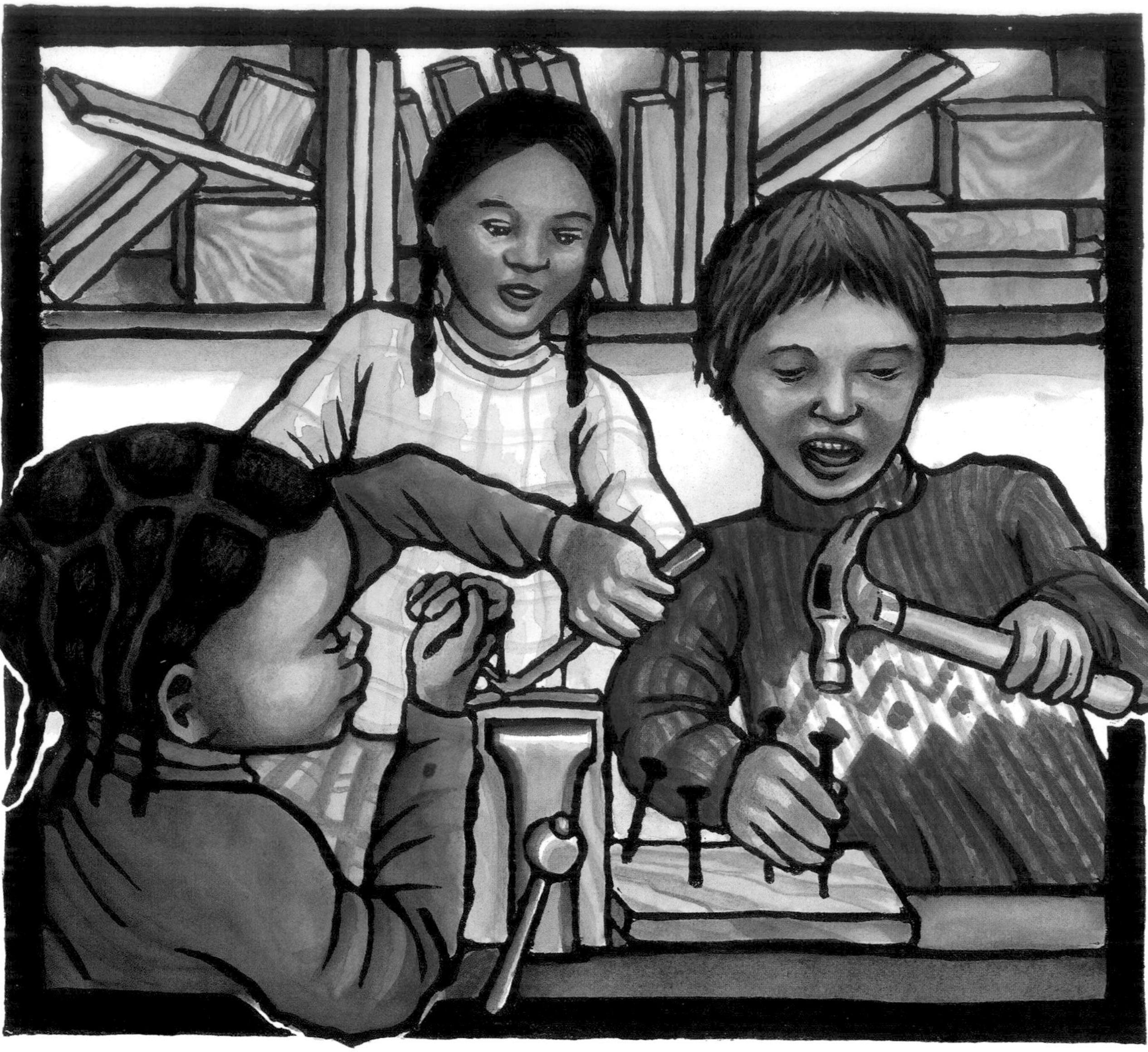

🎵 The Carpenters

Several carpenters are in the center of the circle. They make motions and all the children
imitate them. Additional verses can be added such as farmers, painters, etc.

Puerto Rican Folk Song

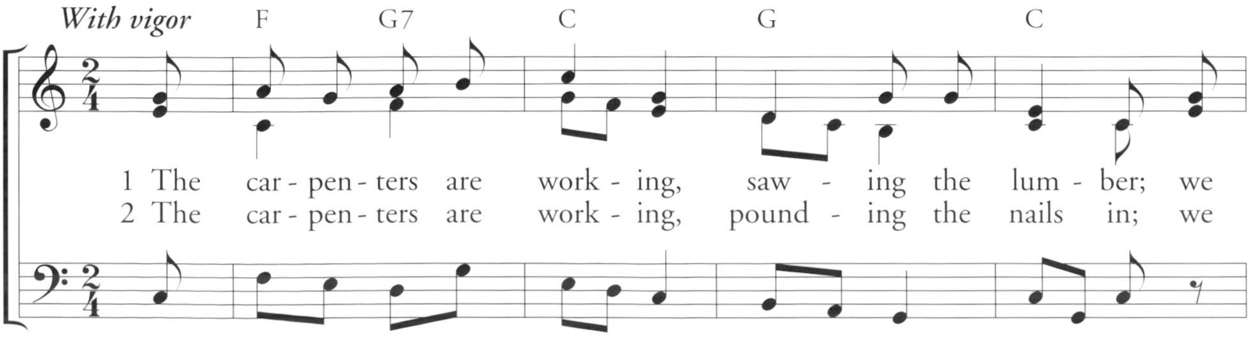

1 The car-pen-ters are work-ing, saw-ing the lum-ber; we
2 The car-pen-ters are work-ing, pound-ing the nails in; we

love to watch them work - ing, saw - ing the lum - ber.
love to watch them work - ing, pound - ing the nails in.

They go *see*, we go *saw*, they go *see*, we go *saw*, un -
They go *bang*, we go *clang*, they go *bang*, we go *clang*, un -

til we've sawed the___ lum - ber. Fin - ished at last!
til we've pound ed the nails in. Fin - ished at last!

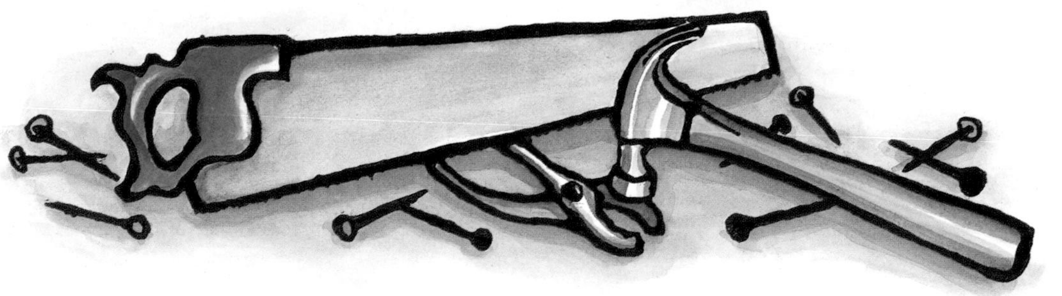

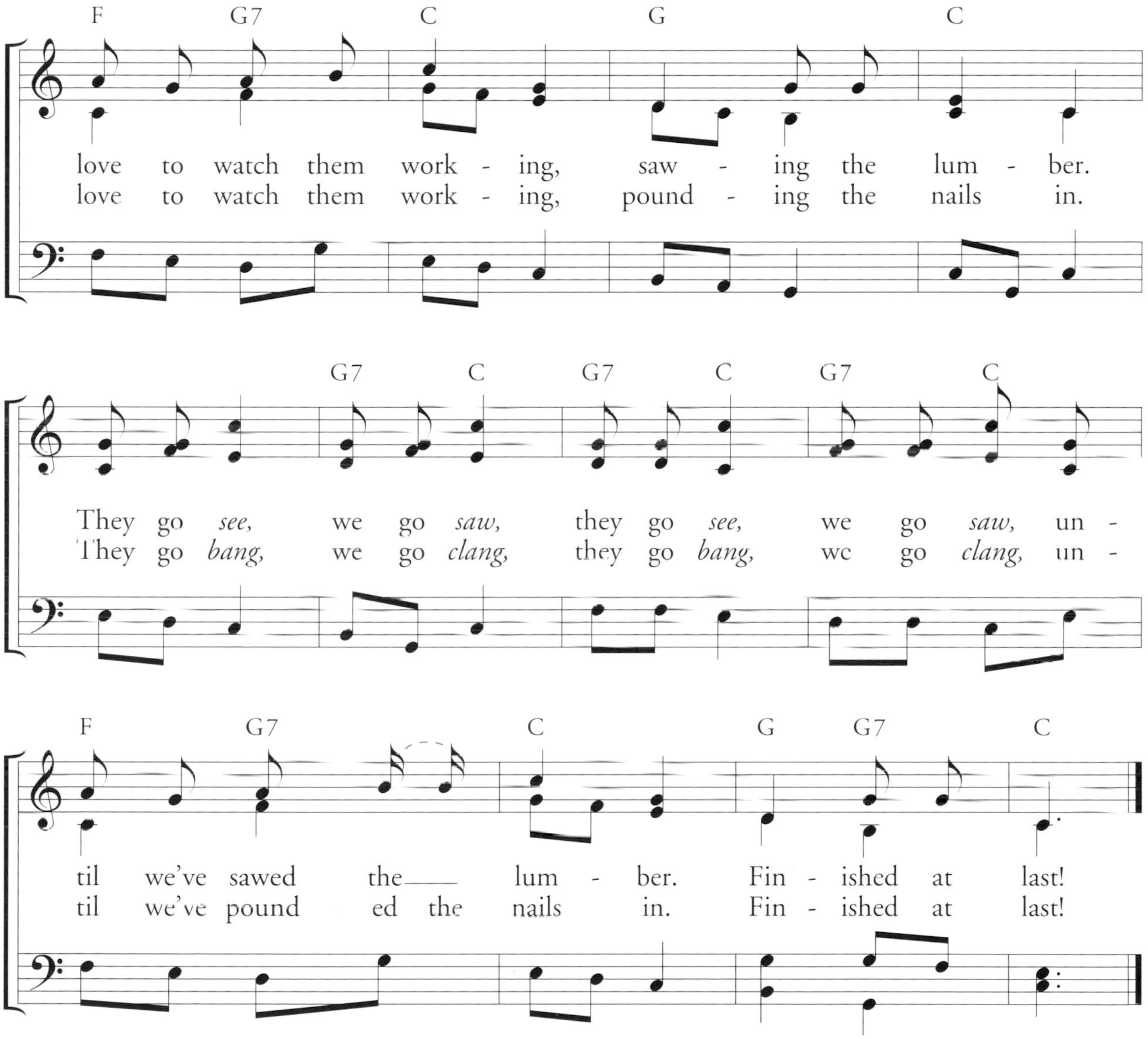

3. O see the masons working,
   mixing the mortar;
   we love to watch them working,
   mixing the mortar.
   They go *swish*, we go *swoosh*,
   they go *swish*, we go *swoosh*,
   until we've mixed the mortar.
   Finished at last!

4. O see the masons working,
   putting the bricks in;
   we love to watch them working,
   putting the bricks in.
   They go *clink*, we go *clank*,
   they go *clink*, we go *clank*,
   until we've put the bricks in.
   Finished at last!

Brother, Come and Dance with Me

Following the text, create a simple partner dance with this song.

From Hansel and Gretel
by Engelbert Humperdinck

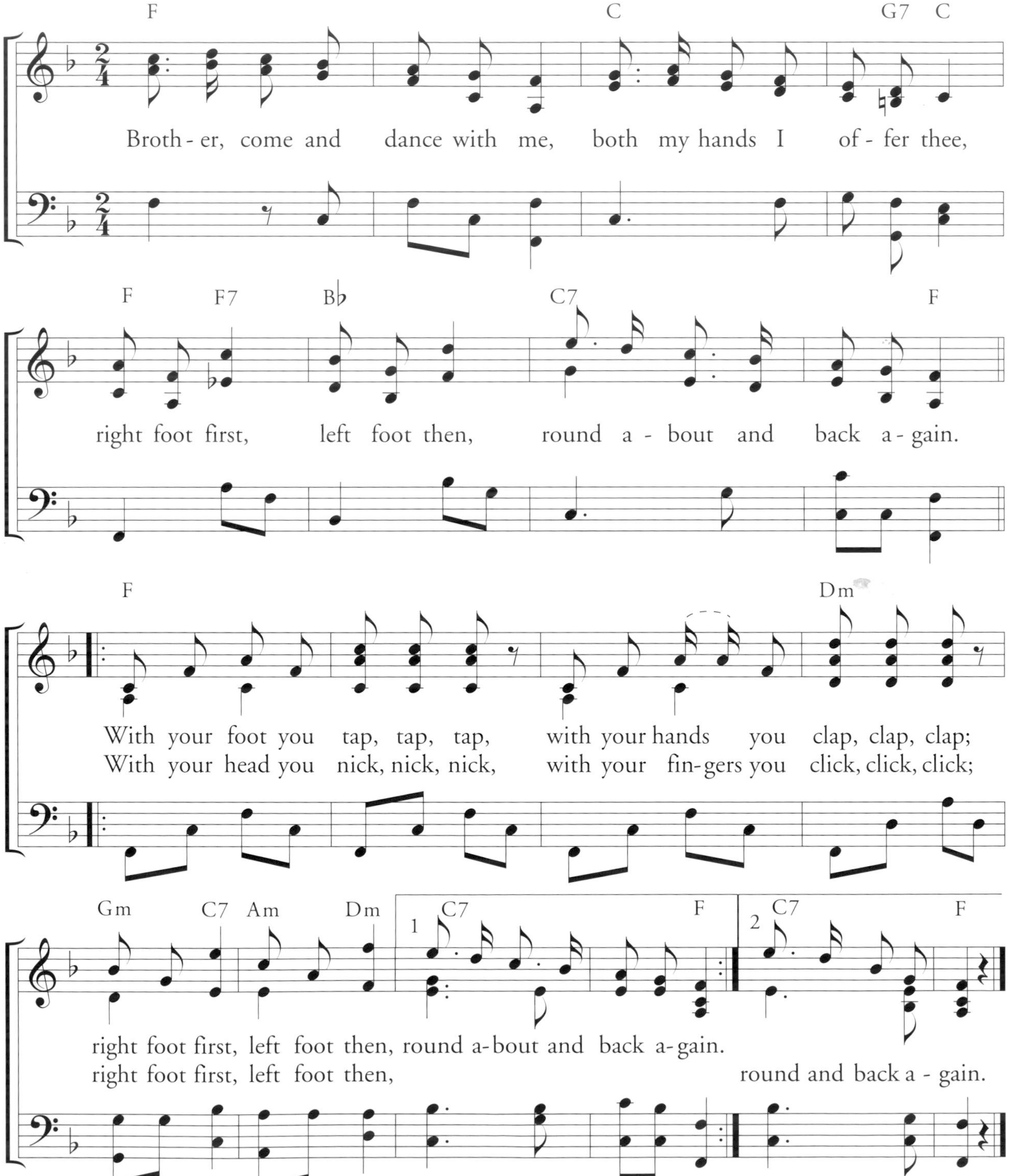

Broth-er, come and dance with me, both my hands I of-fer thee,

right foot first, left foot then, round a-bout and back a-gain.

With your foot you tap, tap, tap, with your hands you clap, clap, clap;
With your head you nick, nick, nick, with your fin-gers you click, click, click;

right foot first, left foot then, round a-bout and back a-gain.
right foot first, left foot then, round and back a-gain.

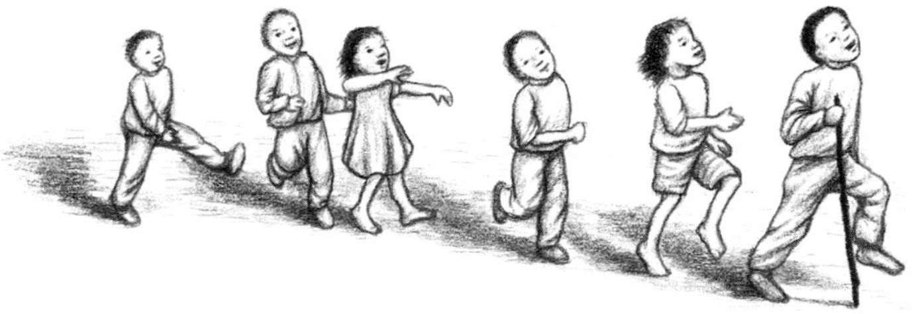

⦿ Stamping Land

Oral Tradition

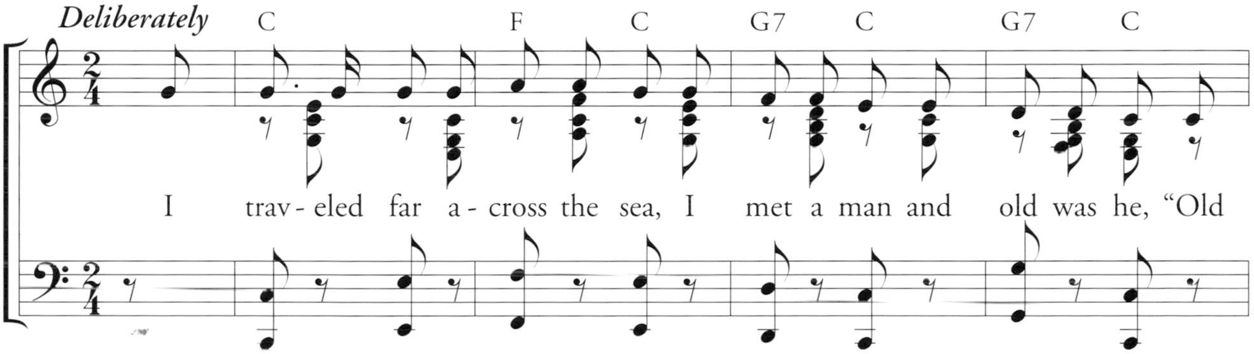

A child chosen to be "it" walks around the inside of the circle. The other children walk around in a circle in the opposite direction.

man," I said, "Where do you live?" And this is what he told me:

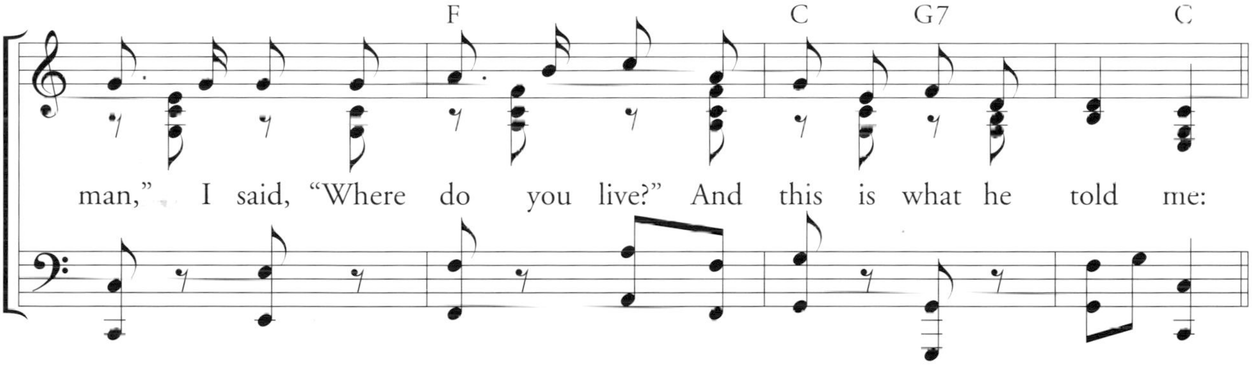

All children stop walking while the "it" shakes his/her finger as if to give instructions.

"Fol - low me to Stamp-ing Land, Stamp-ing Land,— Stamping Land,
All who wish to live with me, Fol - low me to Stamping Land."

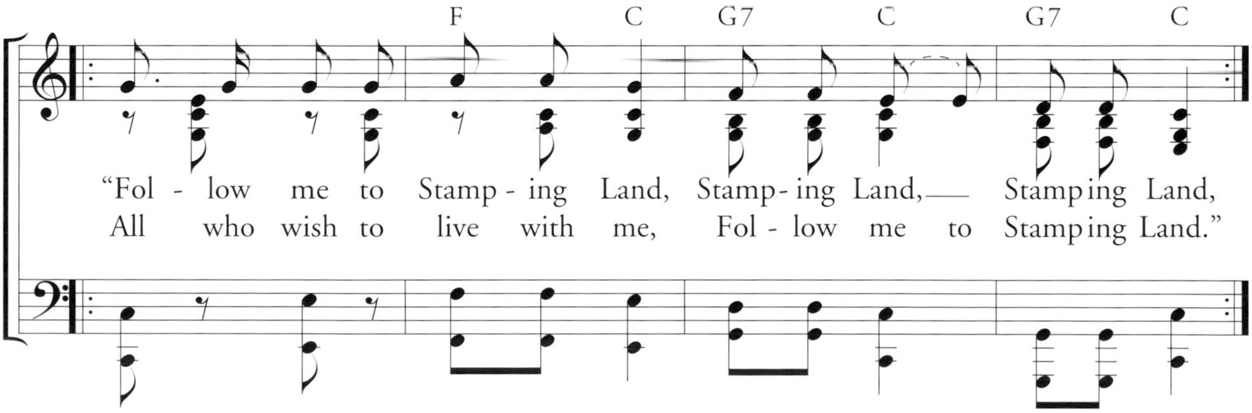

All children go around the circle stamping in the same direction as the "it" in the center.

After you have visited Stamping Land, change the "it" and visit Hopping Land, Tiptoe Land, or whatever the "it" comes up with.

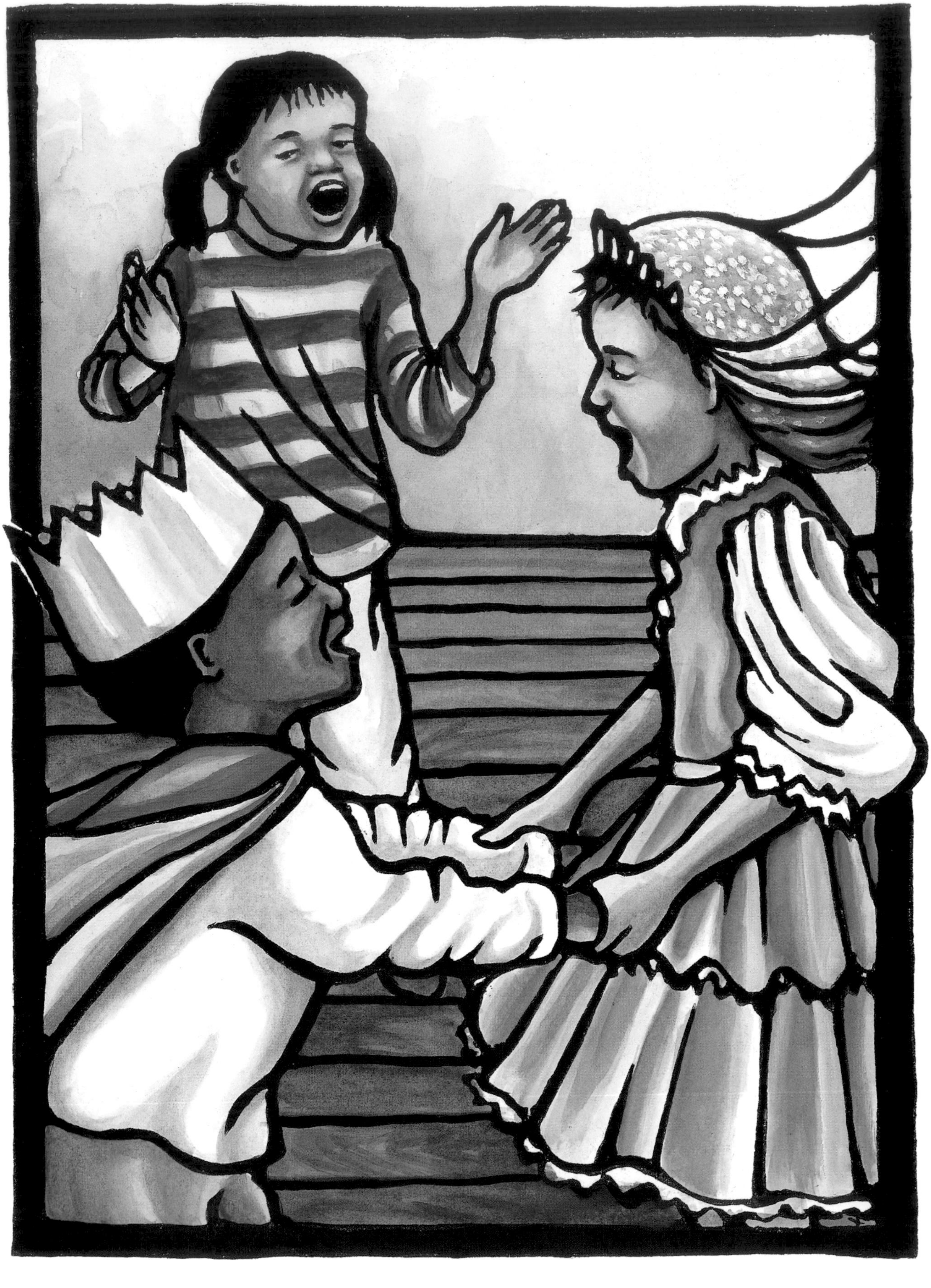

☉ The Princess Was a Lovely Child

Essentially the story of *Sleeping Beauty*, this circle game is a perennial favorite. Add a few simple costumes:
crowns for the prince and princess, a cloak and wand for the wicked fairy.

Old European Singing Game

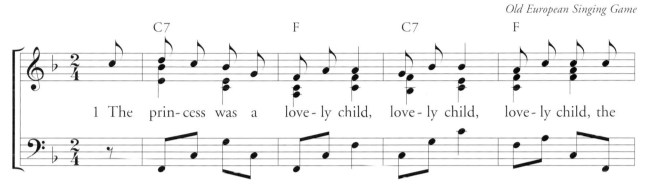

1 The prin-cess was a love-ly child, love-ly child, love-ly child, the

The princess stands alone in the center of the circle of children.

prin-cess was a love-ly child, love-ly child.

2. She lived high in a castle tall, castle tall…

    (Children in circle unclasp hands and raise them high over their heads.)

3. There came a wicked fairy by, fairy by…

    (Children join hands. Child selected to be the wicked fairy goes around the outside of the circle, then enters.)

4. "O princess, sleep a hundred years, hundred years…"

    (Wicked fairy sings and casts spell over the princess, who falls asleep.)

5. A big high hedge grew all around, all around…

    (Children in circle, keeping hands joined, raise arms high.)

6. A gallant prince came riding by, riding by…

    (Child selected to be the prince rides around the outside of the circle.)

7. He chopped down the big high hedge, big high hedge…

    (Prince "chops down hedge" by unclasping the joined hands of the children.)

8. "O princess, wake and be my bride, be my bride…"

    (Prince enters the circle and sings to the princess.)

9. So everybody's happy now, happy now…

    (Prince and princess dance together, while circle around them skips with joined hands.)

In and Out the Bonnie Bluebells

Old English Singing Game

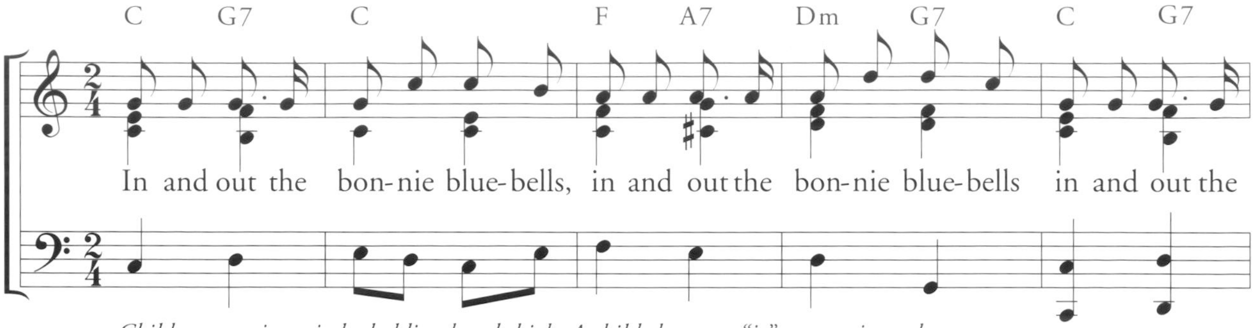

Children start in a circle, holding hands high. A child chosen as "it" weaves in and out.

In and out the bon-nie blue-bells, in and out the bon-nie blue-bells in and out the bon-nie blue-bells, for you are my part-ner. Pit-ter, pat-ter, pit-ter, pat-ter

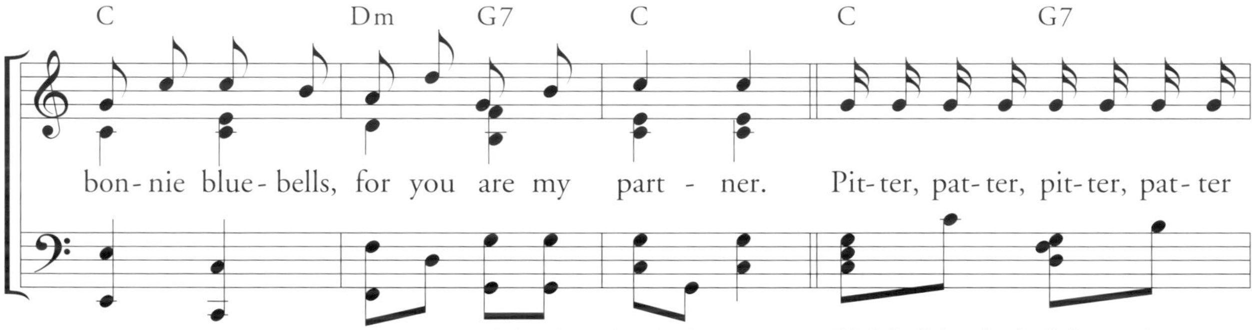

The "it" stops behind another child in the circle.

With both hands, the "it" taps alternate shoulders of the child in front of him/her.

on your shoul-der; pit-ter, pat-ter, pit-ter, pat-ter, on your shoul-der;

pit-ter, pat-ter, pit-ter, pat-ter on your shoul-der, for you are my part-ner.

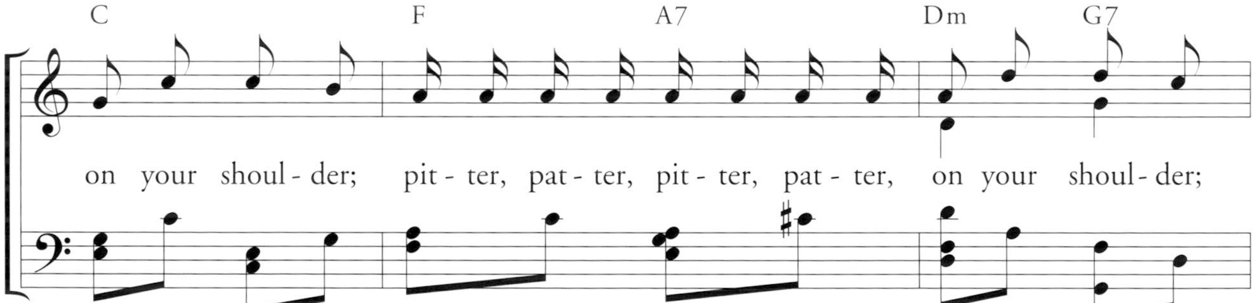

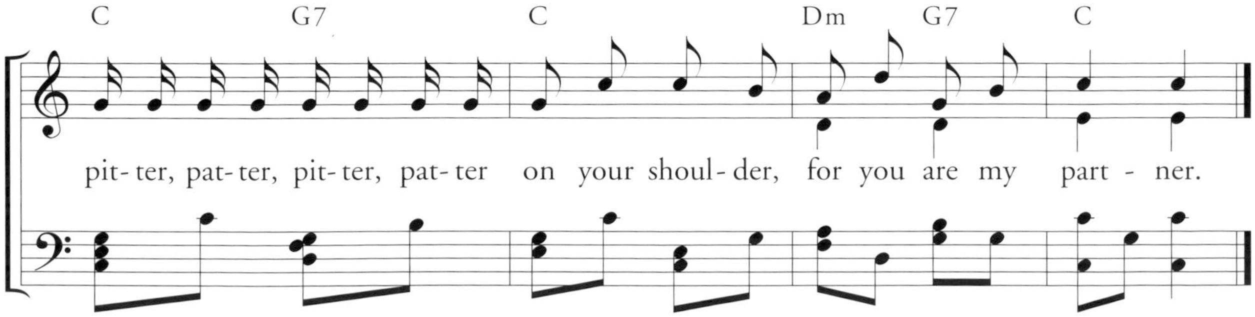

On the repeat of the dance, the two children ("it" and partner holding hands) weave in and out of the circle and step behind two consecutive children. On the next repeat the four children weave in and out. The dance continues until all children are following the "it."

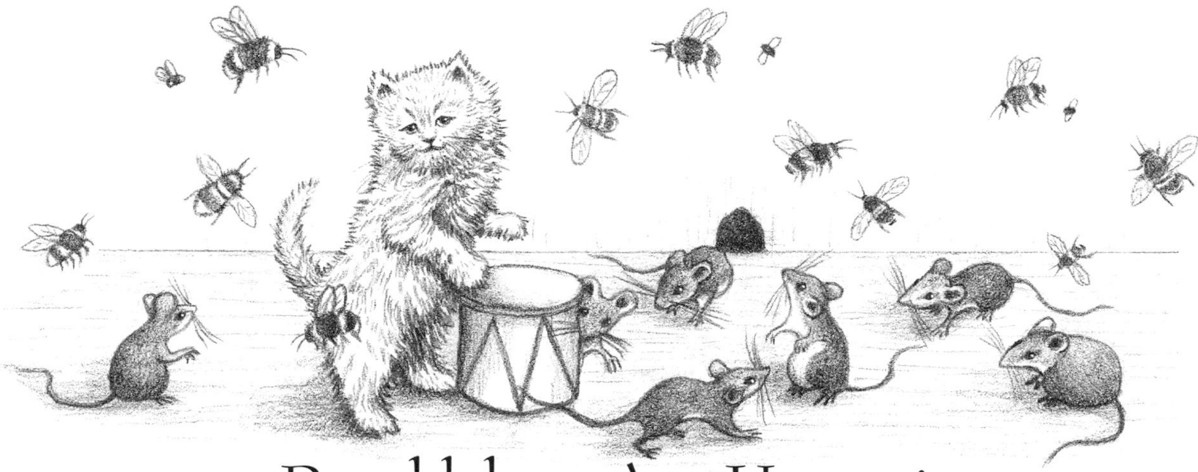

🔘 Bumblebees Are Humming

Let children act out the creature of their choice: a bee, cat, or mouse. Bees buzz to and fro, cats prowl,
and mice scamper. As the dynamic level rises (and it will) have the children dance faster and faster
until BOOM! BOOM! – everyone falls down.

Translated from the Swedish
by Maisie Radford

Words and Music
Alice Tegner

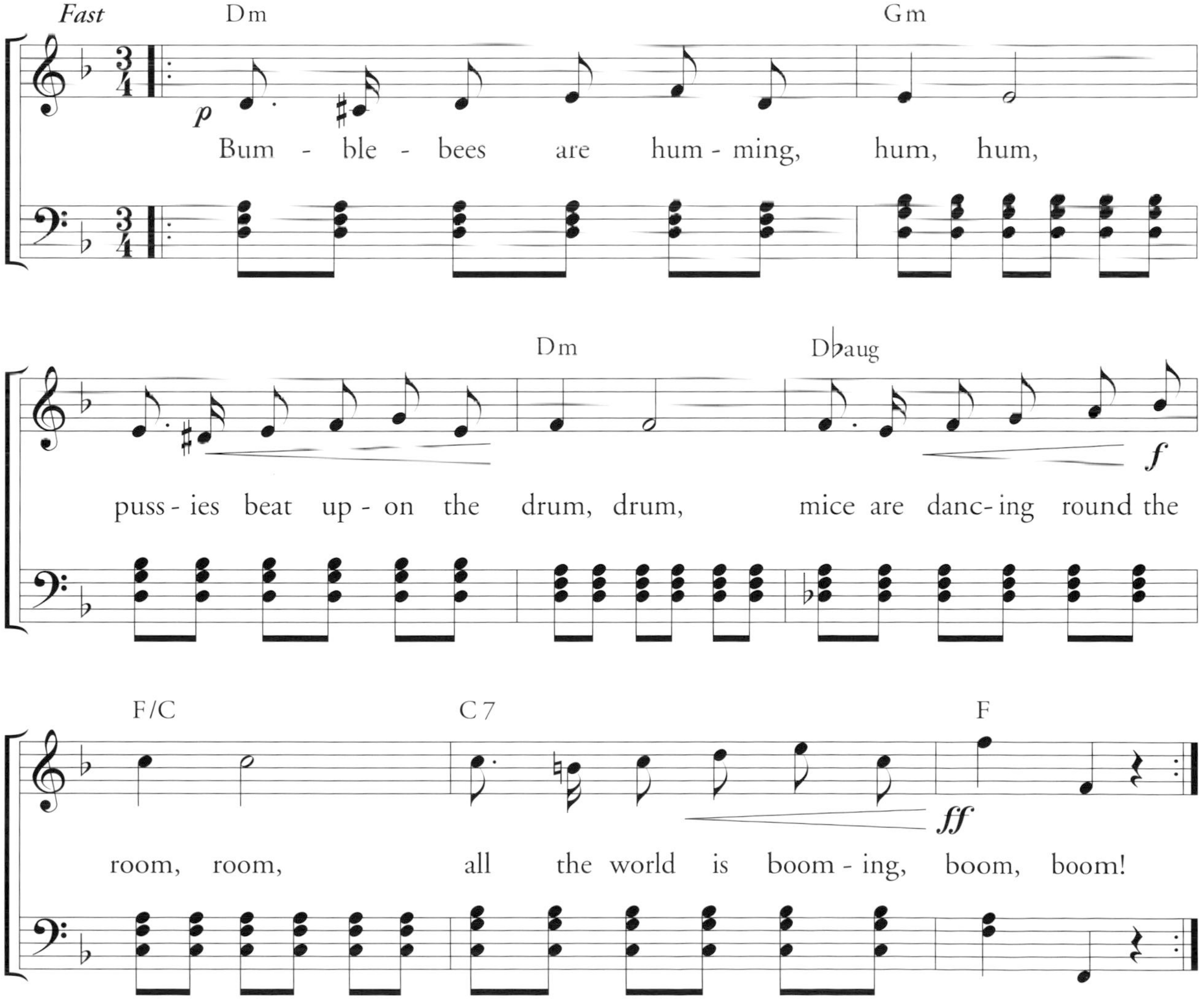

Bum - ble - bees are hum - ming, hum, hum,

puss - ies beat up - on the drum, drum, mice are danc - ing round the

room, room, all the world is boom - ing, boom, boom!

Old Roger Lay Down

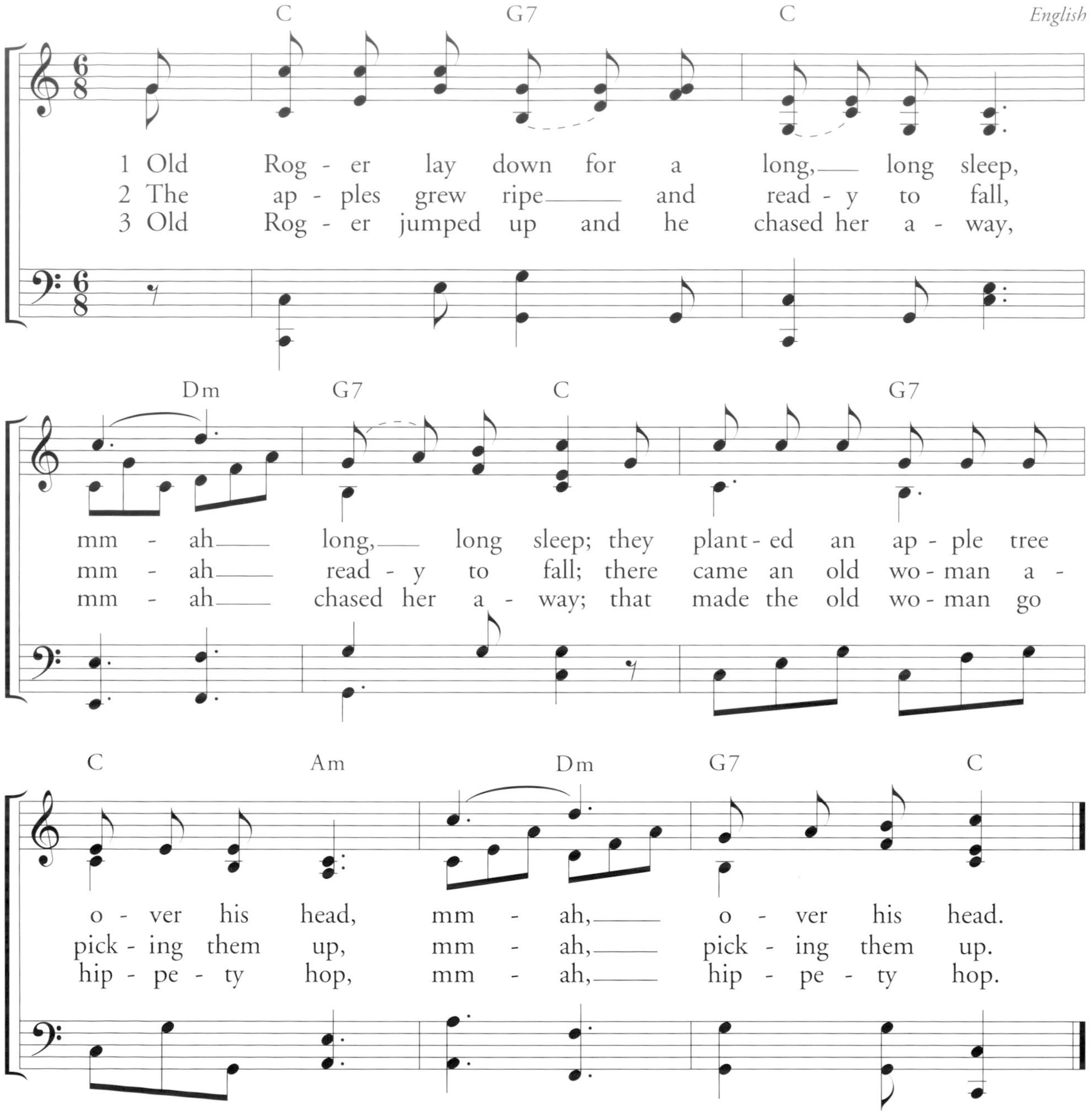

English

1 Old Rog - er lay down for a long,— long sleep,
2 The ap - ples grew ripe—— and read - y to fall,
3 Old Rog - er jumped up and he chased her a - way,

mm - ah—— long,— long sleep; they plant - ed an ap - ple tree
mm - ah—— read - y to fall; there came an old wo - man a -
mm - ah—— chased her a - way; that made the old wo - man go

o - ver his head, mm - ah,—— o - ver his head.
pick - ing them up, mm - ah,—— pick - ing them up.
hip - pe - ty hop, mm - ah,—— hip - pe - ty hop.

1. *Children hold hands and walk in a circle while a child chosen to be old Roger lies down in the center.*

2. *A child chosen to be the apple tree stands at old Roger's head, spreading his/her arms like branches. An old woman waits outside the circle, then comes and pretends to pick up apples off the ground.*

3. *Old Roger jumps up and chases her around the circle.(Remind children that elderly people do not run, but hobble.)*

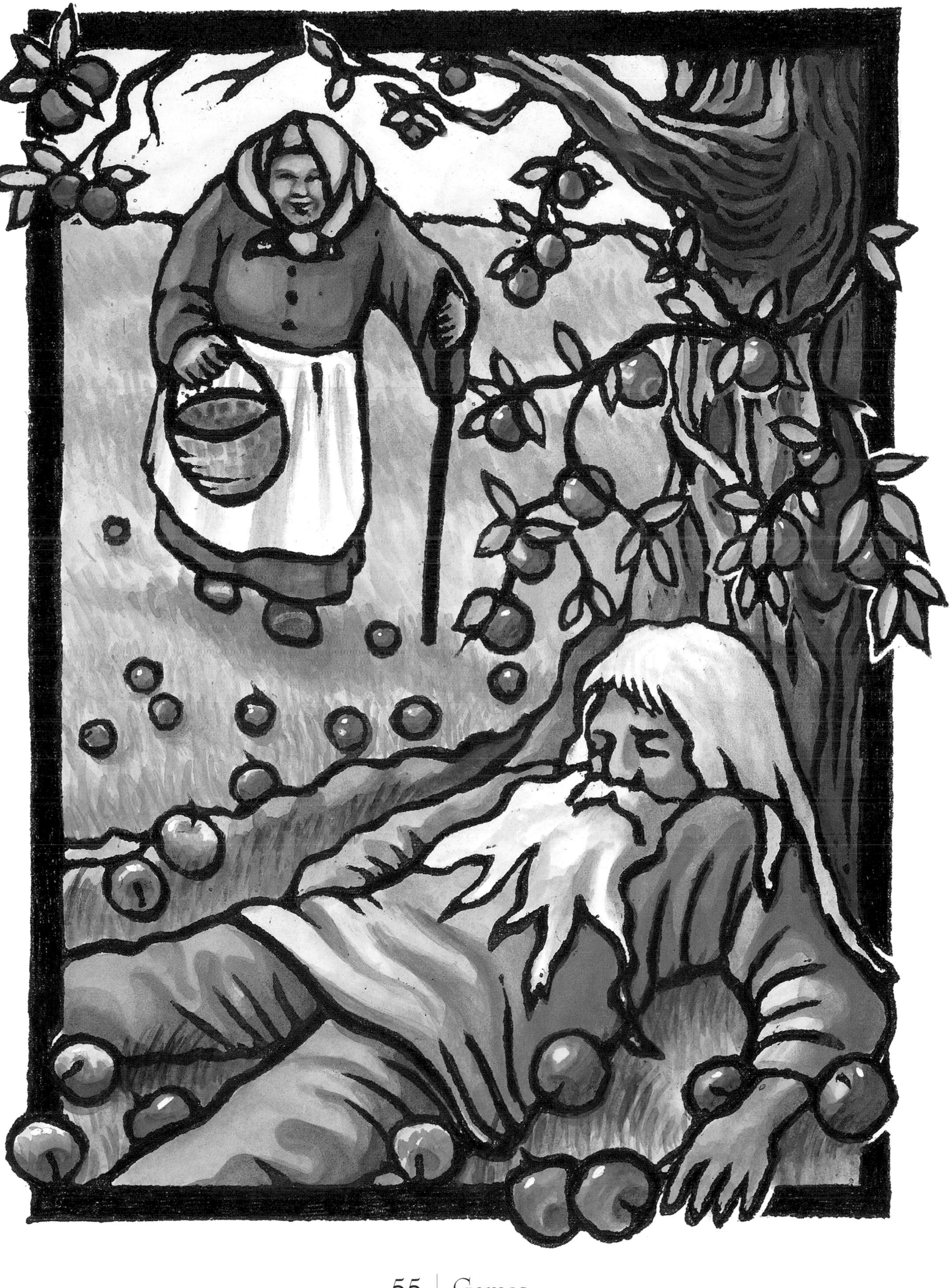

All Who Born in January

This song makes a perfect circle game. Have the birthday children for each month
step to the center for their verse and dance while the rest of the class stands
and claps. Make up a different musical movement for each month.

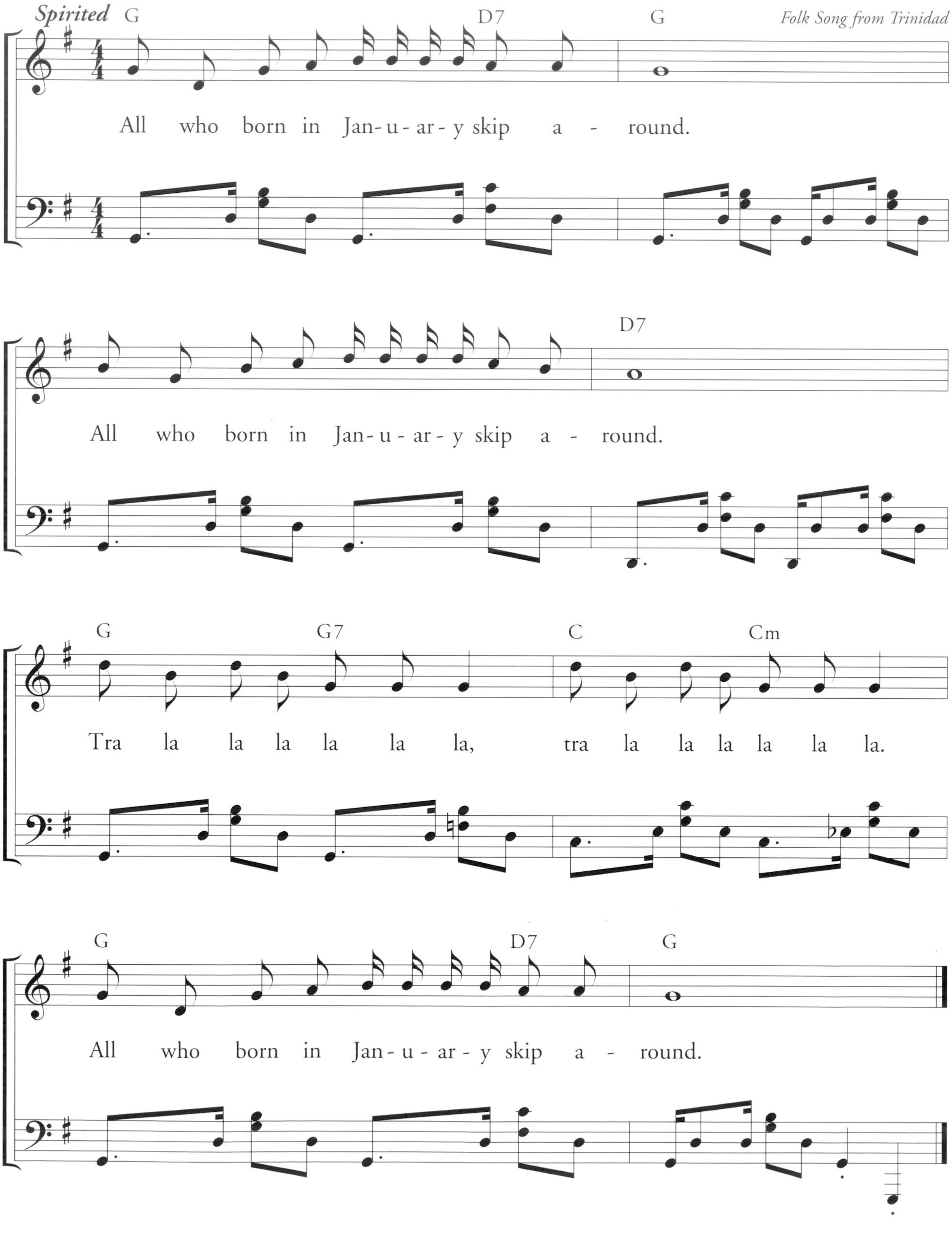

Spirited   *Folk Song from Trinidad*

All who born in Jan-u-ar-y skip a - round.

All who born in Jan-u-ar-y skip a - round.

Tra la la la la la la, tra la la la la la la.

All who born in Jan-u-ar-y skip a - round.

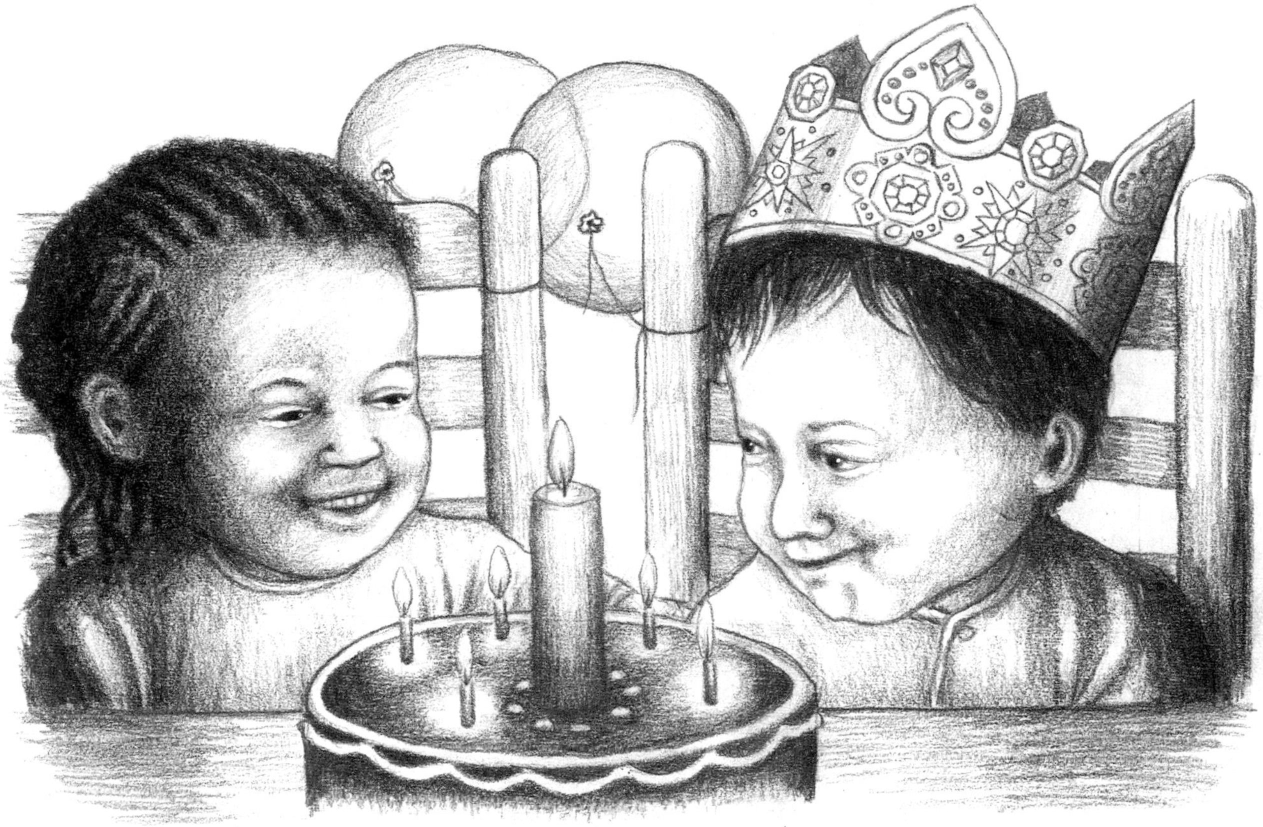

The Counting Birthday Song

Oral Tradition

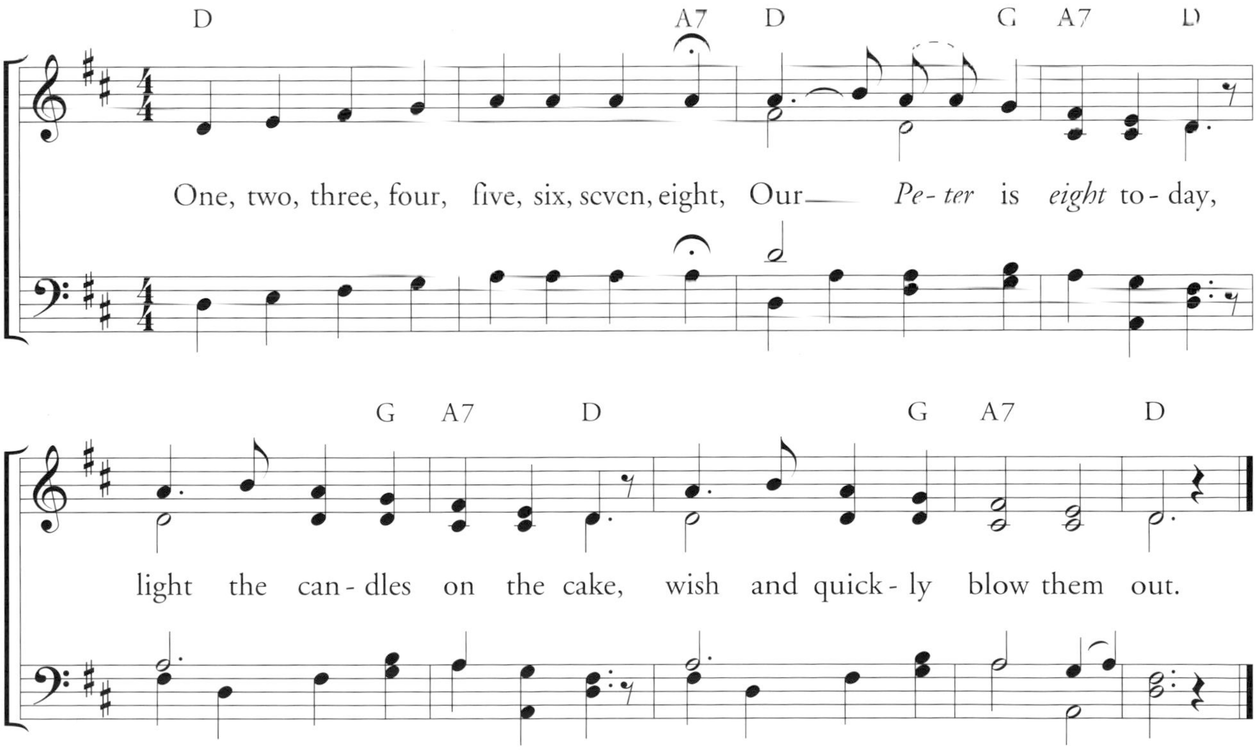

One, two, three, four, five, six, seven, eight, Our— Pe-ter is eight to-day,

light the can-dles on the cake, wish and quick-ly blow them out.

Count until you reach the birthday child's age. After "holding"
on that number, finish the song while the candles are blown out.

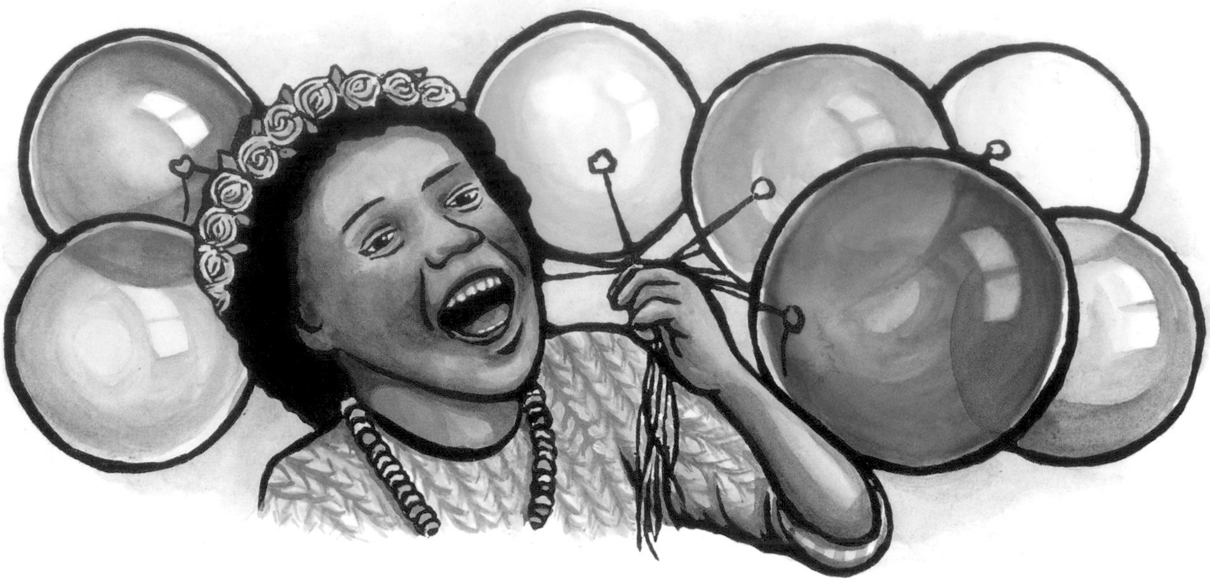

Happy Birthday

Oral Tradition

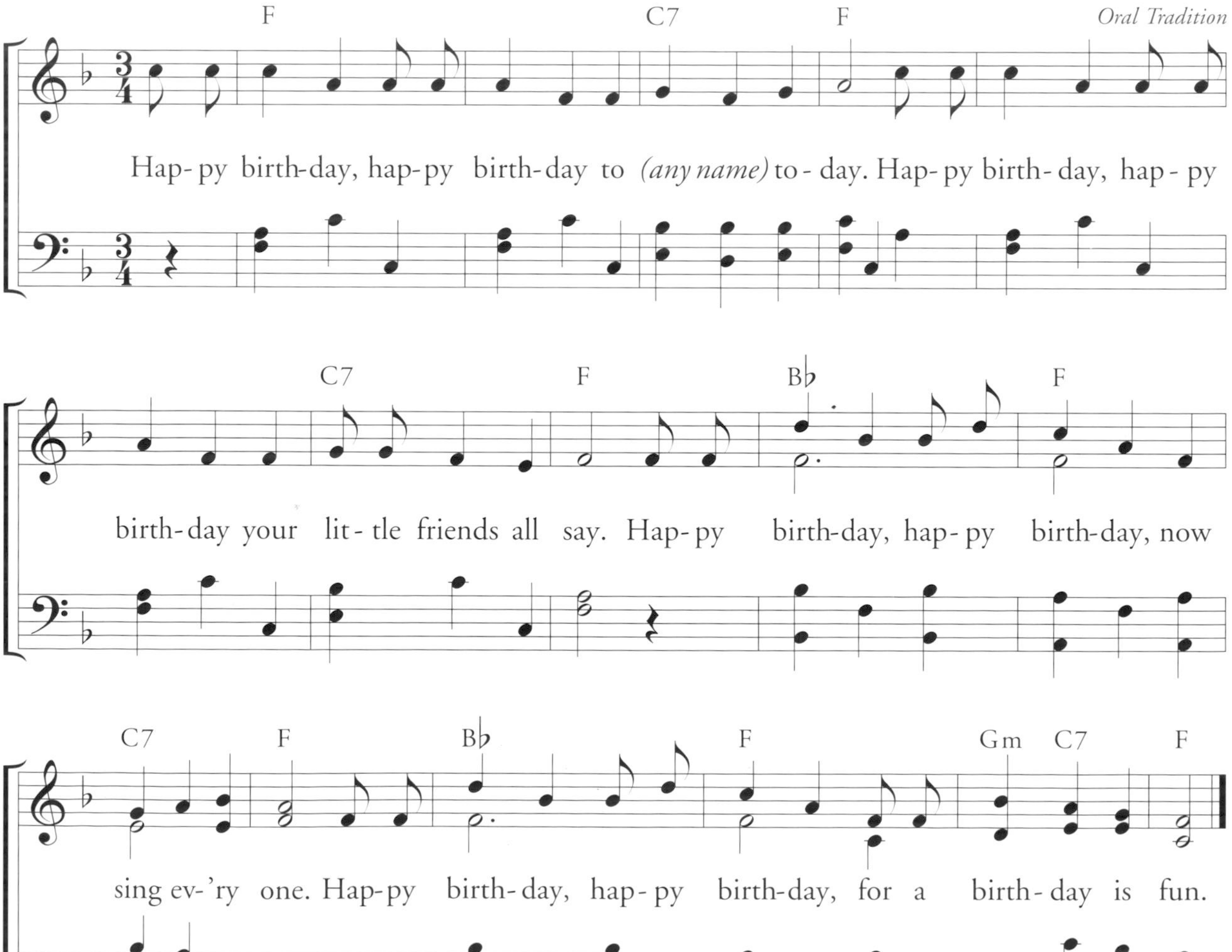

Hap-py birth-day, hap-py birth-day to *(any name)* to-day. Hap-py birth-day, hap-py

birth-day your lit-tle friends all say. Hap-py birth-day, hap-py birth-day, now

sing ev-'ry one. Hap-py birth-day, hap-py birth-day, for a birth-day is fun.

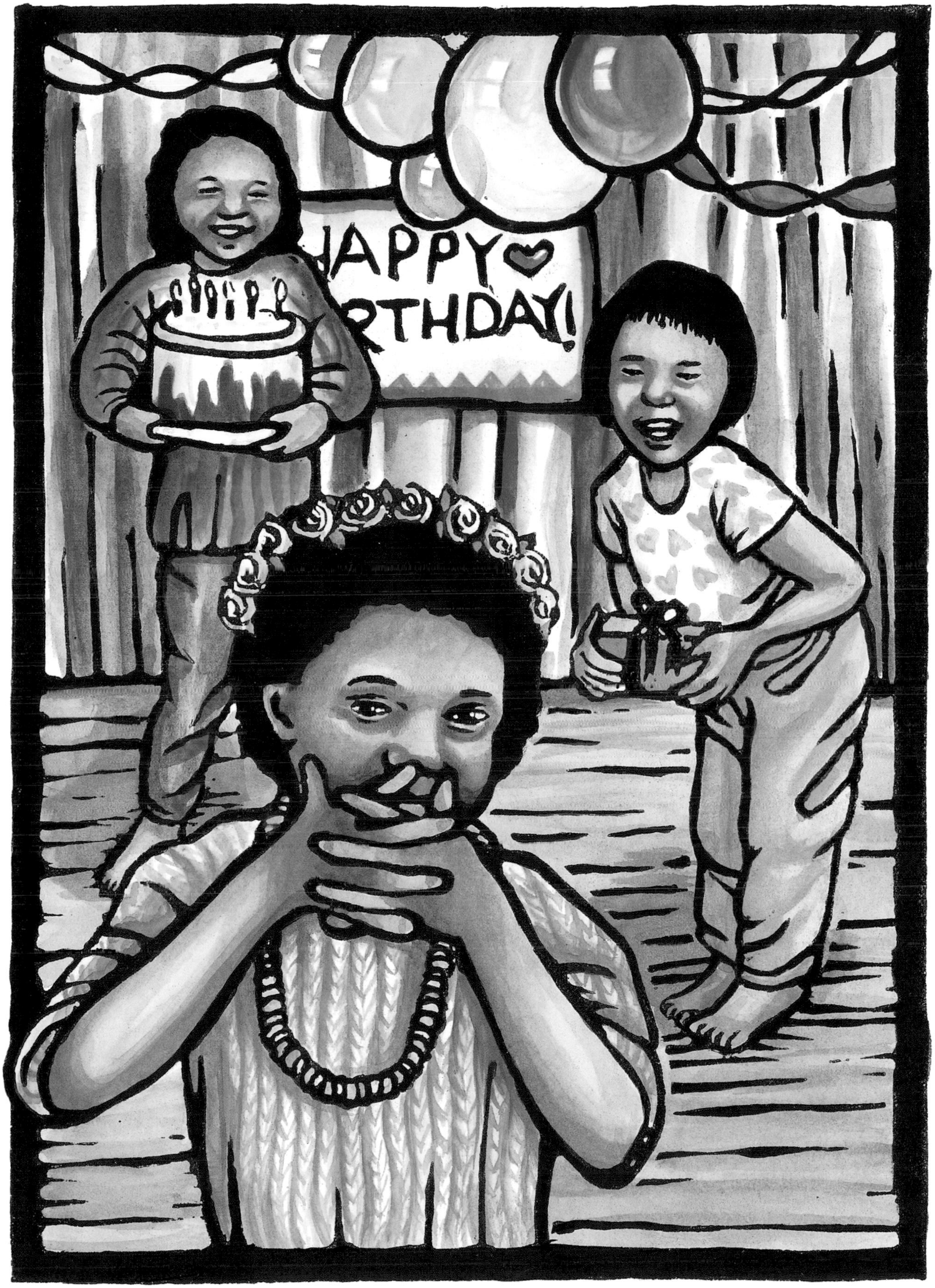
HAPPY
RTHDAY!

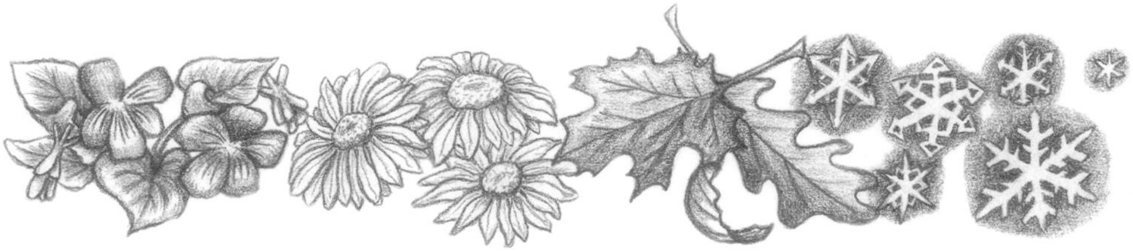

Seasons Birthday Song

Jane Tyson Clement

Marlys Swinger

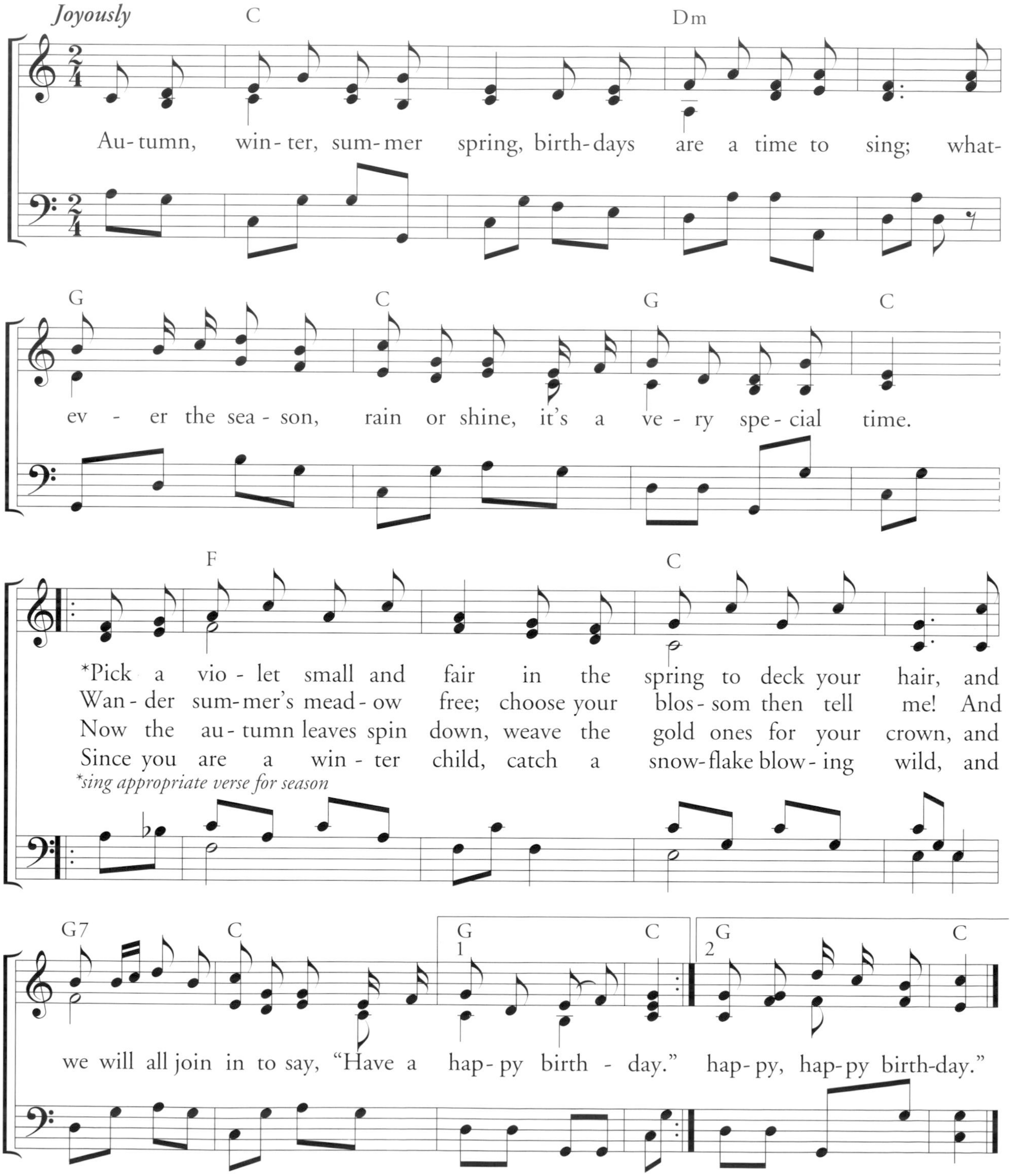

Joyously

Au-tumn, win-ter, sum-mer spring, birth-days are a time to sing; what-

ev-er the sea-son, rain or shine, it's a ve-ry spe-cial time.

*Pick a vio-let small and fair in the spring to deck your hair, and
Wan-der sum-mer's mead-ow free; choose your blos-som then tell me! And
Now the au-tumn leaves spin down, weave the gold ones for your crown, and
Since you are a win-ter child, catch a snow-flake blow-ing wild, and

*sing appropriate verse for season

we will all join in to say, "Have a hap-py birth-day." hap-py, hap-py birth-day."

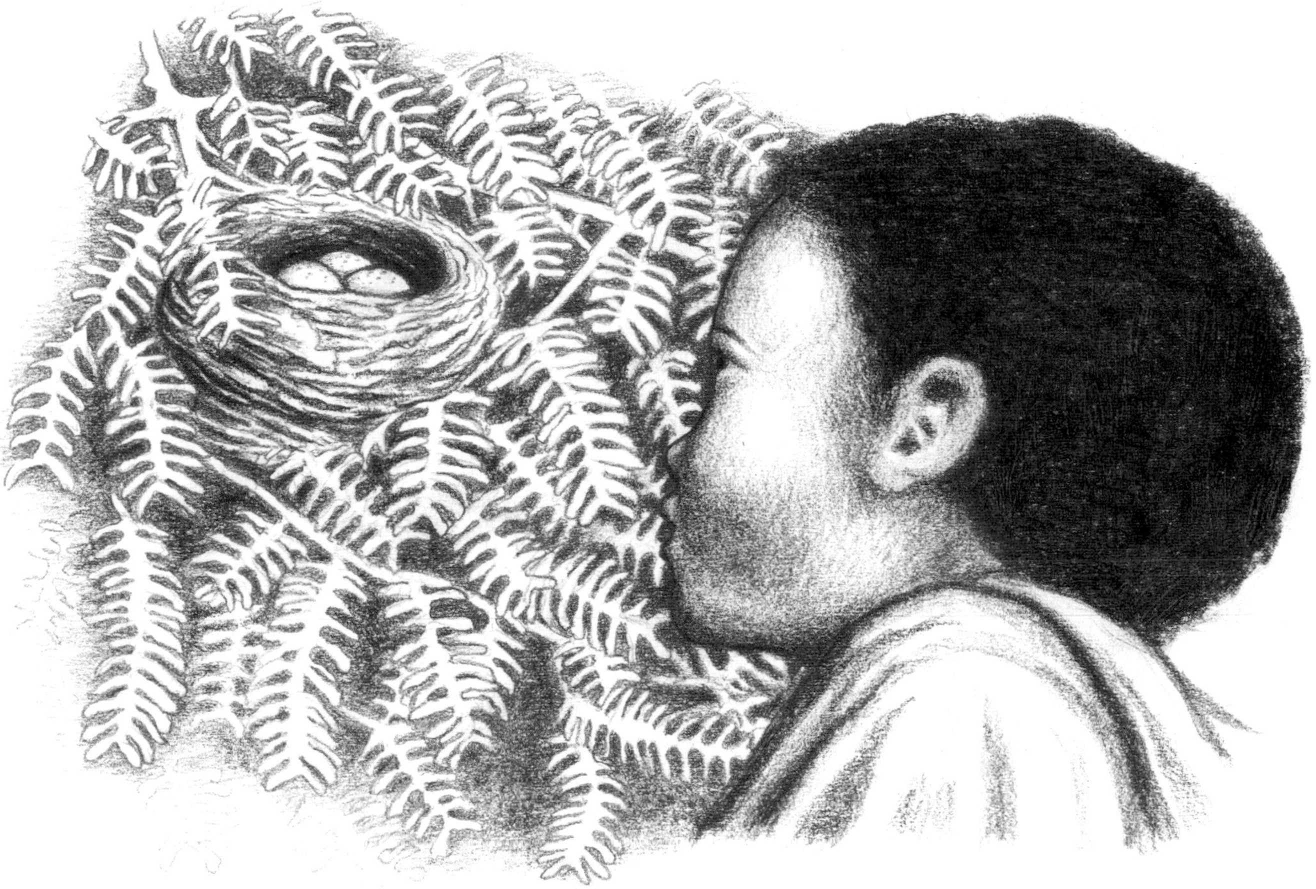

The Earth Needs the Raindrops

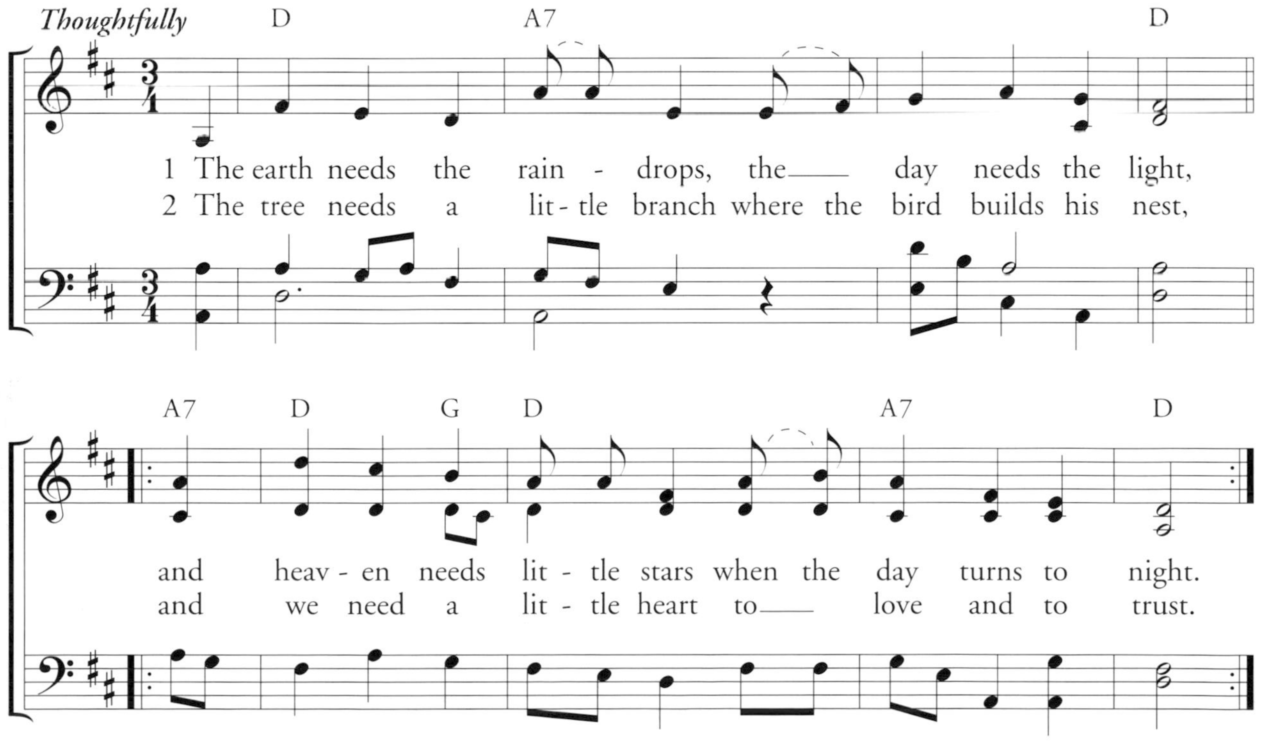

J. Kurtsch

A. Wagner

Thoughtfully

1 The earth needs the rain - drops, the___ day needs the light,
2 The tree needs a lit - tle branch where the bird builds his nest,

and heav - en needs lit - tle stars when the day turns to night.
and we need a lit - tle heart to__ love and to trust.

Pit, Pat, Pat

*Translated from the Swedish
by Maisie Radford*

Alice Tegner

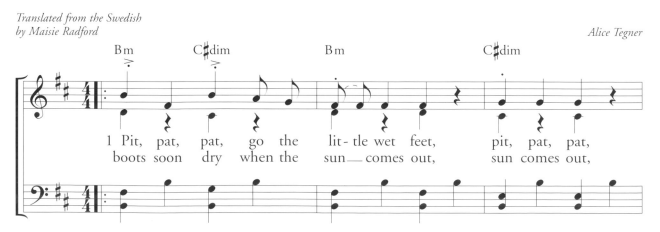

1 Pit, pat, pat, go the lit-tle wet feet,
boots soon dry when the sun— comes out,
pit, pat, pat,
sun comes out,

pit, pat, pat; to be out in the rain, what a treat, treat, treat,
sun comes out;_____ moth-er is wait-ing and hears us shout,

pit, pat, pat. For the wet, for the wet, does the chil-dren good,
hears us shout. When we come in at last from a long, long day,

chil-dren good, chil-dren good, when they sing as they walk as all
long, long day, long, long day, we get brown bread and but-ter and

chil-dren should, chil-dren should. 2 Our
curds and whey, curds and whey.

◉ It Rained on Anne

Ivy O. Eastwick   *Marlys Swinger*

It rained on Anne, it rained on Fan, it rained and rained on Ar-a - bel-la,— but it

did not rain on Mar - y Jane, she had a HUGE um - brel-la.——

Repeat ad lib using the names of children in your class.

🎵 Japanese Rain Song

The Japanese origins of this folk song make a perfect opening for discussing Japan and its contribution to our culture. Add bells and rhythm sticks for raindrops, and show your class a globe or map.

Japanese Folk Song

1 Un-der-neath my big um-brel-la I can hear the rain,
2 Un-der-neath my big um-brel-la I can see the sun;

un-der-neath my roof of yel-low sing-ing down the lane.
down I bring my roof of yel-low for the rain is done.

Pi - chi, pi - chi, cha - pu, cha - pu, ran, ran, ran.
Pi - chi, pi - chi, cha - pu, cha - pu, ran, ran, ran.

Rain in the Night

Raise a pansy or another potted flower with your class and assign each child a day to water it.

Amelia Josephine Burr   *Marlys Swinger*

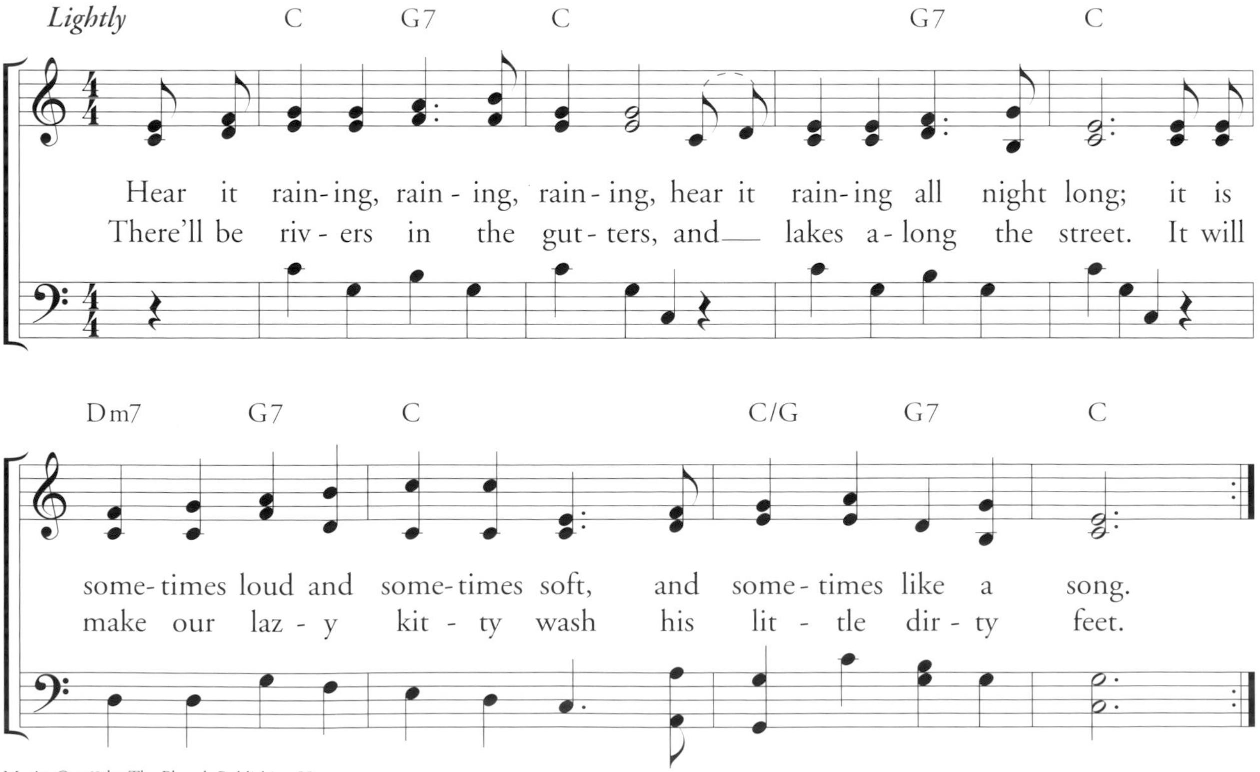

Lightly

Hear it rain-ing, rain-ing, rain-ing, hear it rain-ing all night long; it is
There'll be riv-ers in the gut-ters, and— lakes a-long the street. It will

some-times loud and some-times soft, and some-times like a song.
make our laz-y kit-ty wash his lit-tle dir-ty feet.

E7 Am E7 Am E7 Am
The ros - es will—wear dia-monds like kings and queens—at court; but the
Dm G7 C F G7 C G7
pan-sies all—get mud - dy be - cause they are so short. I will sail my boat to-
C F Dm7 C Dm G7
mor-row in won - der - ful new plac - es, but first I'll take— my
C F Dm7 G7 C F G7 C
wa - t'ring can and wash the pan-sies' fac - es, and wash the pan - sies' fac-es.

The Sun

John Drinkwater

Marlys Swinger

Cheerily

I told the Sun that I was glad, I'm sure I don't know why; some-how the pleas-ant way he had of shin-ing in the sky, just put a no-tion in my head that would-n't it be fun if, walk-ing on the hill, I said, "I'm hap-py" to the Sun.

Music: © 1968 by The Plough Publishing House.

🎵 White Sheep

If clouds can be sheep, they can surely be other things as well. Study the sky
with your children and discover other animals and shapes.

Unknown   *Marlys Swinger*

White sheep, white sheep, on a blue hill, when the wind stops

you all stand still. When the wind blows you walk a-way slow.

White sheep, white sheep, where do you go?

☉ Boats Sail on the Rivers

All children love rainbows. After learning this song, spend some time coloring rainbows.

Christina Rossetti   *Marlys Swinger*

Smoothly C

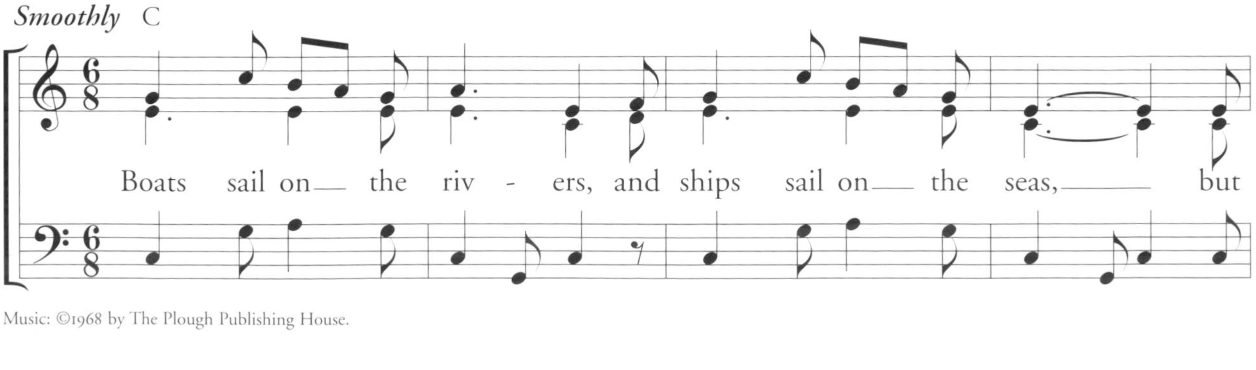

Boats   sail on — the   riv - ers,   and ships   sail on — the   seas, ____ but

Music: ©1968 by The Plough Publishing House.

Dm7 G7 C Am C/G G7 C
clouds that sail a - cross the sky are pret - ti - er far than these. There are
bridg - es on the riv - ers as pret ty as you please, but the
Dm7 G7 C F
bow that bridg - es heav - en and o - ver - tops the trees and
Dm7 C/G Am Dm7 G7 C
builds a road from earth to sky is pret - ti - er far than these.

⊙ Who Loves the Wind on a Stormy Night

Have children bring in scarves to twirl as they dance around the room and enact a whistling wind.

Mysteriously   Dm   A7   *Unknown*

mp

1 Who   loves   the   wind   on   a   storm - y   night,   when
2 He   rocks   the   nests   in   the   tree - tops   high   and
3 When   snow - drops make   their   tim - id   show   and

Dm A7
curtains are drawn and fires are bright? He
blows the kites right up in the sky; he
cold March winds be - gin to blow, we
Dm Cdim Gm A
cresc.
roars down the chim - ney, the win - dows he shakes, and
fills the sails of the ships so fine and
know that in spite of the wind and the rain that
Dm Gm Dm A Dm
ff
all round the house such an up - roar he makes. Ooh
dries the wash - ing hung out on the line.
sum - mer will soon be here a - gain.
A7 Dm Dm/A A7 Dm
dim.
p
ooh ooh ooh says the wind.

Hi, Thunder! 'Lo, Thunder!

*Words and music
by children of the
Macedonia Community*

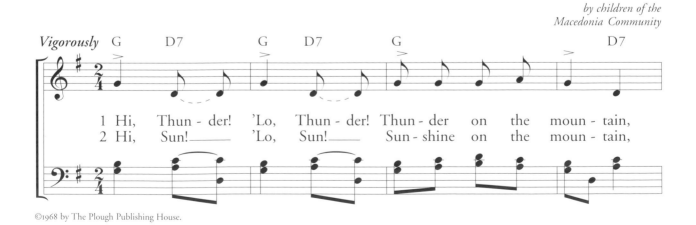

1 Hi, Thun-der! 'Lo, Thun-der! Thun-der on the moun-tain,
2 Hi, Sun! 'Lo, Sun! Sun-shine on the moun-tain,

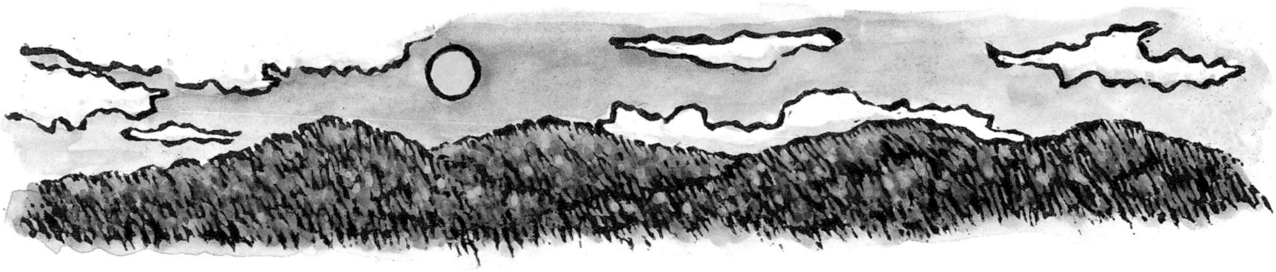

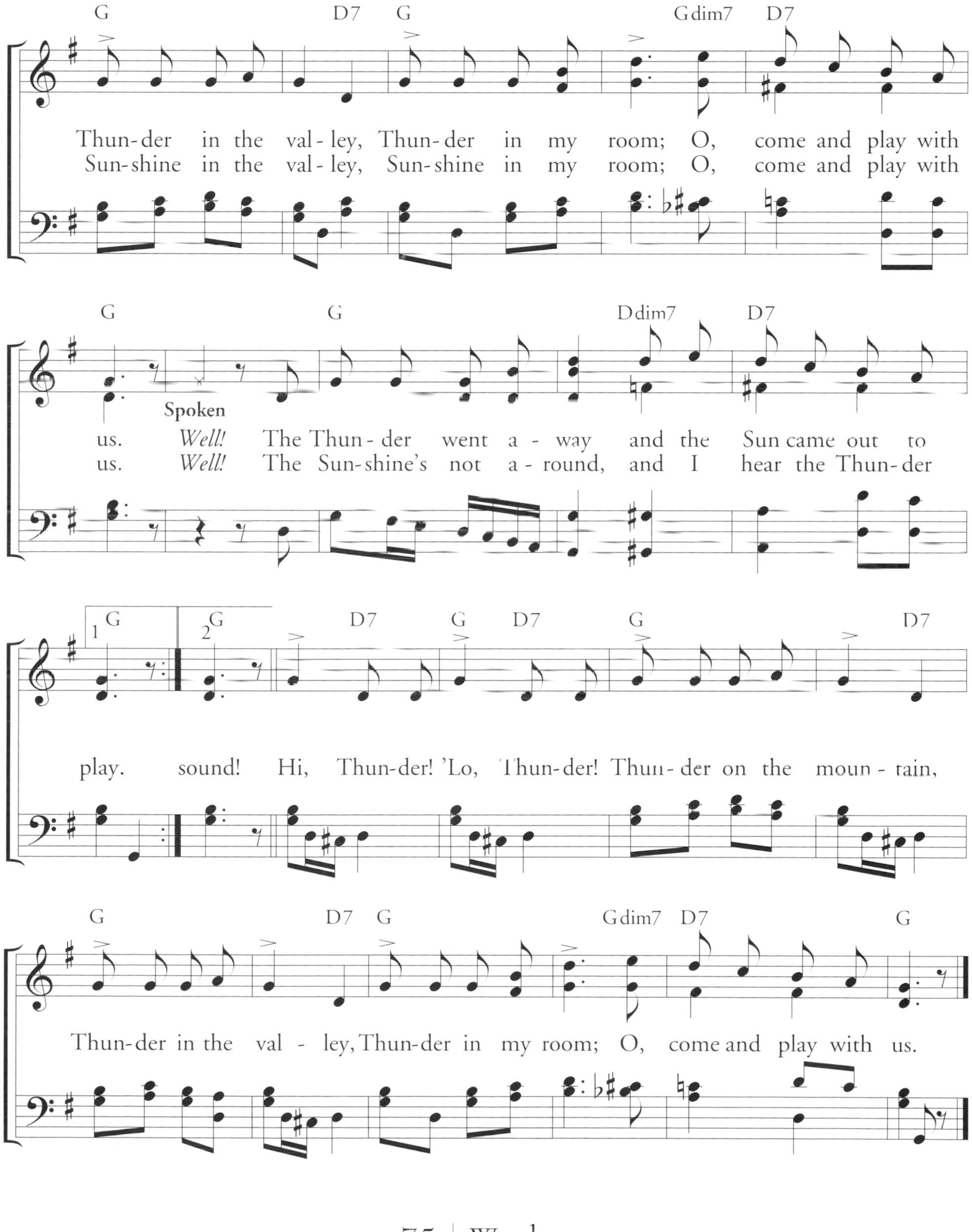

G D7 G Gdim7 D7
Thun-der in the val-ley, Thun-der in my room; O, come and play with
Sun-shine in the val-ley, Sun-shine in my room; O, come and play with
G G Ddim7 D7
Spoken
us. Well! The Thun-der went a - way and the Sun came out to
us. Well! The Sun-shine's not a - round, and I hear the Thun-der
1 G 2 G D7 G D7 G D7
play. sound! Hi, Thun-der! 'Lo, Thun-der! Thun-der on the moun - tain,
G D7 G Gdim7 D7 G
Thun-der in the val - ley, Thun-der in my room; O, come and play with us.

Sunshine and Rain

Lithuanian

Margarete Derlein

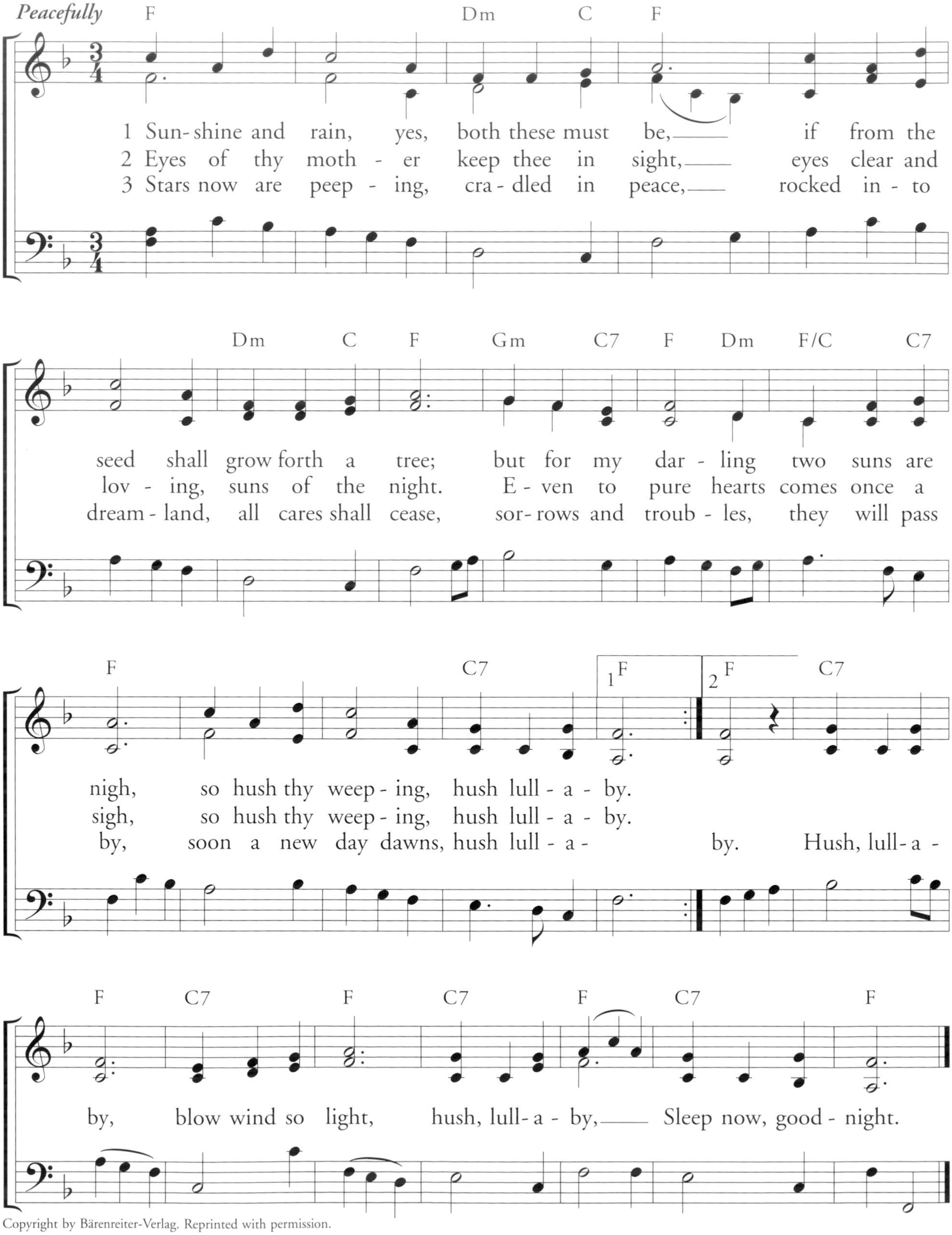

1 Sun-shine and rain, yes, both these must be,____ if from the
2 Eyes of thy moth - er keep thee in sight,____ eyes clear and
3 Stars now are peep - ing, cra - dled in peace,____ rocked in - to

seed shall grow forth a tree; but for my dar - ling two suns are
lov - ing, suns of the night. E - ven to pure hearts comes once a
dream - land, all cares shall cease, sor - rows and troub - les, they will pass

nigh, so hush thy weep - ing, hush lull - a - by.
sigh, so hush thy weep - ing, hush lull - a - by.
by, soon a new day dawns, hush lull - a - by. Hush, lull - a -

by, blow wind so light, hush, lull - a - by,____ Sleep now, good - night.

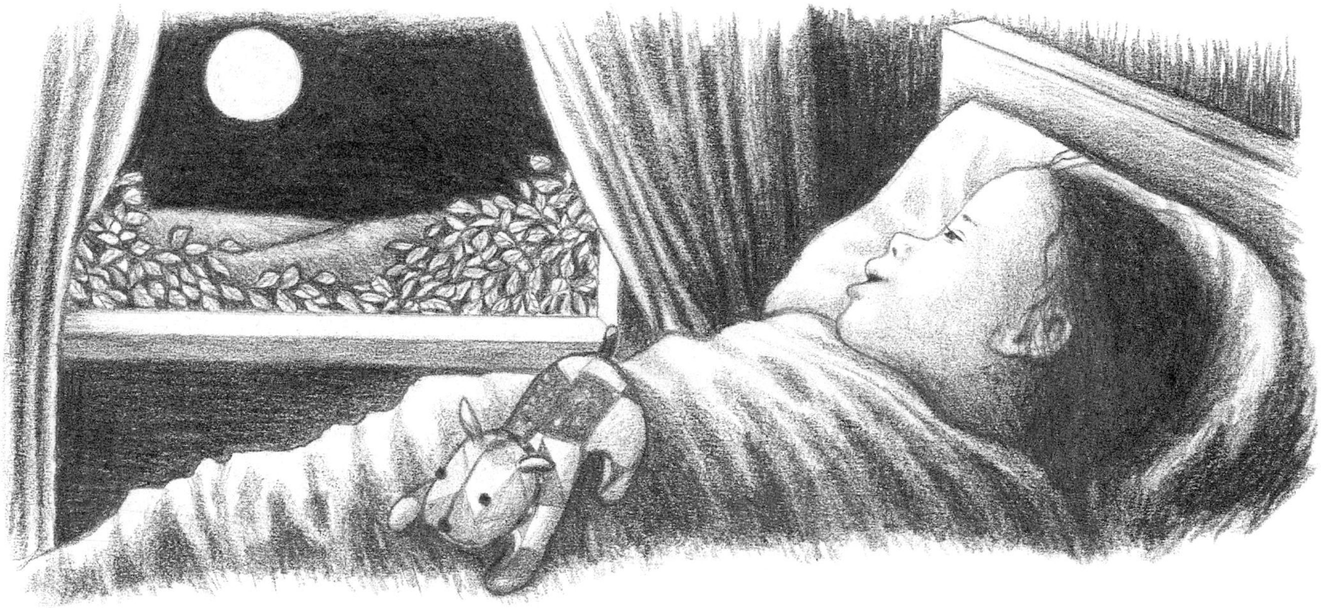

🎵 Good Evening, Shining Silver Moon!

German Folk Song

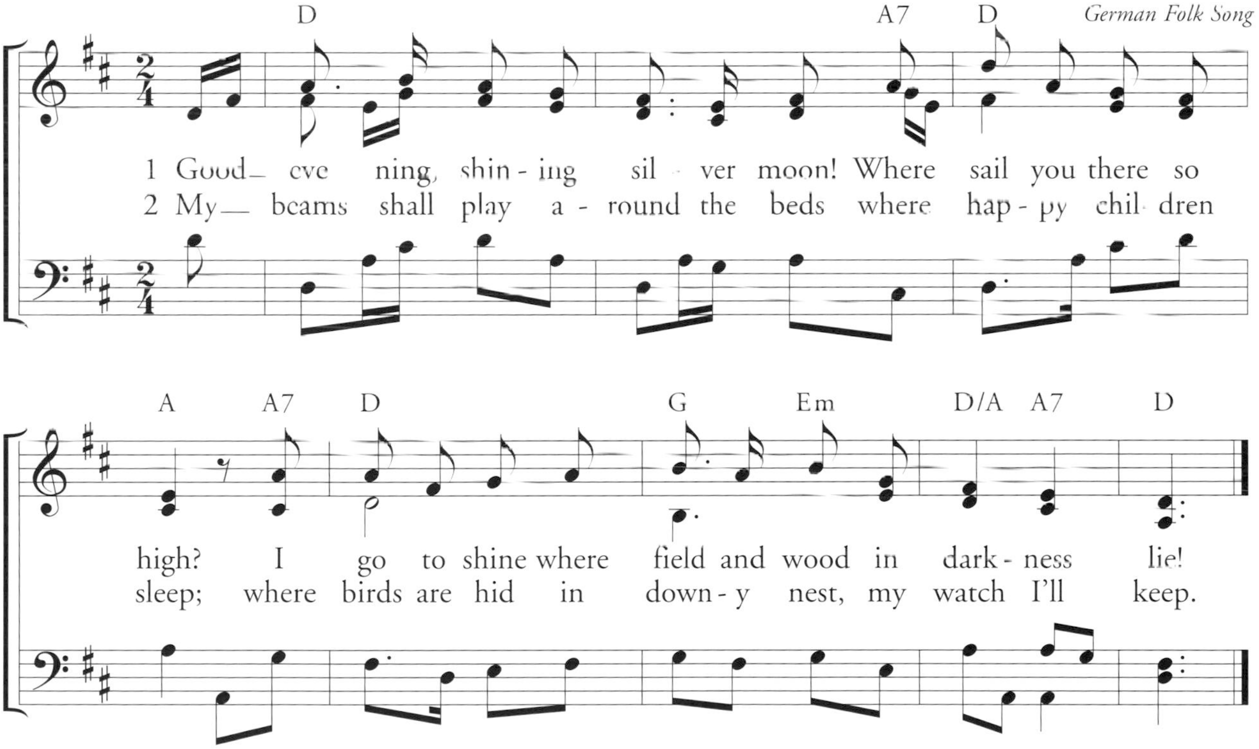

1 Good— eve — ning, shin - ing sil - ver moon! Where sail you there so
2 My— beams shall play a - round the beds where hap - py chil - dren

high? I go to shine where field and wood in dark - ness lie!
sleep; where birds are hid in down - y nest, my watch I'll keep.

3. Across the wand'rer's lonely path I'll send my cheering ray;
   I'll twinkle where the merry elves and fairies play.

4. I sail, dear child, across the sky that I each night may show
   the great Creator's tender love for all below!

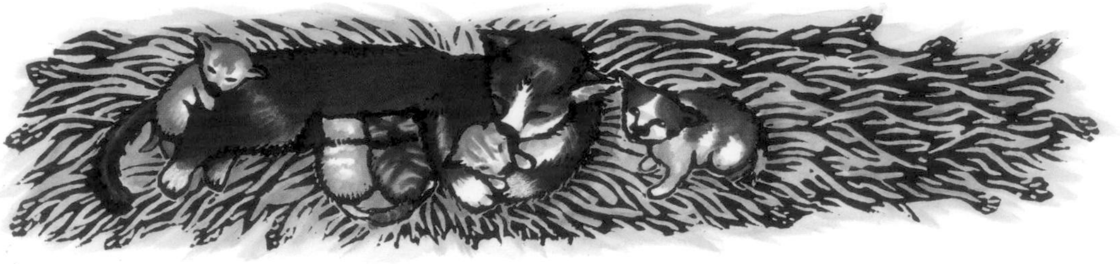

⊚ Little Donkey, Close Your Eyes

Have you ever stopped to think that little donkeys, cats, pigs, and monkeys might also have to be sung to sleep at bedtime? A good story to accompany this favorite is Margaret Wise Brown's *Good Night Moon*.

Margaret Wise Brown   *Marlys Swinger*

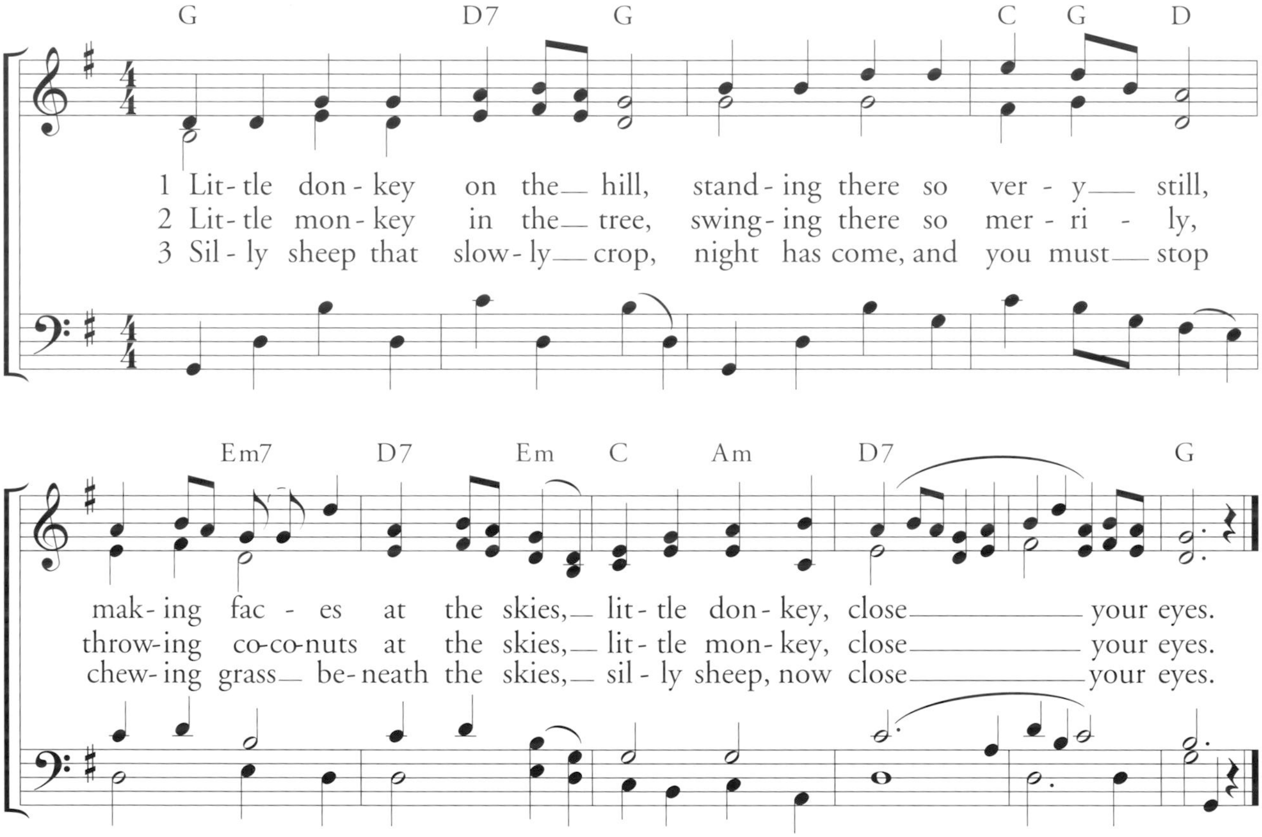

1 Lit-tle don-key on the— hill, stand-ing there so ver-y— still,
2 Lit-tle mon-key in the— tree, swing-ing there so mer-ri-ly,
3 Sil-ly sheep that slow-ly— crop, night has come, and you must— stop

mak-ing fac-es at the skies,— lit-tle don-key, close————— your eyes.
throw-ing co-co-nuts at the skies,— lit-tle mon-key, close————— your eyes.
chew-ing grass be-neath the skies,— sil-ly sheep, now close————— your eyes.

4. Little pig that squeals about,
   make no noises with your snout,
   no more squealing to the skies;
   little pig, now close your eyes.

5. Wild young birds that sweetly sing,
   curve your heads beneath your wings;
   dark night covers all the skies,
   wild young birds, now close your eyes.

6. Old black cat down in the barn,
   keeping five small kittens warm,
   let the wind blow in the skies,
   dear old black cat, close your eyes.

7. Little child all tucked in bed,
   looking such a sleepyhead,
   stars are quiet in the skies,
   little child, now close your eyes.

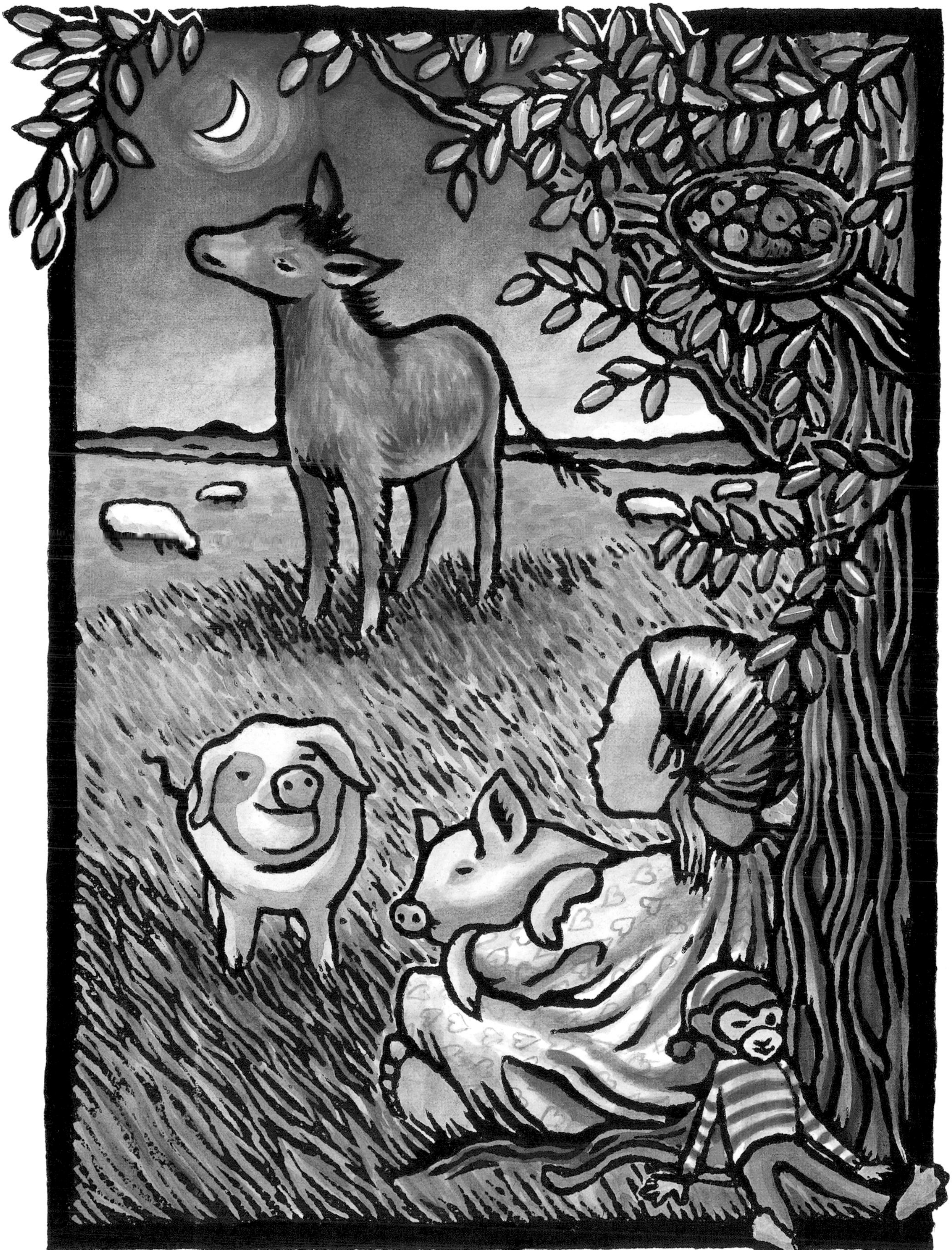

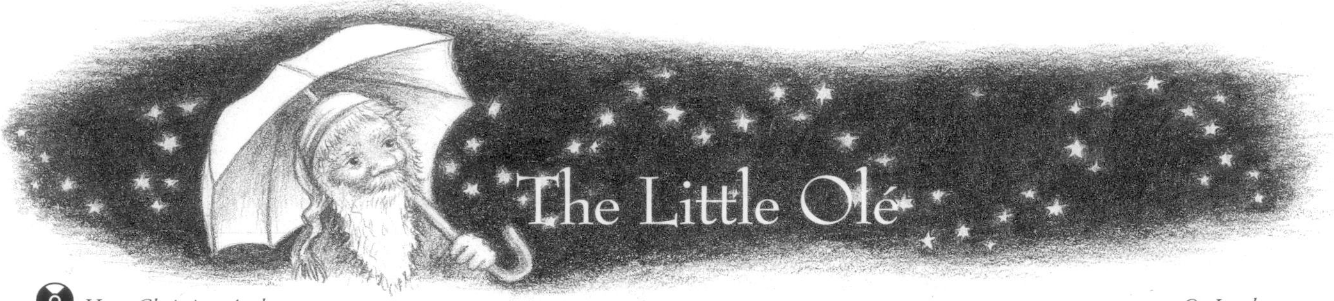

The Little Olé

Hans Christian Andersen

O. Jacobsen

Imaginatively

1 The lit-tle O-lé with his um-brel-la, all chil-dren
2 This strange um-brel-la he spreads a-bove them, it's full of
3 He tells of beau-ti-ful stars that guide us, and love-ly

love him, the friend-ly fel-low. He comes un-seen and he makes no
pic-tures and chil-dren love them, and when the child in-to dream-land
an-gels that walk be-side us, and fair-ies danc-ing so mer-ri-

noise; he puts to bed lit-tle girls and boys.
sails, he tells them won-der-ful fair-y tales.
ly that ev-'ry-bod-y would like to see.

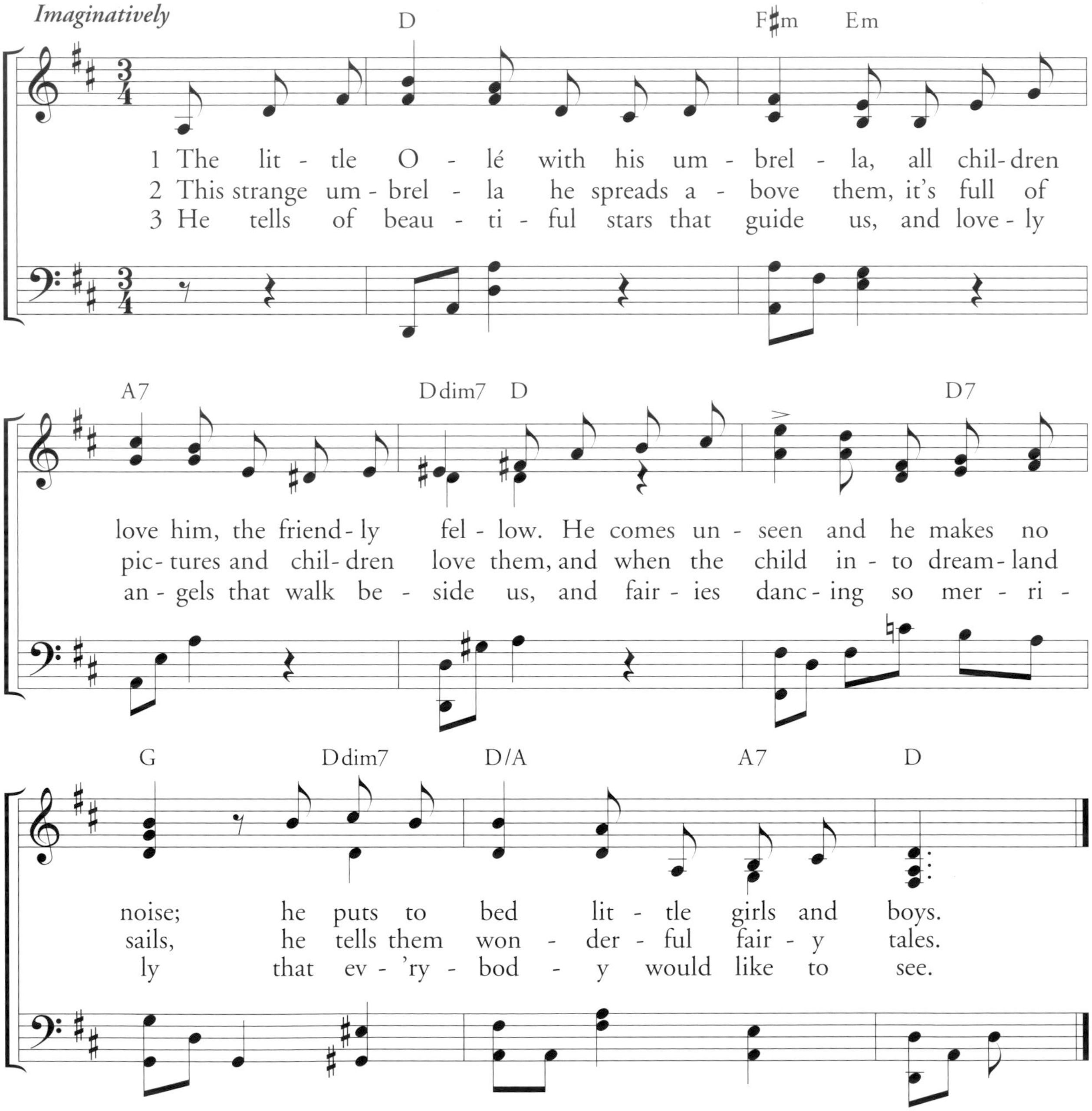

4. And all the children who mind their mothers
and always try to be good to others,
shall under Olé's umbrella hear
sweet angel voices so soft and clear.

5. When night is over and day is breaking,
with rosy cheek and with smile they waken;
a kiss for mother and a hug for dad
and thanks to God for the dreams they had.

By'm By

Assign each child a number to sing out
as it comes in the song, but let everyone shout out the *ten* at the end.

Freely

American Folk Song

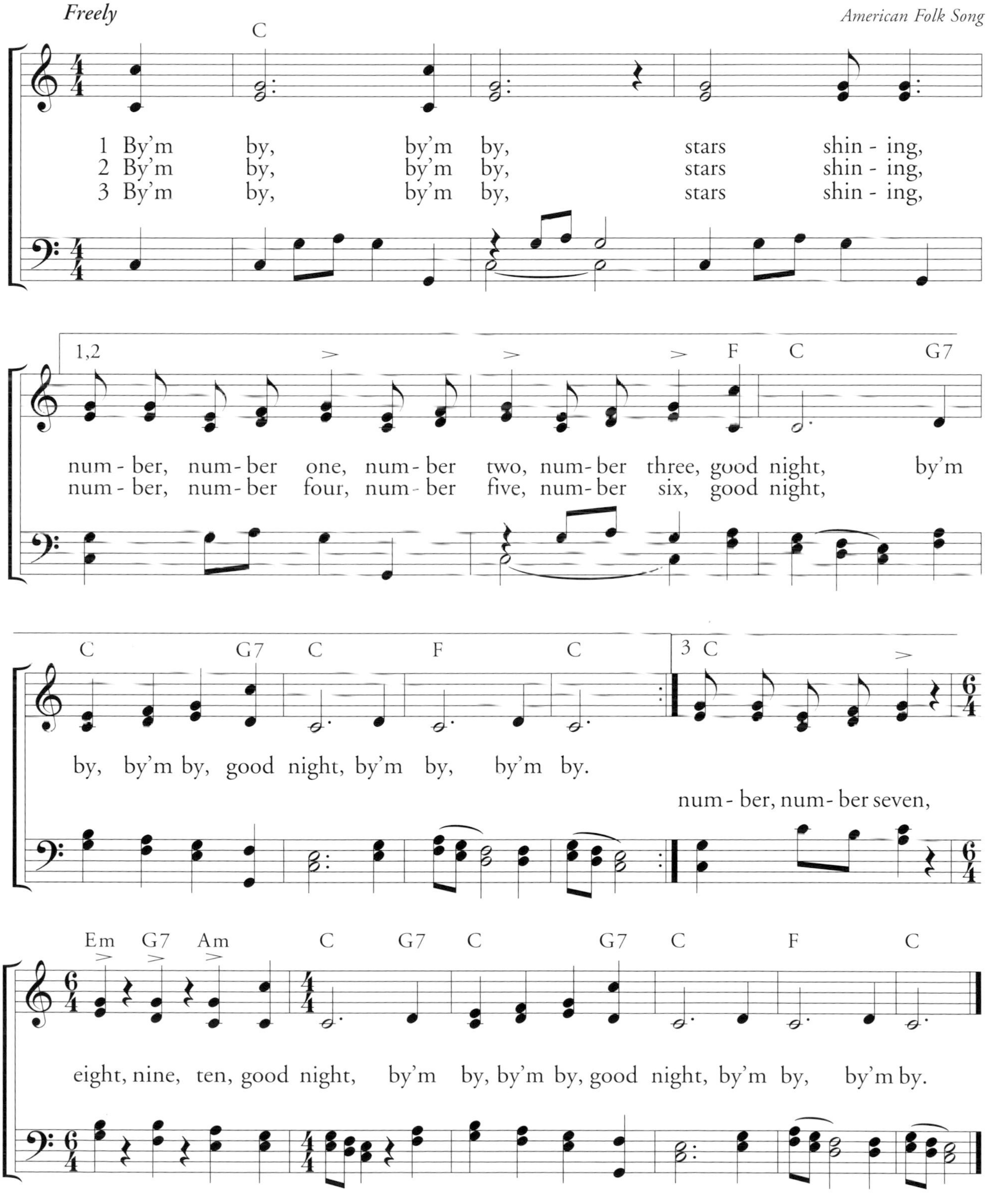

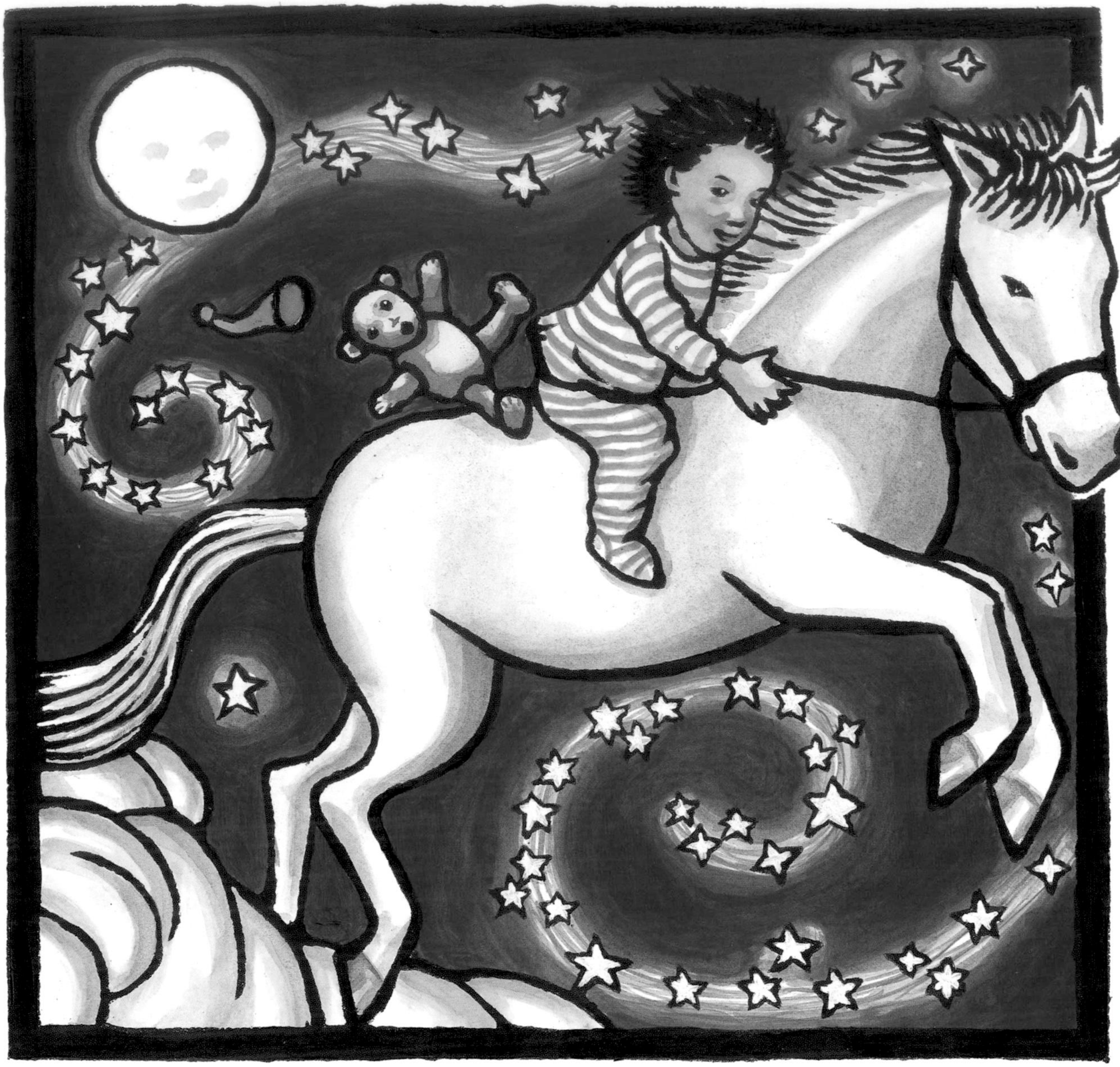

⊙ Heidschi Bum Beidschi

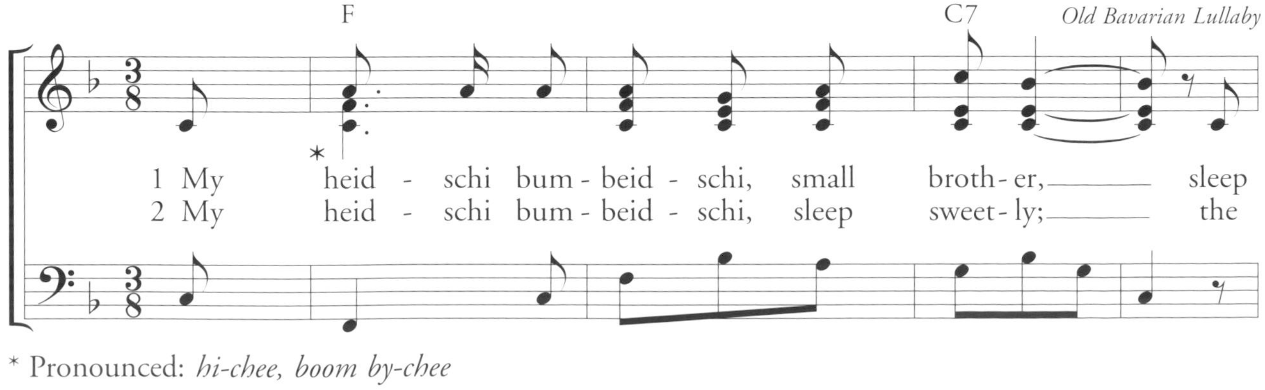

F   C7   *Old Bavarian Lullaby*

              *

1 My   heid - schi bum - beid - schi,   small   broth - er,_____   sleep

2 My   heid - schi bum - beid - schi,   sleep   sweet - ly;_____   the

* Pronounced: *hi-chee, boom by-chee*

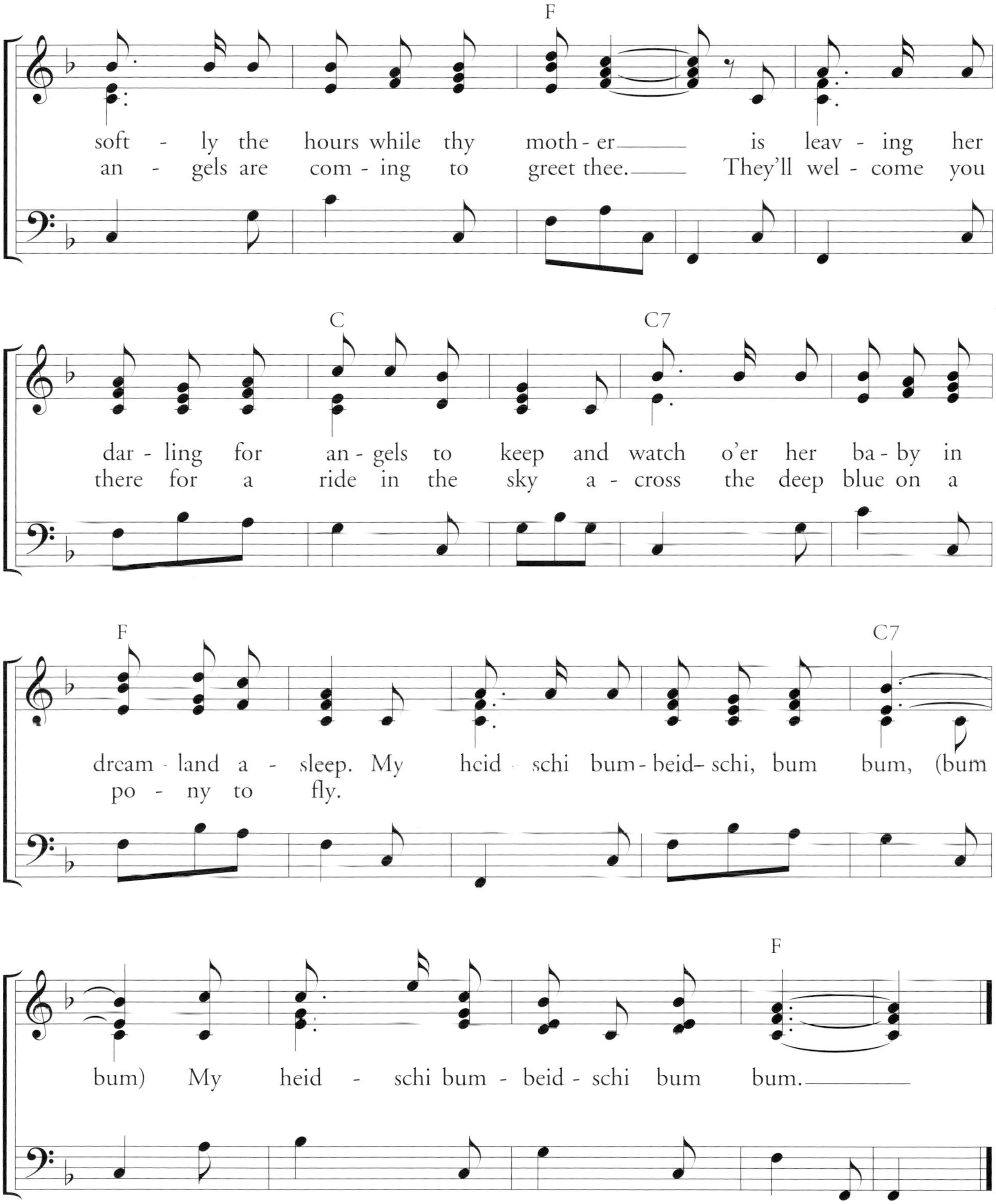

3. My heidschi bumbeidschi, in heaven,
   a pony snow-white you'll be given,
   and on it an angel with lantern so bright,
   the loveliest star in the darkness of night.
   My…

4. The heidschi bumbeidschi comes riding,
   my little one into sleep guiding,
   he's taking him up to the star-dotted sky;
   good night, now, my baby, and sweet lullaby.
   My…

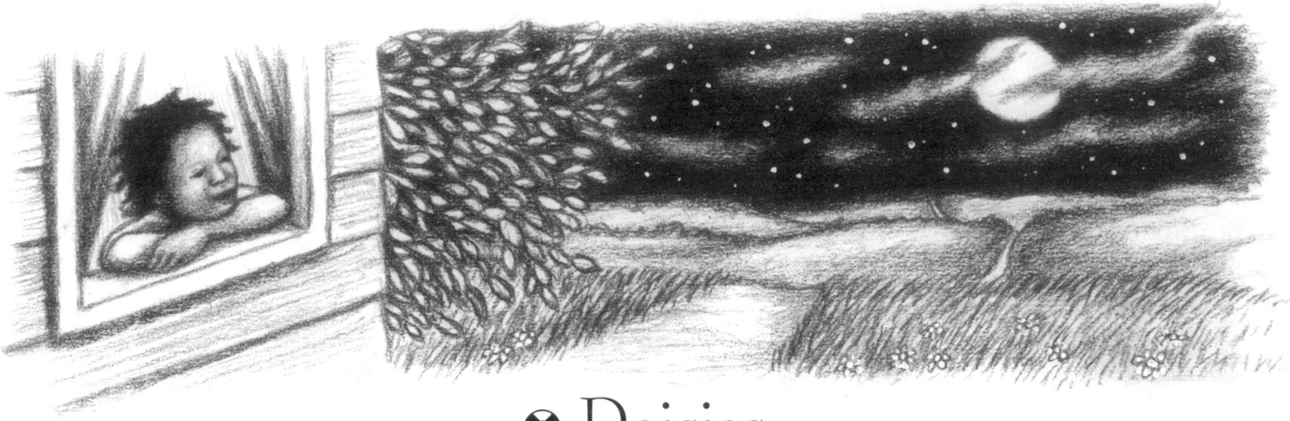

☉ Daisies

Frank Dempster Sherman   *Winifred Dyroff*

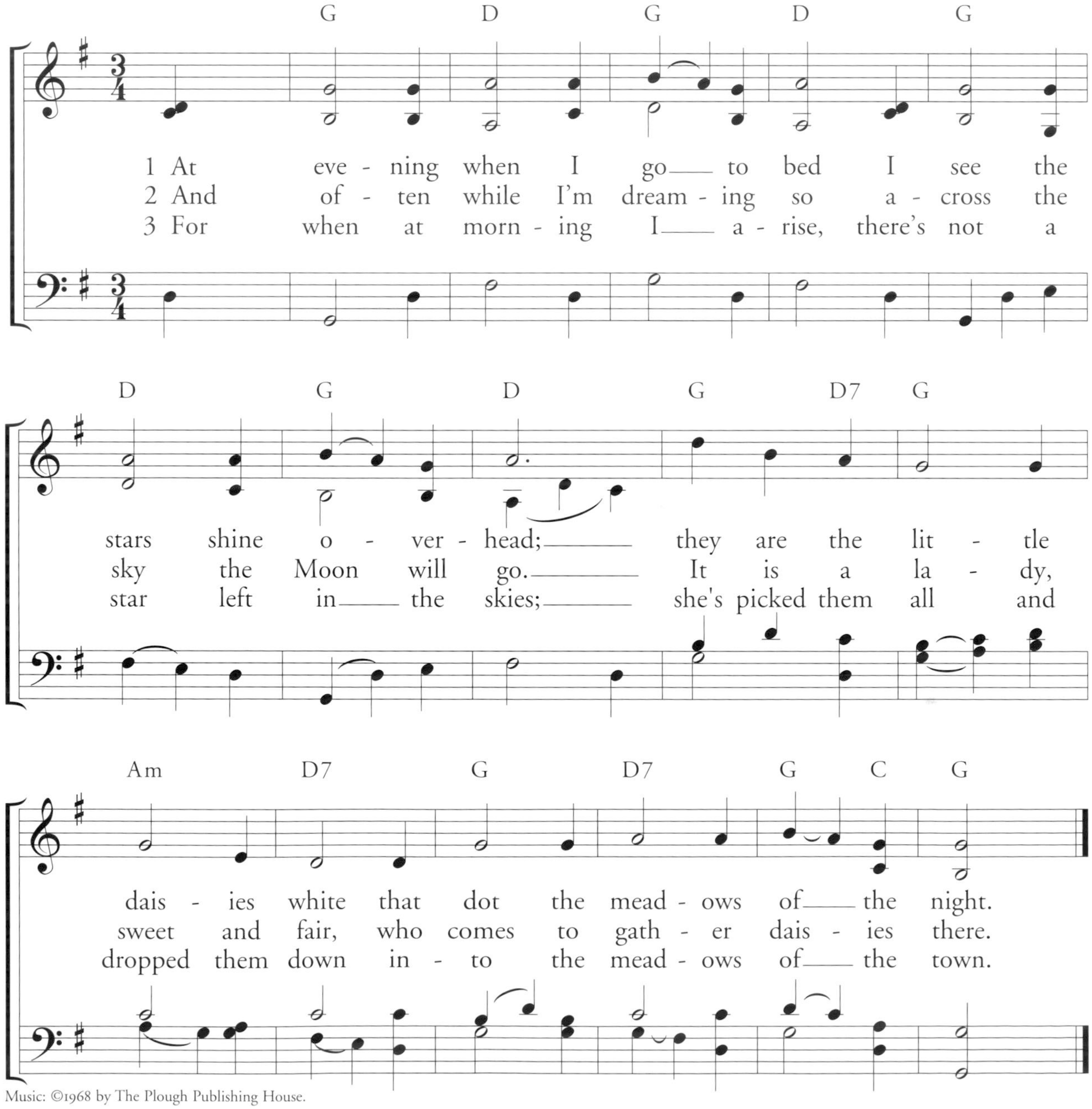

1 At eve - ning when I go — to bed I see the
2 And of - ten while I'm dream - ing so a - cross the
3 For when at morn - ing I — a - rise, there's not a

stars shine o - ver - head; —— they are the lit - tle
sky the Moon will go. —— It is a la - dy,
star left in — the skies; —— she's picked them all and

dais - ies white that dot the mead - ows of —— the night.
sweet and fair, who comes to gath - er dais - ies there.
dropped them down in - to the mead - ows of —— the town.

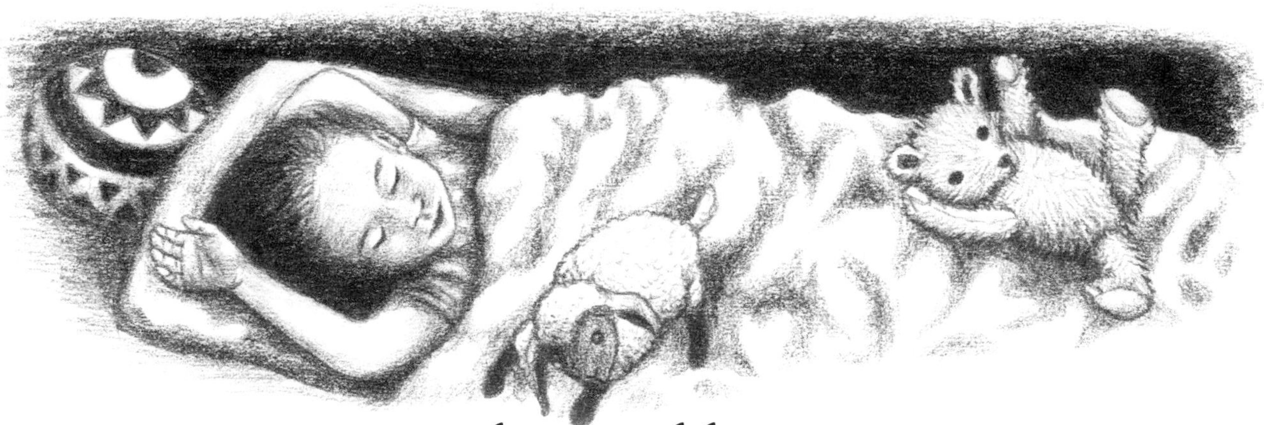

Little Lambkin Sweet

Jane Tyson Clement   *Marlys Swinger*

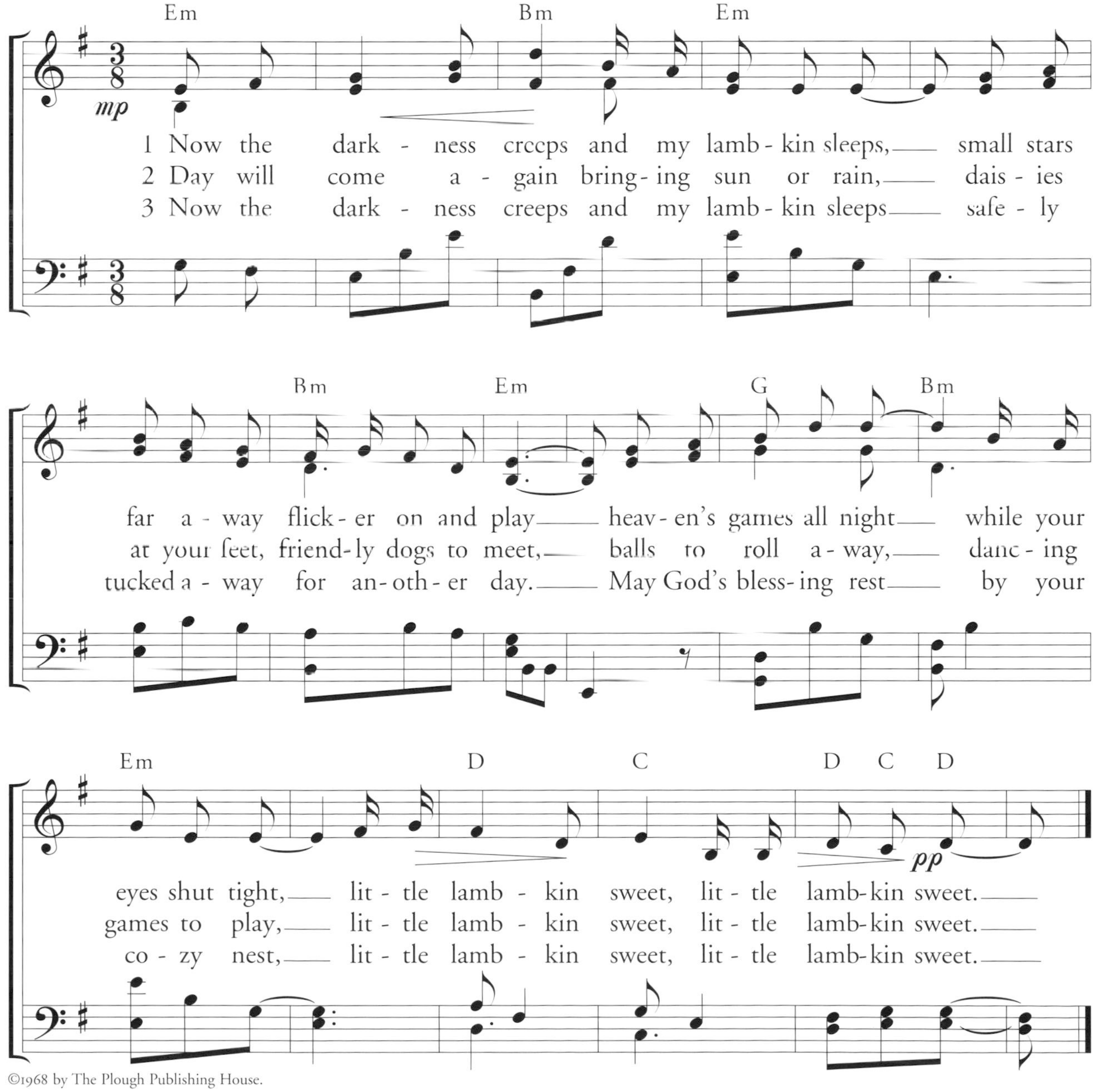

1 Now the dark - ness creeps and my lamb - kin sleeps,____ small stars
2 Day will come a - gain bring - ing sun or rain,____ dais - ies
3 Now the dark - ness creeps and my lamb - kin sleeps____ safe - ly

far a - way flick - er on and play____ heav - en's games all night____ while your
at your feet, friend - ly dogs to meet,____ balls to roll a - way,____ danc - ing
tucked a - way for an - oth - er day.____ May God's bless - ing rest____ by your

eyes shut tight,____ lit - tle lamb - kin sweet, lit - tle lamb - kin sweet.____
games to play,____ lit - tle lamb - kin sweet, lit - tle lamb - kin sweet.____
co - zy nest,____ lit - tle lamb - kin sweet, lit - tle lamb - kin sweet.____

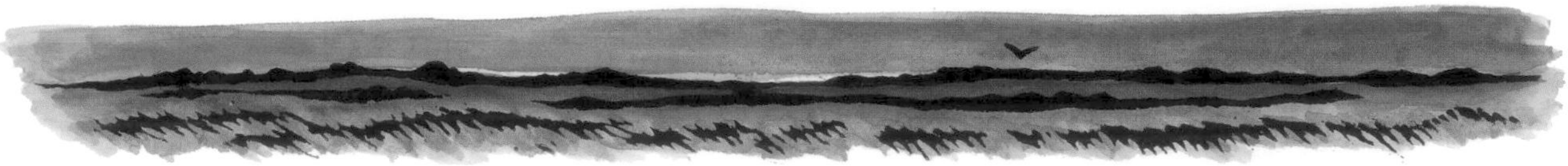

Little Red Bird

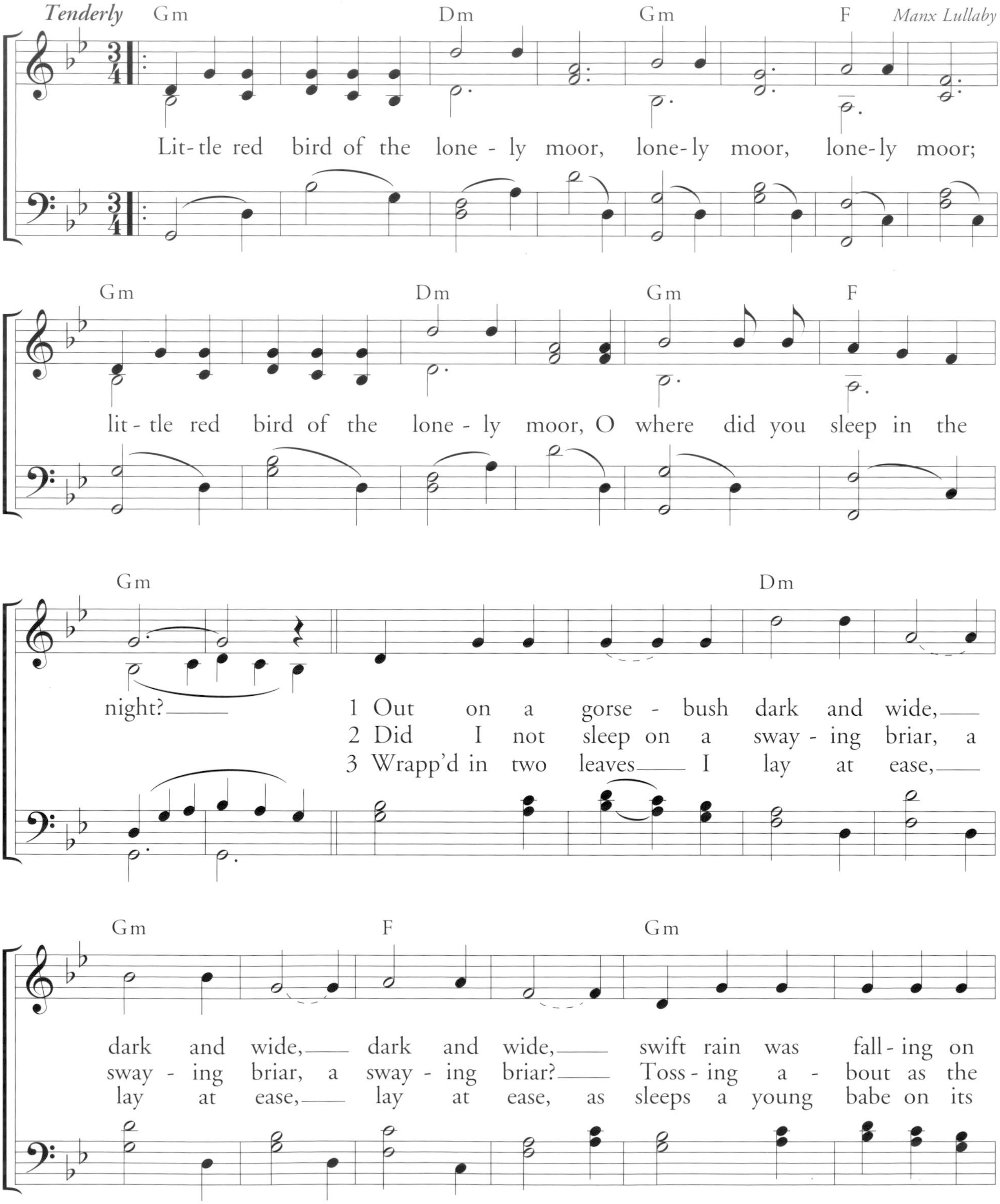

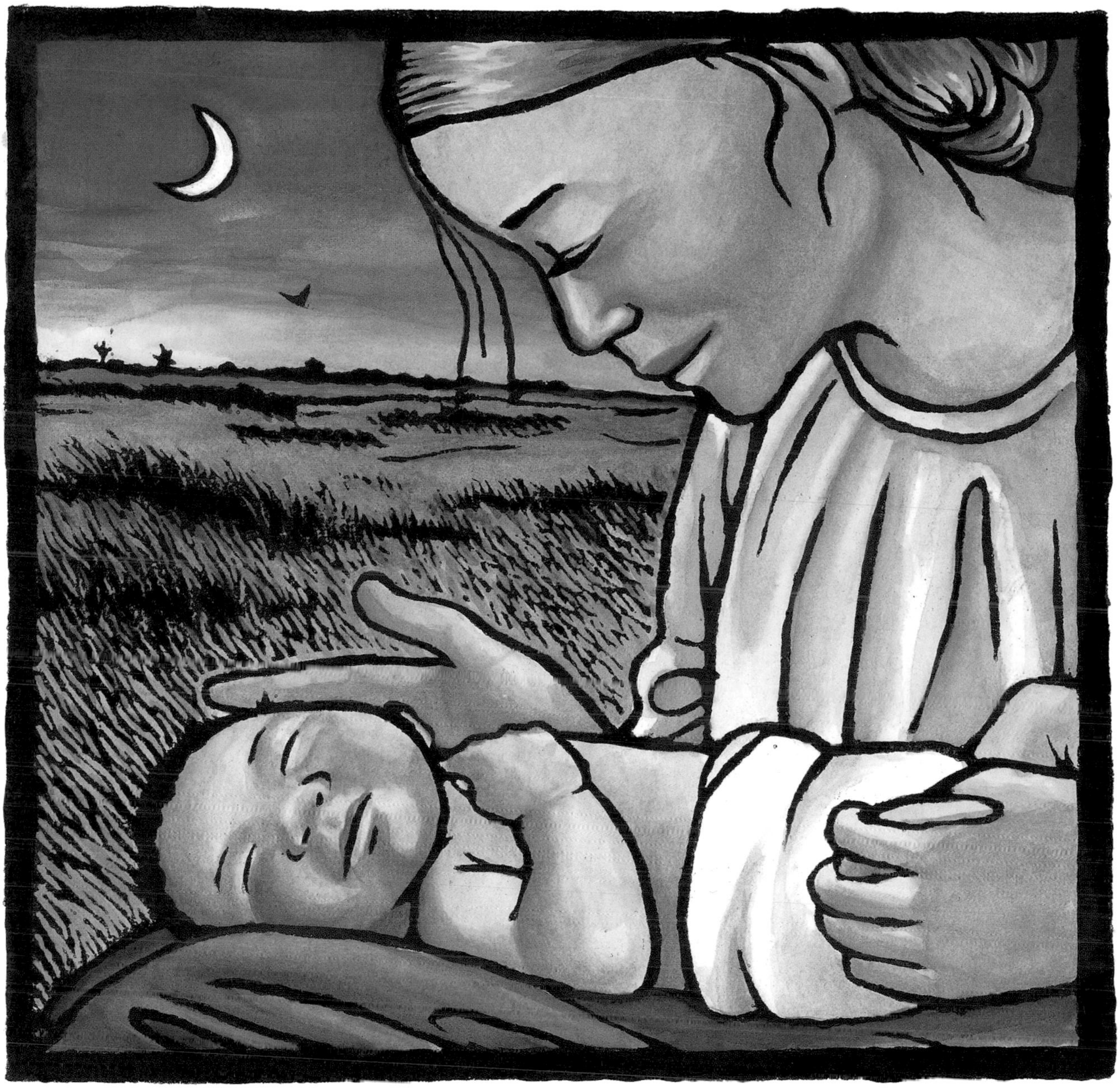

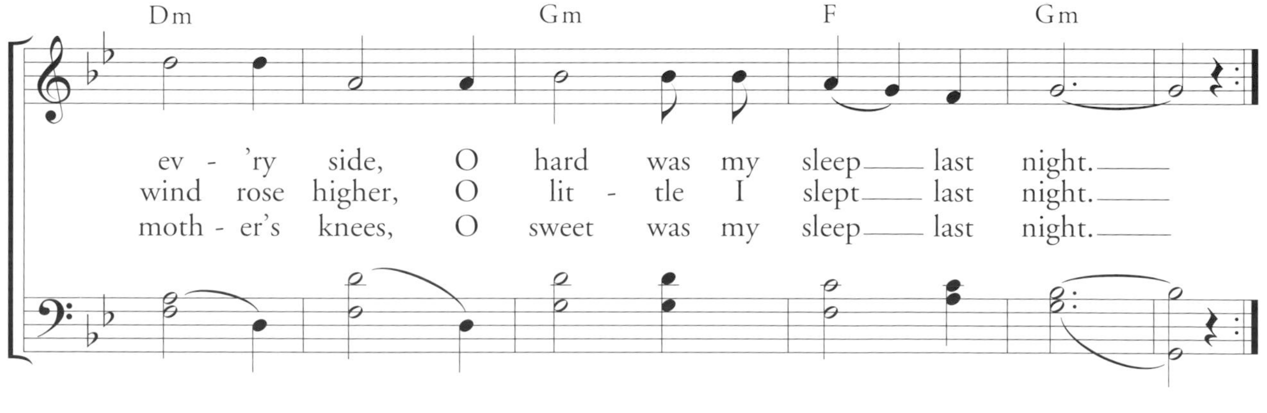

| Dm | Gm | F | Gm |

ev - 'ry side, O hard was my sleep—— last night.——
wind rose higher, O lit - tle I slept—— last night.——
moth - er's knees, O sweet was my sleep—— last night.——

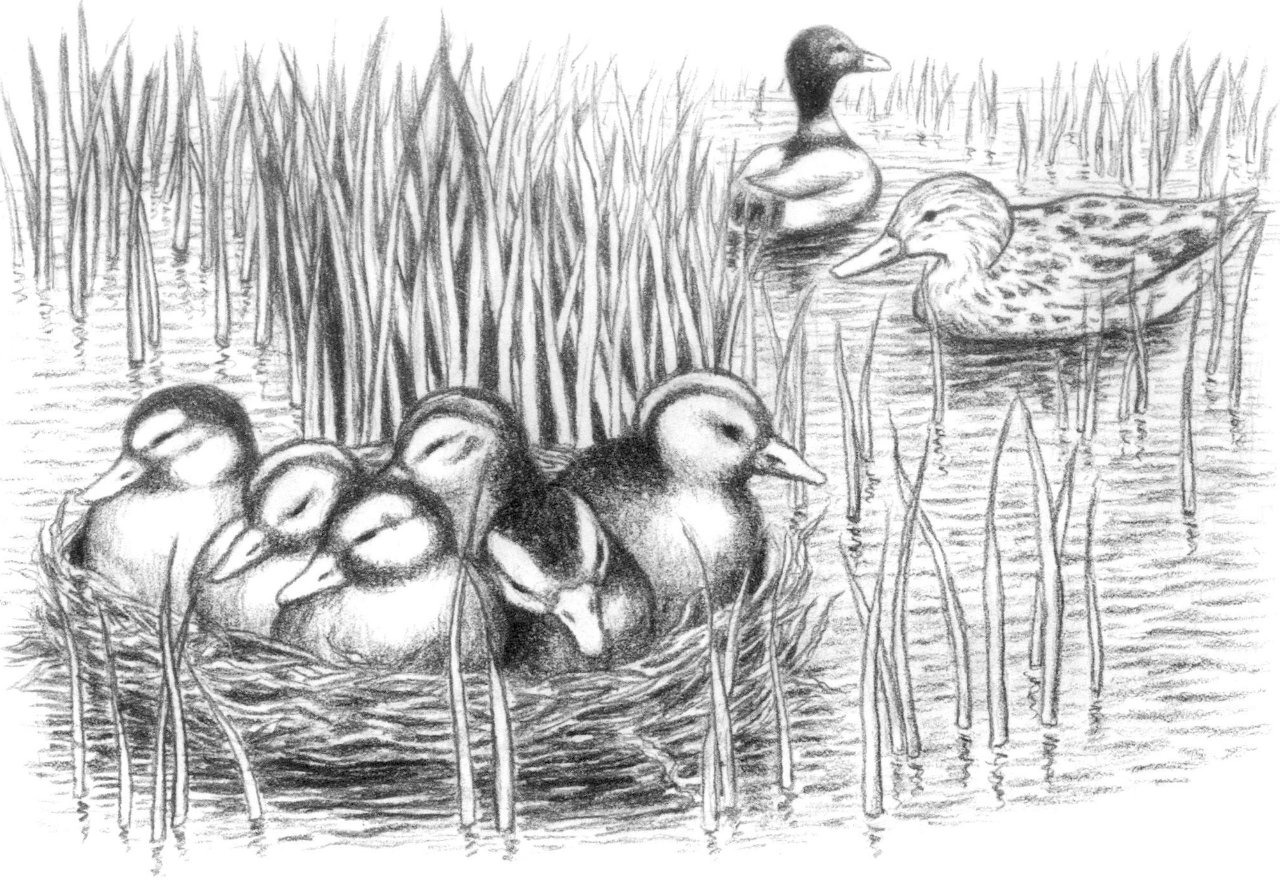

Sleep, My Duckling

This lullaby voices an often unspoken question of children at bedtime: Where's Dad? Where's Mom?
Maybe that's why they ask for this beautiful song over and over again.

Finnish Folk Song

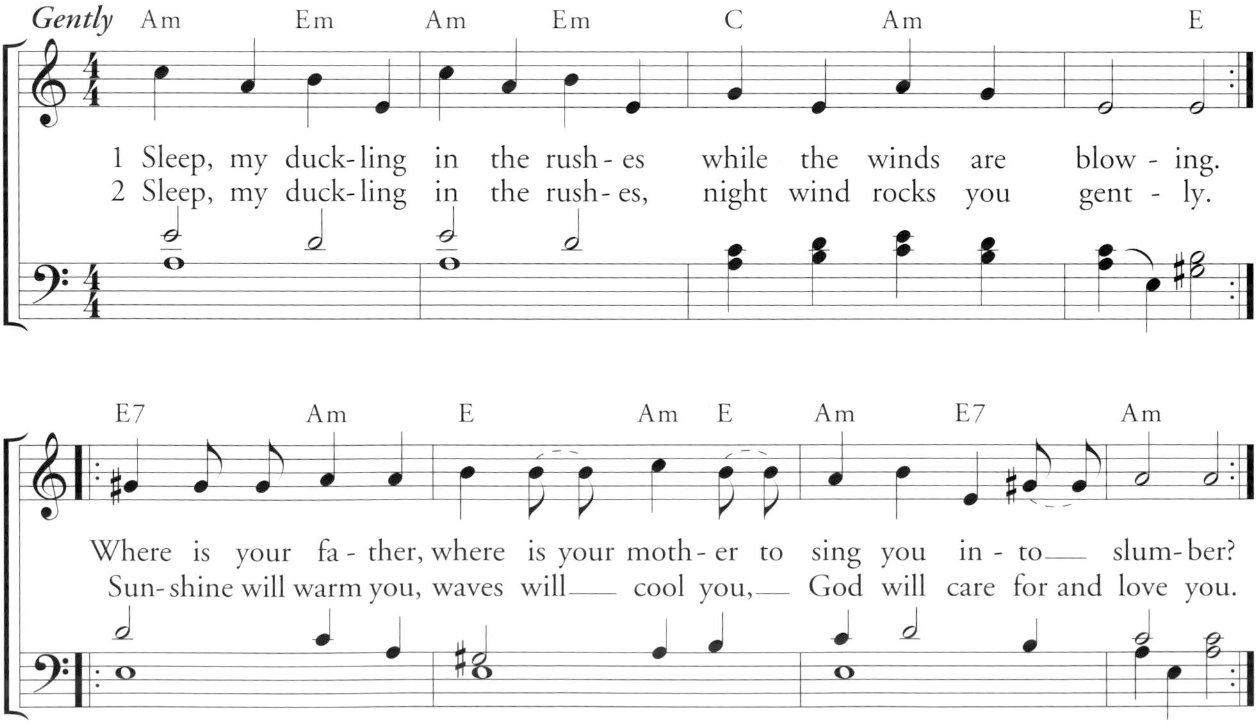

1 Sleep, my duck-ling in the rush-es while the winds are blow-ing.
2 Sleep, my duck-ling in the rush-es, night wind rocks you gent-ly.

Where is your fa-ther, where is your moth-er to sing you in-to slum-ber?
Sun-shine will warm you, waves will cool you, God will care for and love you.

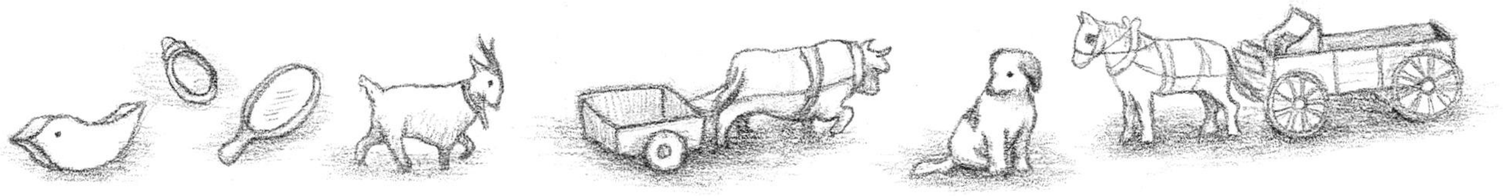

⊚ Hush Little Baby

Like any folk song that's been passed down from generation to generation, this song can be sung as you like – with "Mama," "Papa," "Mommy," or "Daddy." Alter the words as they suit you best.

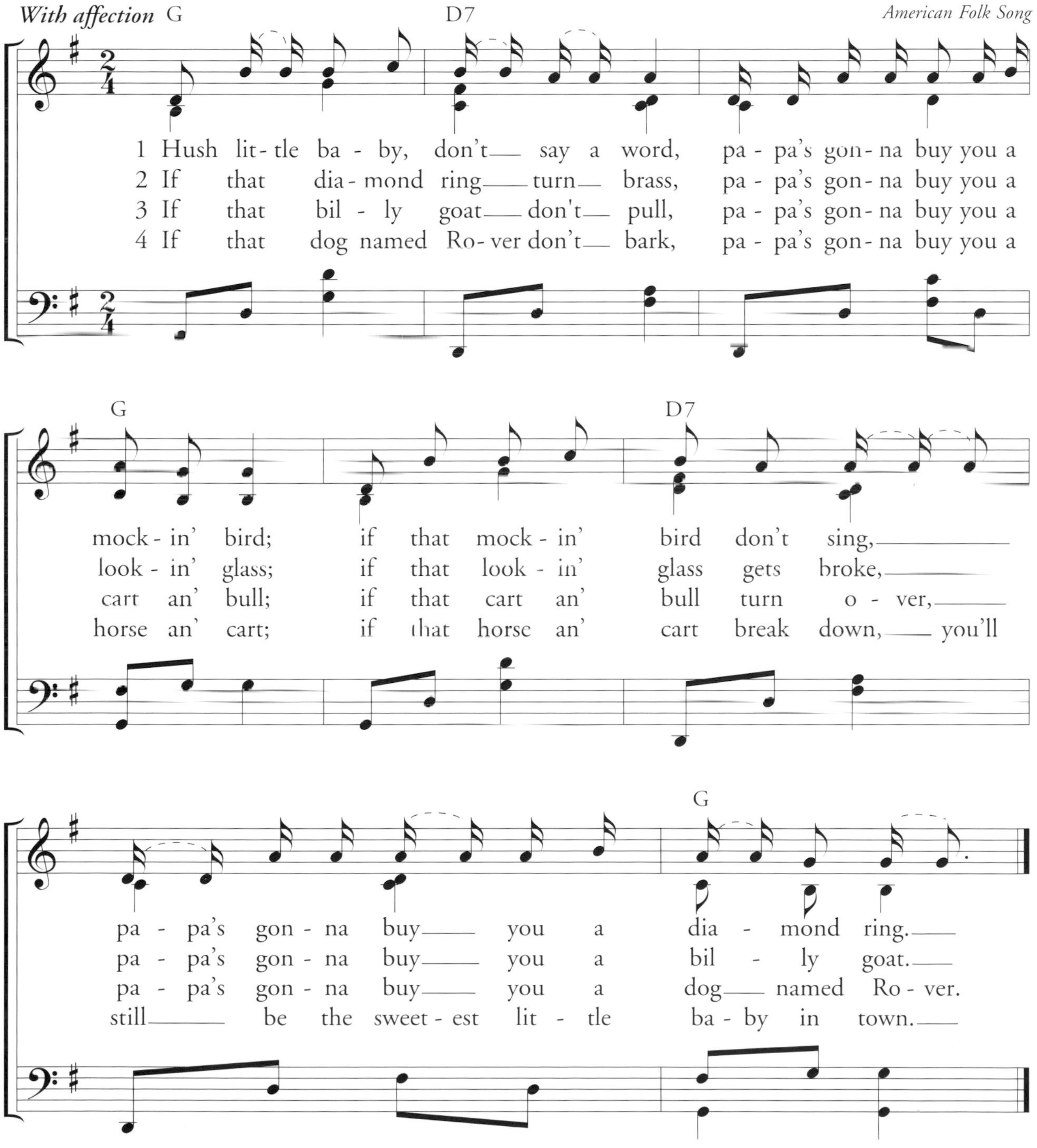

With affection G

American Folk Song

1 Hush lit-tle ba-by, don't say a word, pa-pa's gon-na buy you a
2 If that dia-mond ring turn brass, pa-pa's gon-na buy you a
3 If that bil-ly goat don't pull, pa-pa's gon-na buy you a
4 If that dog named Ro-ver don't bark, pa-pa's gon-na buy you a

mock-in' bird; if that mock-in' bird don't sing,
look-in' glass; if that look-in' glass gets broke,
cart an' bull; if that cart an' bull turn o-ver,
horse an' cart; if that horse an' cart break down, you'll

pa-pa's gon-na buy you a dia-mond ring.
pa-pa's gon-na buy you a bil-ly goat.
pa-pa's gon-na buy you a dog named Ro-ver.
still be the sweet-est lit-tle ba-by in town.

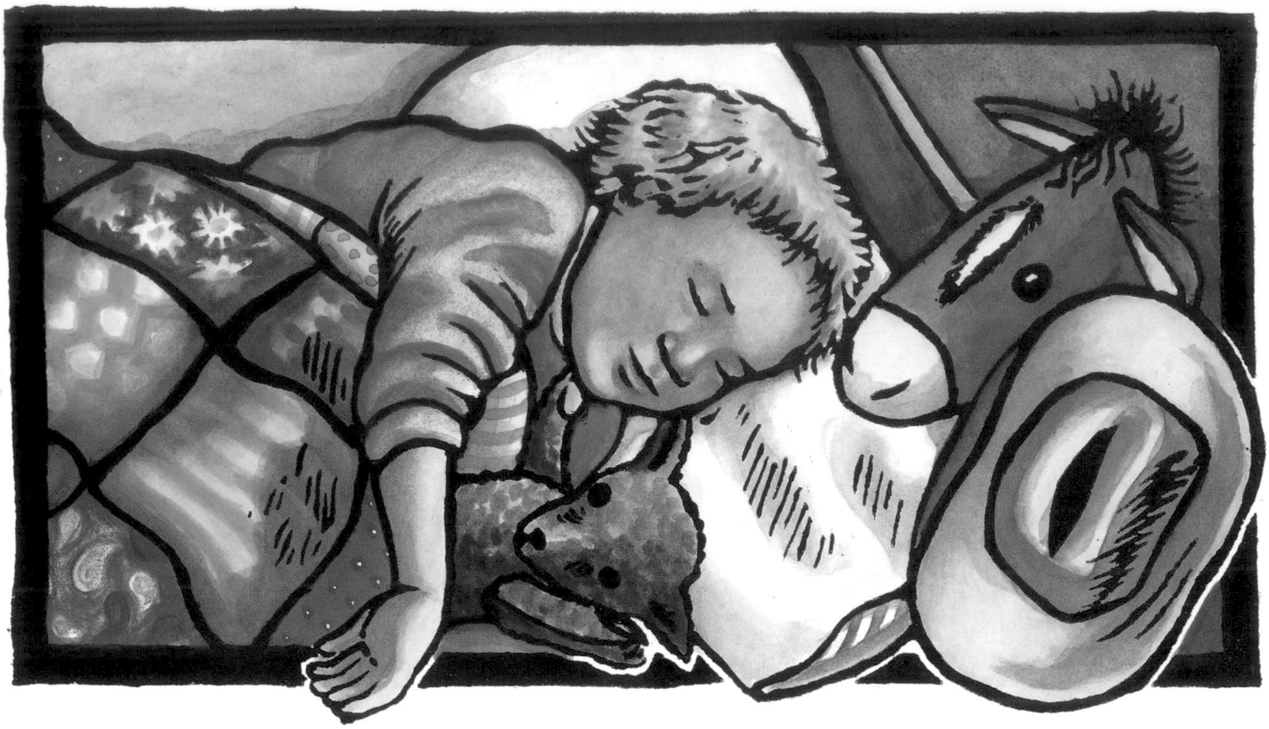

🔊 Time to Go to Sleep

Turn your class into cowboys, each with their own made-to-order pony. A long stick,
an old sock stuffed with rags, and two button eyes make a wonderful friend,
first to ride, and then to lay next to the mat at nap time.

Words and Music
Marlys Swinger

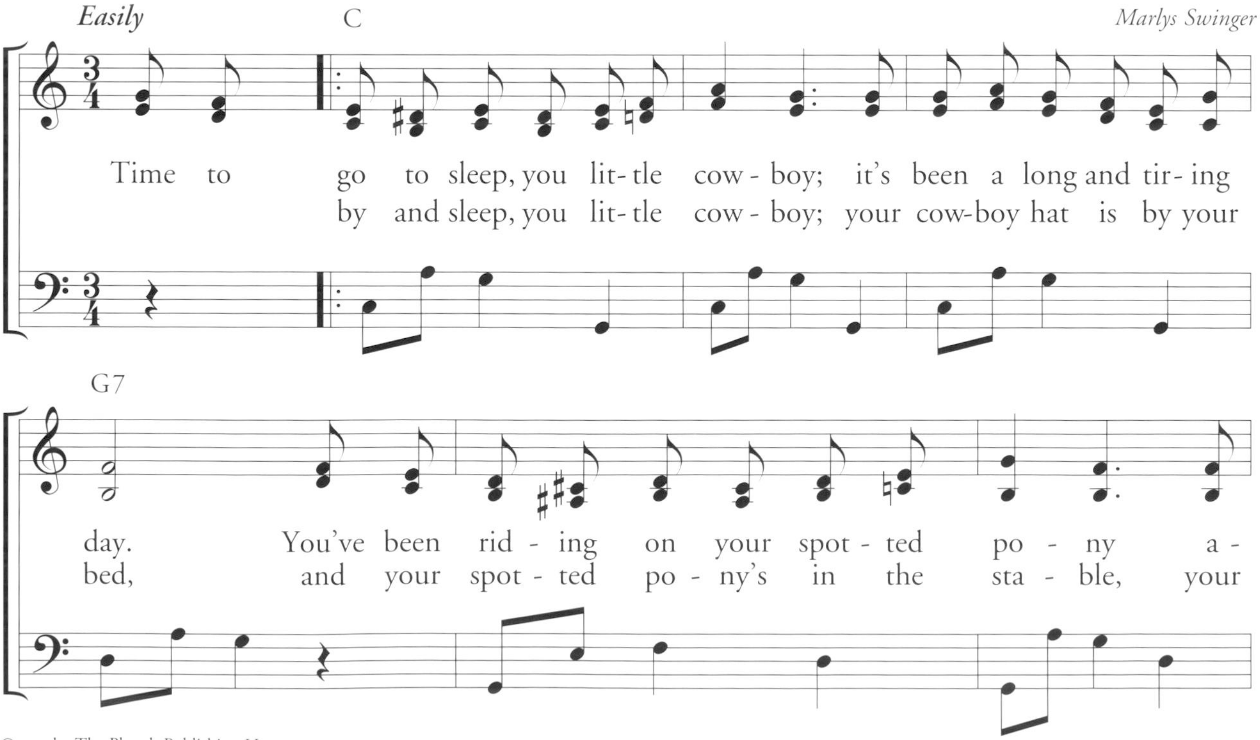

Time to go to sleep, you lit-tle cow-boy; it's been a long and tir-ing
by and sleep, you lit-tle cow-boy; your cow-boy hat is by your

day. You've been rid-ing on your spot-ted po-ny a-
bed, and your spot-ted po-ny's in the sta-ble, your

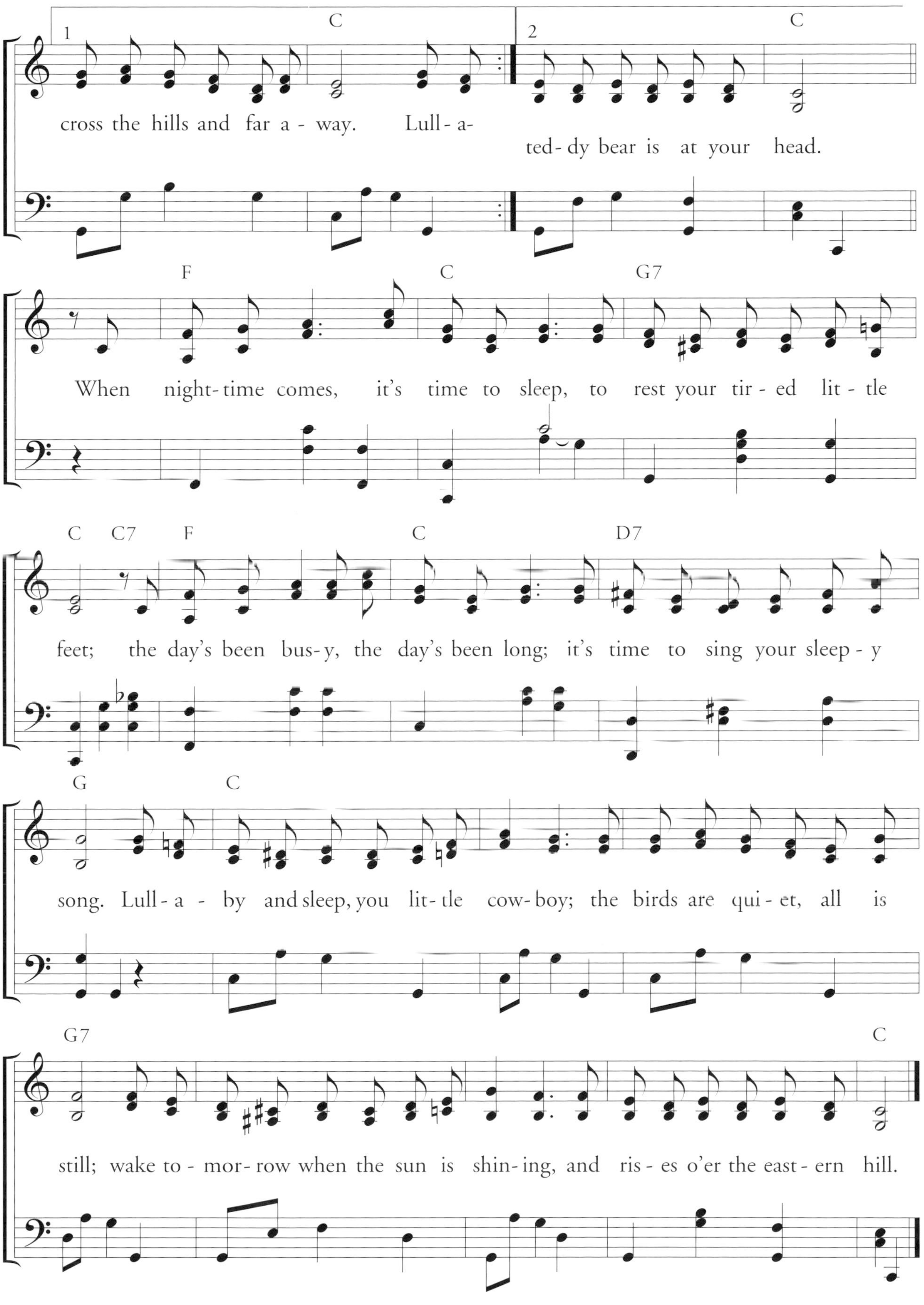
1
C
2
C
cross the hills and far a - way. Lull - a-
ted - dy bear is at your head.
F
C
G7
When night - time comes, it's time to sleep, to rest your tir - ed lit - tle
C
C7
F
C
D7
feet; the day's been bus - y, the day's been long; it's time to sing your sleep - y
G
C
song. Lull - a - by and sleep, you lit - tle cow - boy; the birds are qui - et, all is
G7
C
still; wake to - mor - row when the sun is shin - ing, and ris - es o'er the east - ern hill.

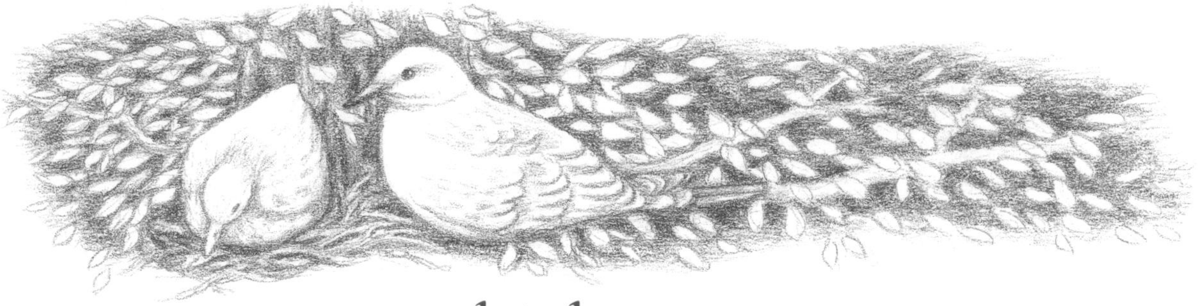

O Hush Thee, My Dove

Manx Lullaby

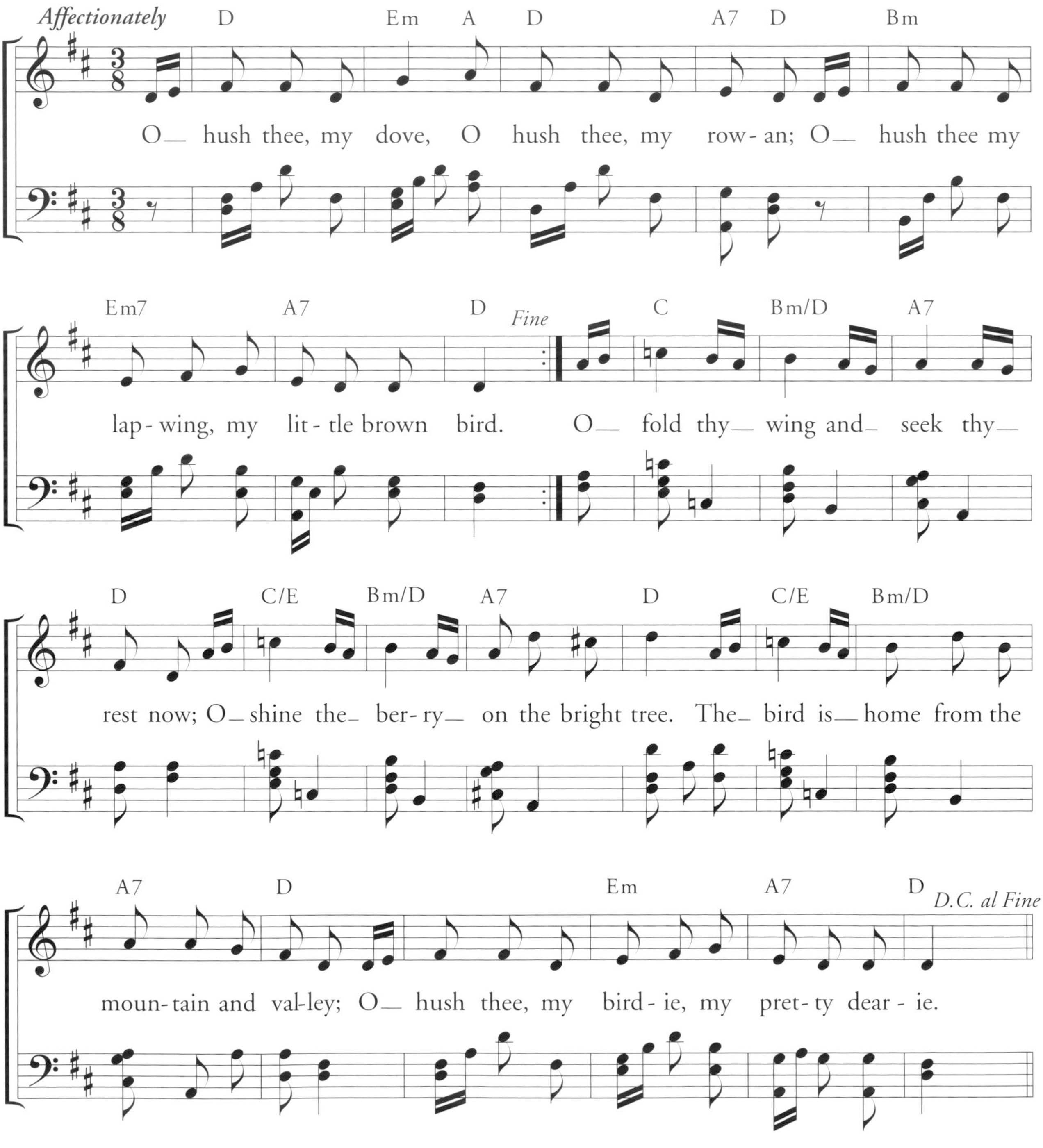

O— hush thee, my dove, O hush thee, my row-an; O— hush thee my lap-wing, my lit-tle brown bird. O— fold thy— wing and— seek thy— rest now; O— shine the— ber-ry— on the bright tree. The— bird is— home from the moun-tain and val-ley; O— hush thee, my bird-ie, my pret-ty dear-ie.

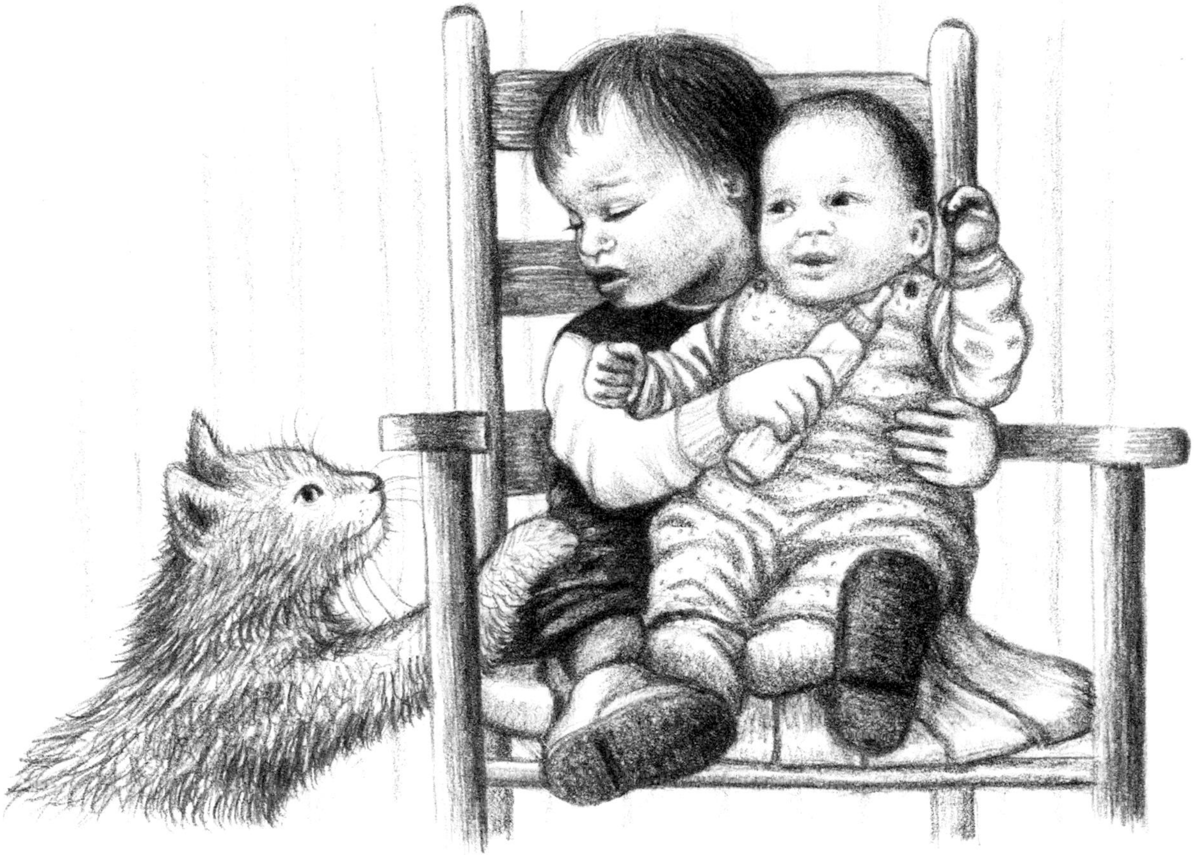

🎵 Old Gray Cat

Cajun Lullaby

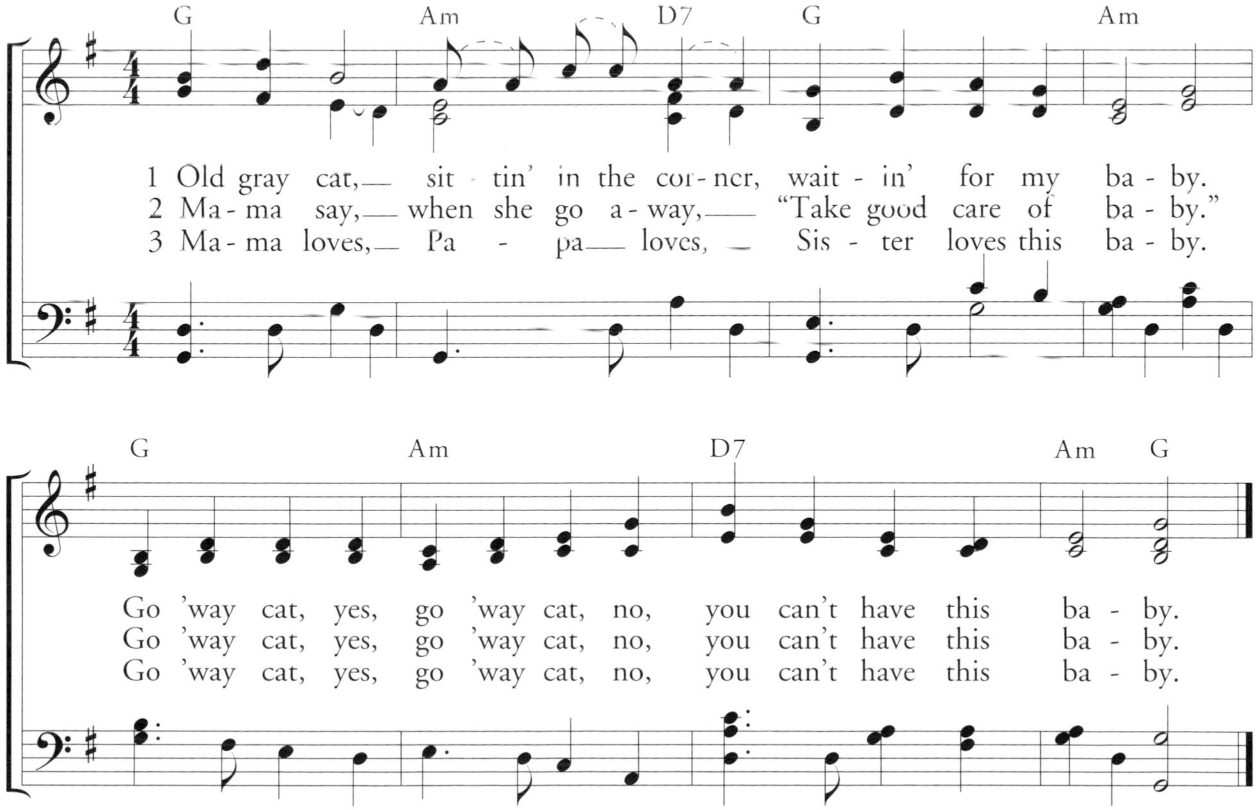

1 Old gray cat,— sit-tin' in the cor-ner, wait-in' for my ba-by.
2 Ma-ma say,— when she go a-way,— "Take good care of ba-by."
3 Ma-ma loves,— Pa-pa— loves,— Sis-ter loves this ba-by.

Go 'way cat, yes, go 'way cat, no, you can't have this ba-by.
Go 'way cat, yes, go 'way cat, no, you can't have this ba-by.
Go 'way cat, yes, go 'way cat, no, you can't have this ba-by.

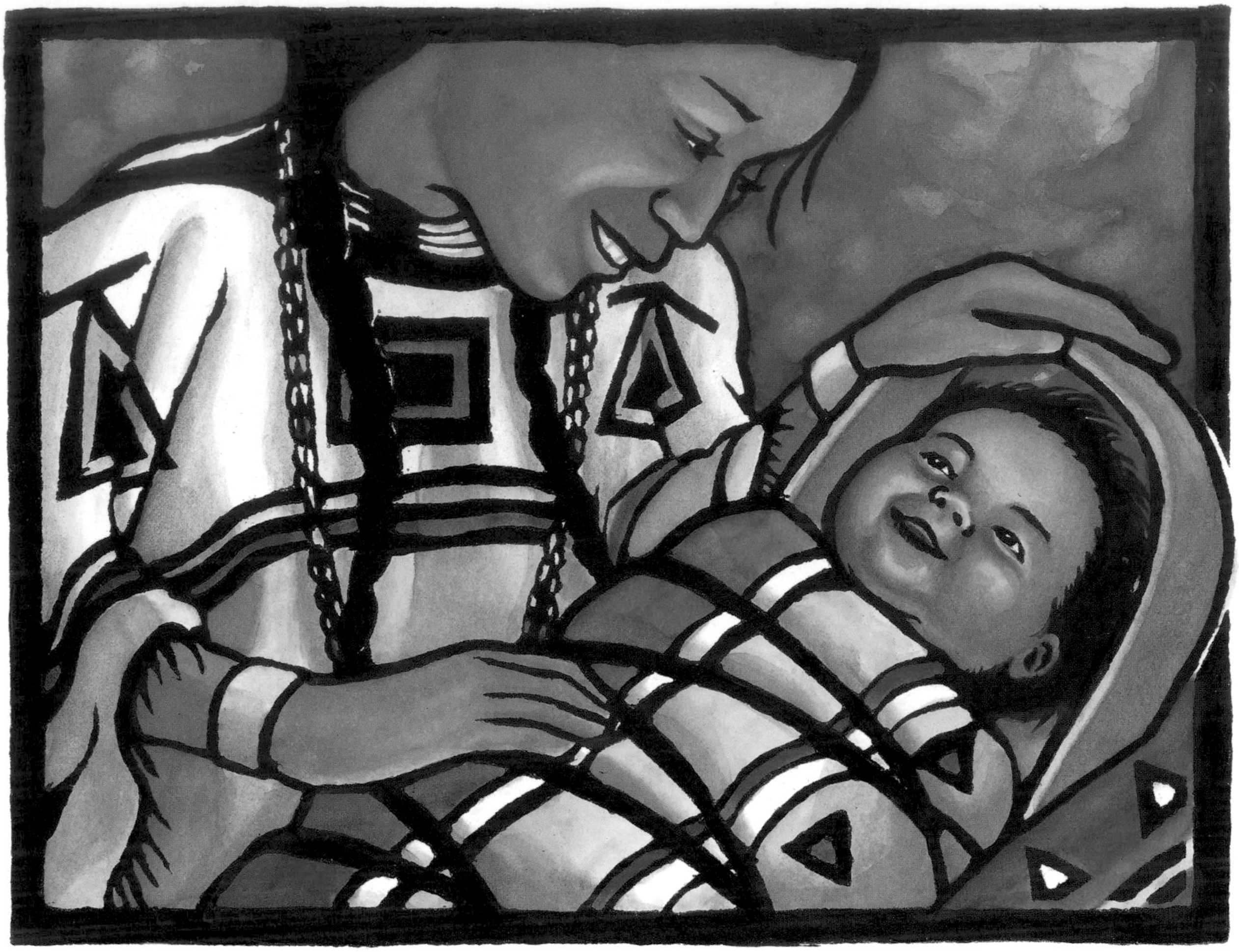

🎵 Indian Lullaby

With cardboard and string you can make a simple cradleboard large enough to carry a papoose.
Then learn this beautiful lullaby and sing the doll to sleep.

Henry W. Longfellow   *Walter H. Aiken*

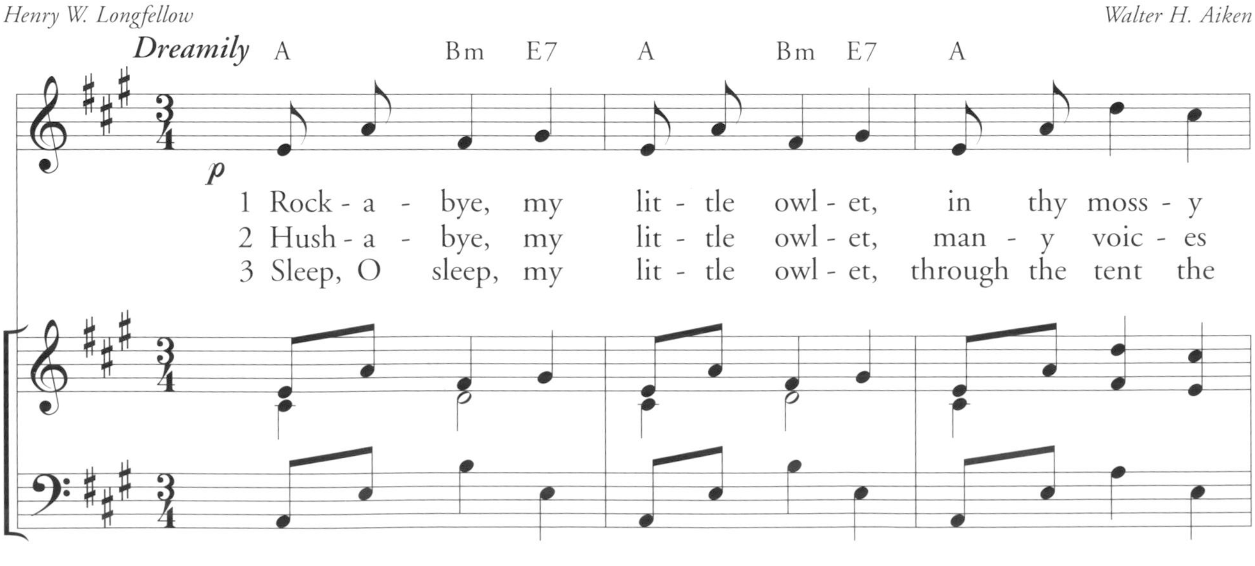

1 Rock - a - bye, my   lit - tle owl - et,   in   thy moss - y
2 Hush - a - bye, my   lit - tle owl - et,   man - y   voic - es
3 Sleep, O   sleep, my   lit - tle owl - et, through the tent the

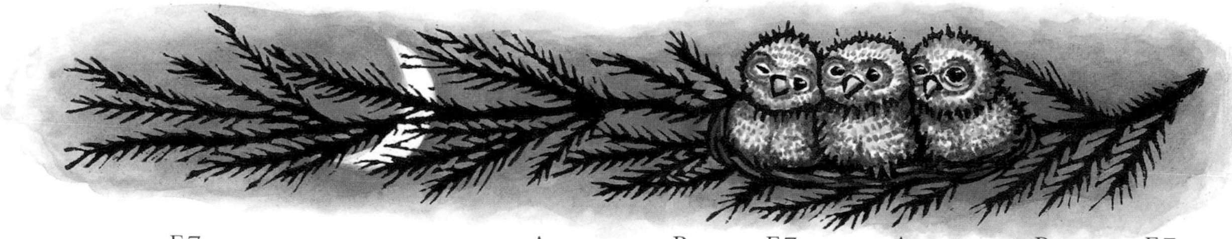

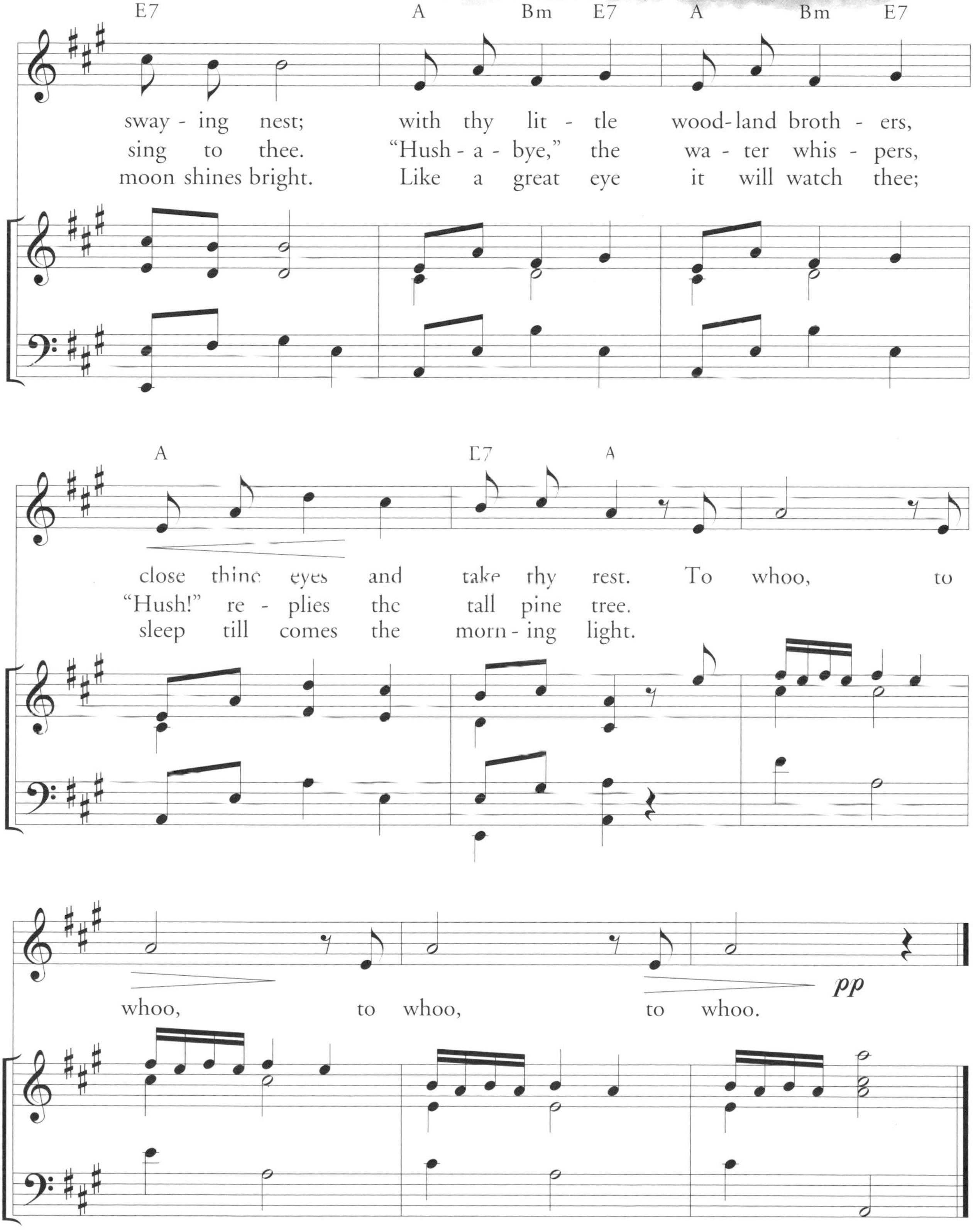

swaying nest; with thy little woodland brothers,
sing to thee. "Hush - a - bye," the water whispers,
moon shines bright. Like a great eye it will watch thee;

close thine eyes and take thy rest. To whoo, to
"Hush!" replies the tall pine tree.
sleep till comes the morning light.

whoo, to whoo, to whoo.

The Children's Prayer

This beloved song comes from the story of Hansel and Gretel. Read it aloud,
or better yet, find and play a recording of Humperdinck's operetta of the same title.

From Hansel and Gretel *by*
Engelbert Humperdinck

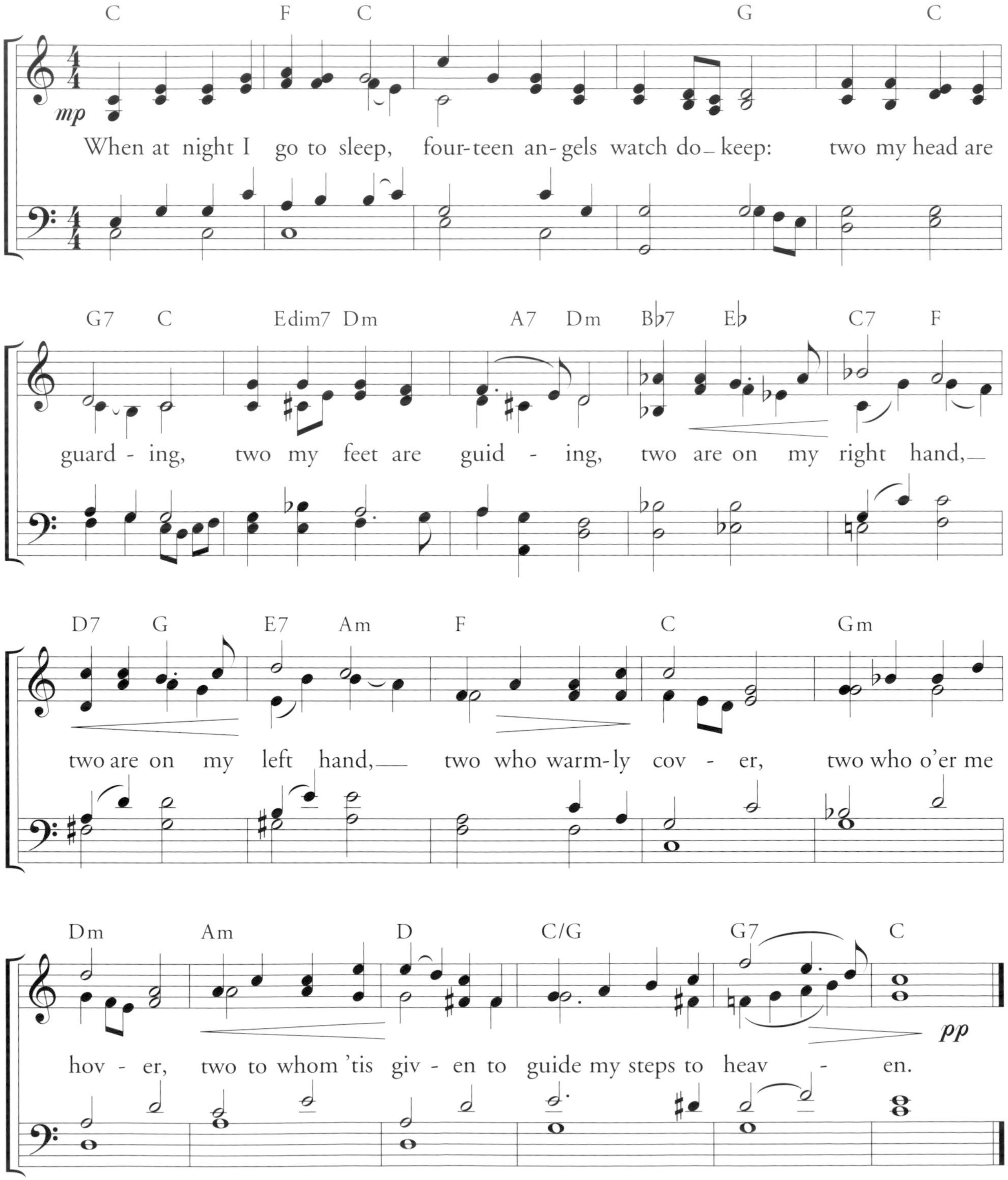

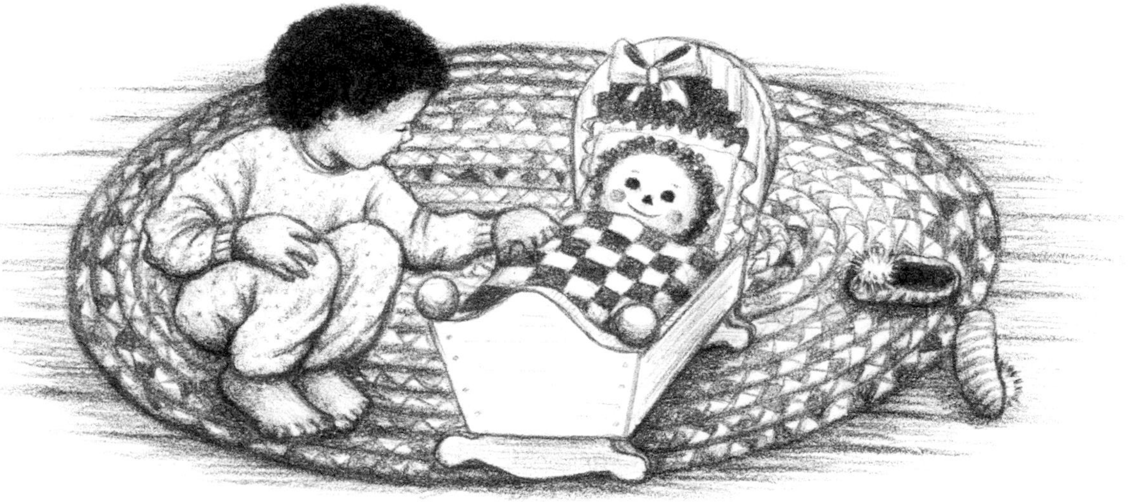

Rickety, Rockety, Hush-a-bye

Unknown

Winifred Hildel

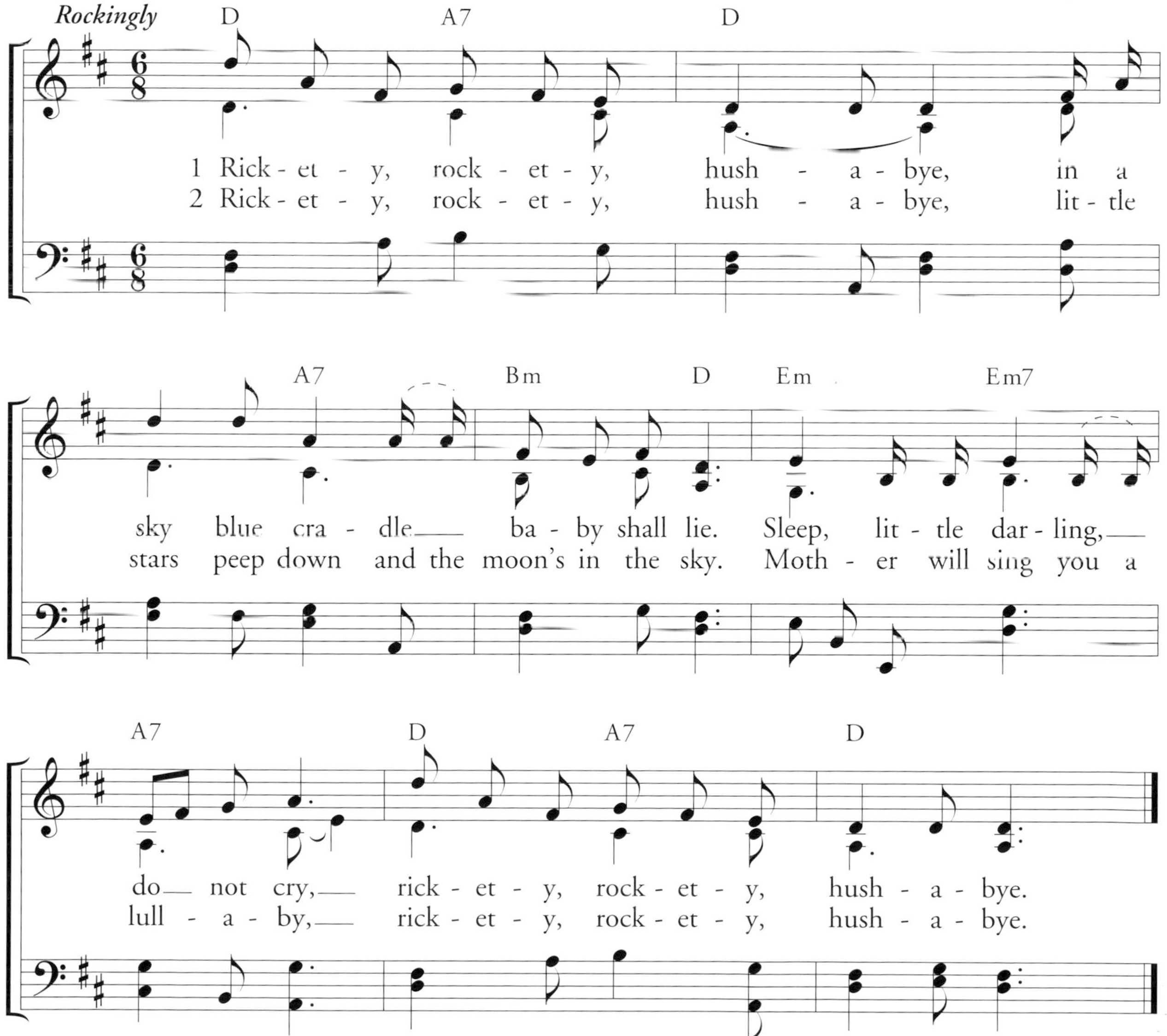

Rockingly

1 Rick-et-y, rock-et-y, hush-a-bye, in a
2 Rick-et-y, rock-et-y, hush-a-bye, lit-tle

sky blue cra-dle___ ba-by shall lie. Sleep, lit-tle dar-ling,___
stars peep down and the moon's in the sky. Moth-er will sing you a

do___ not cry,___ rick-et-y, rock-et-y, hush-a-bye.
lull-a-by,___ rick-et-y, rock-et-y, hush-a-bye.

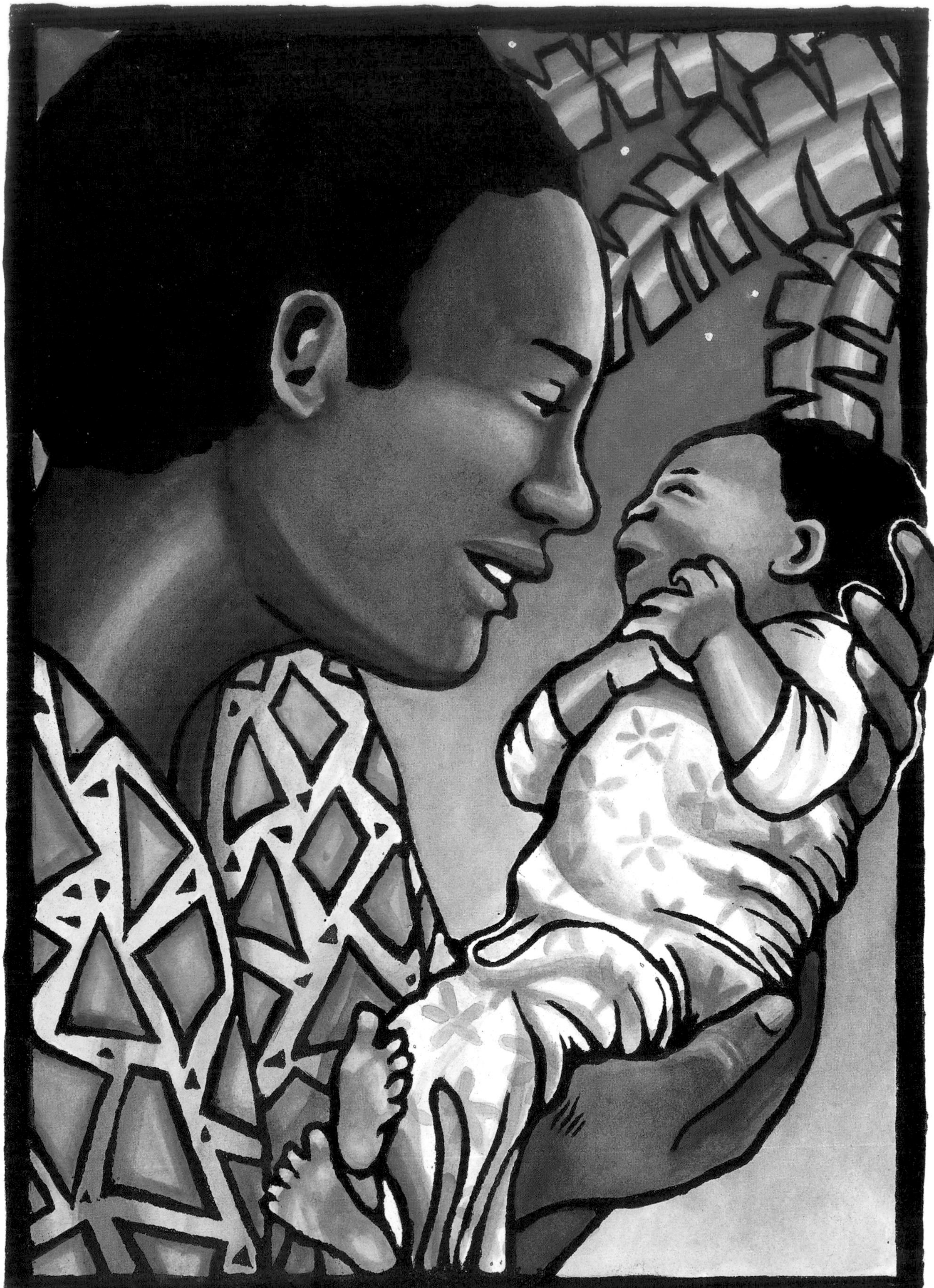

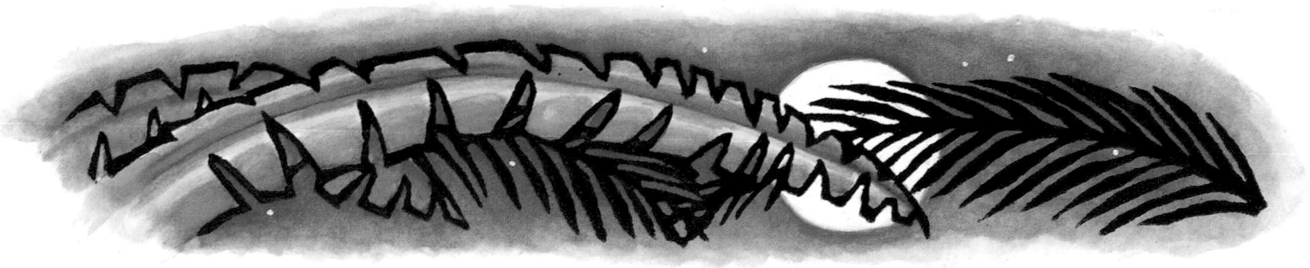

All Me Rock, Me Rock

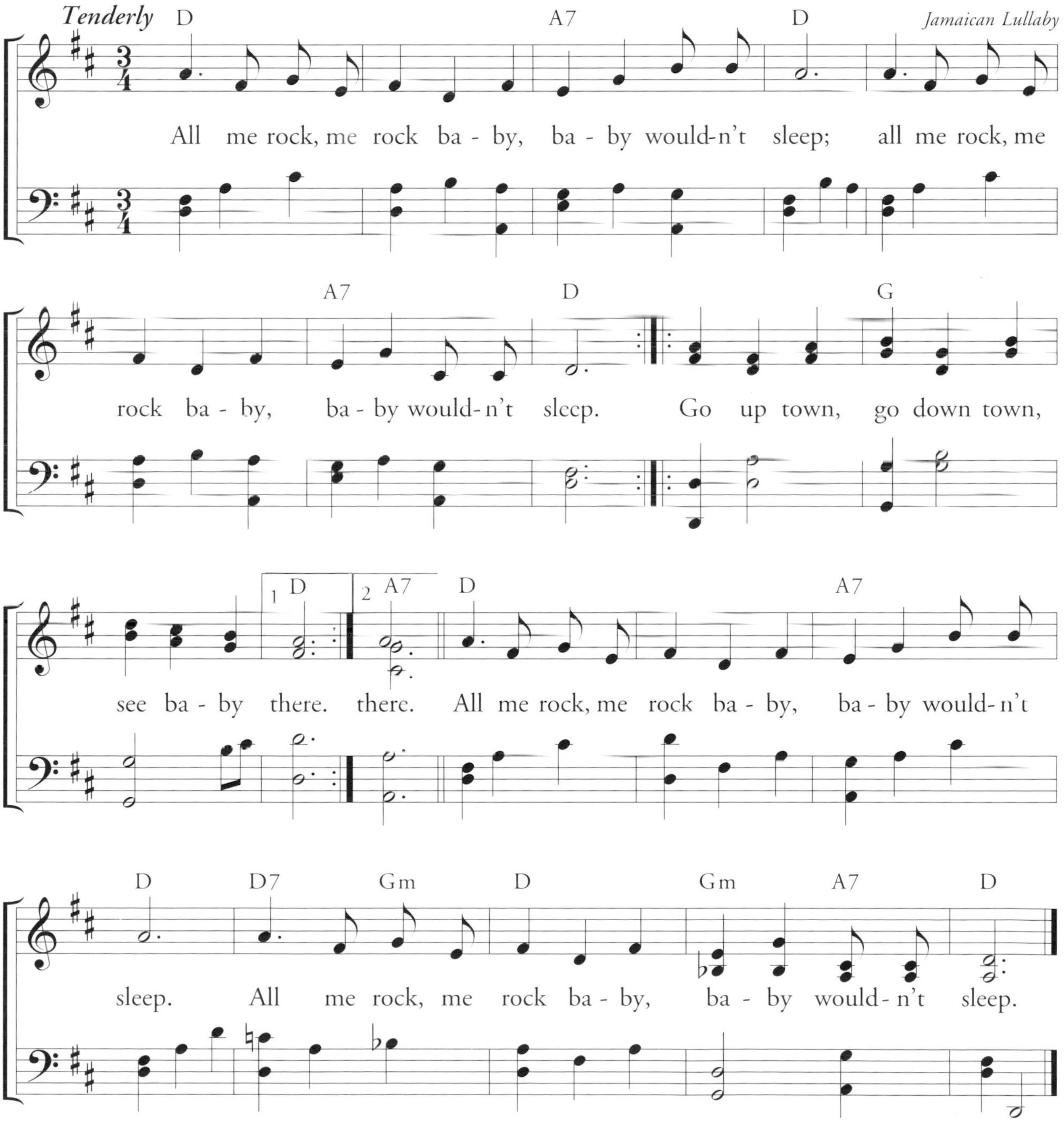

Tenderly   *Jamaican Lullaby*

All me rock, me rock ba - by, ba - by would-n't sleep; all me rock, me

rock ba - by, ba - by would-n't sleep. Go up town, go down town,

see ba - by there. there. All me rock, me rock ba - by, ba - by would-n't

sleep. All me rock, me rock ba - by, ba - by would-n't sleep.

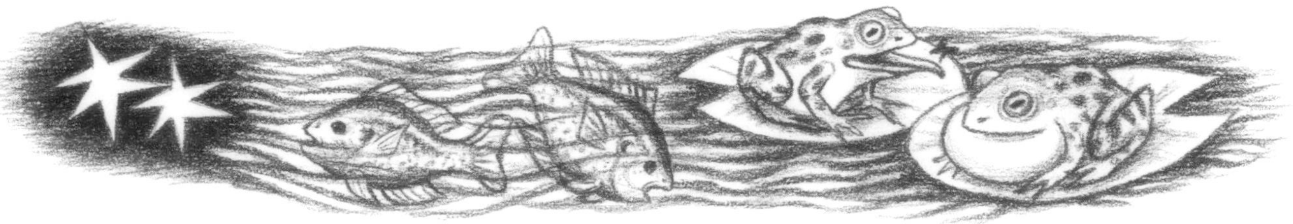

Come to the Window

Unknown   *Marlys Swinger*

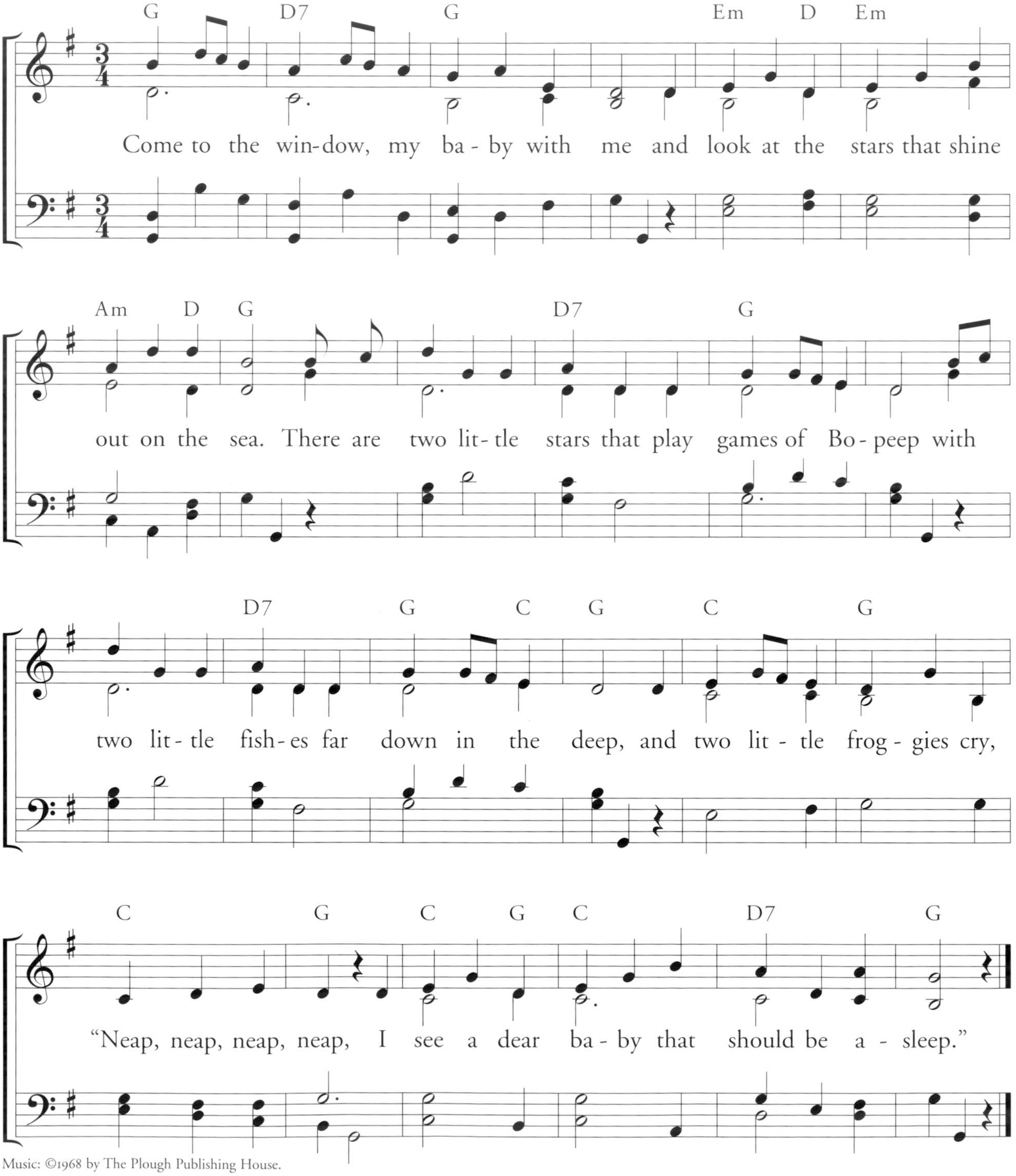

Come to the win-dow, my ba-by with me and look at the stars that shine

out on the sea. There are two lit-tle stars that play games of Bo-peep with

two lit-tle fish-es far down in the deep, and two lit-tle frog-gies cry,

"Neap, neap, neap, neap, I see a dear ba-by that should be a-sleep."

Oro, My Little Boat

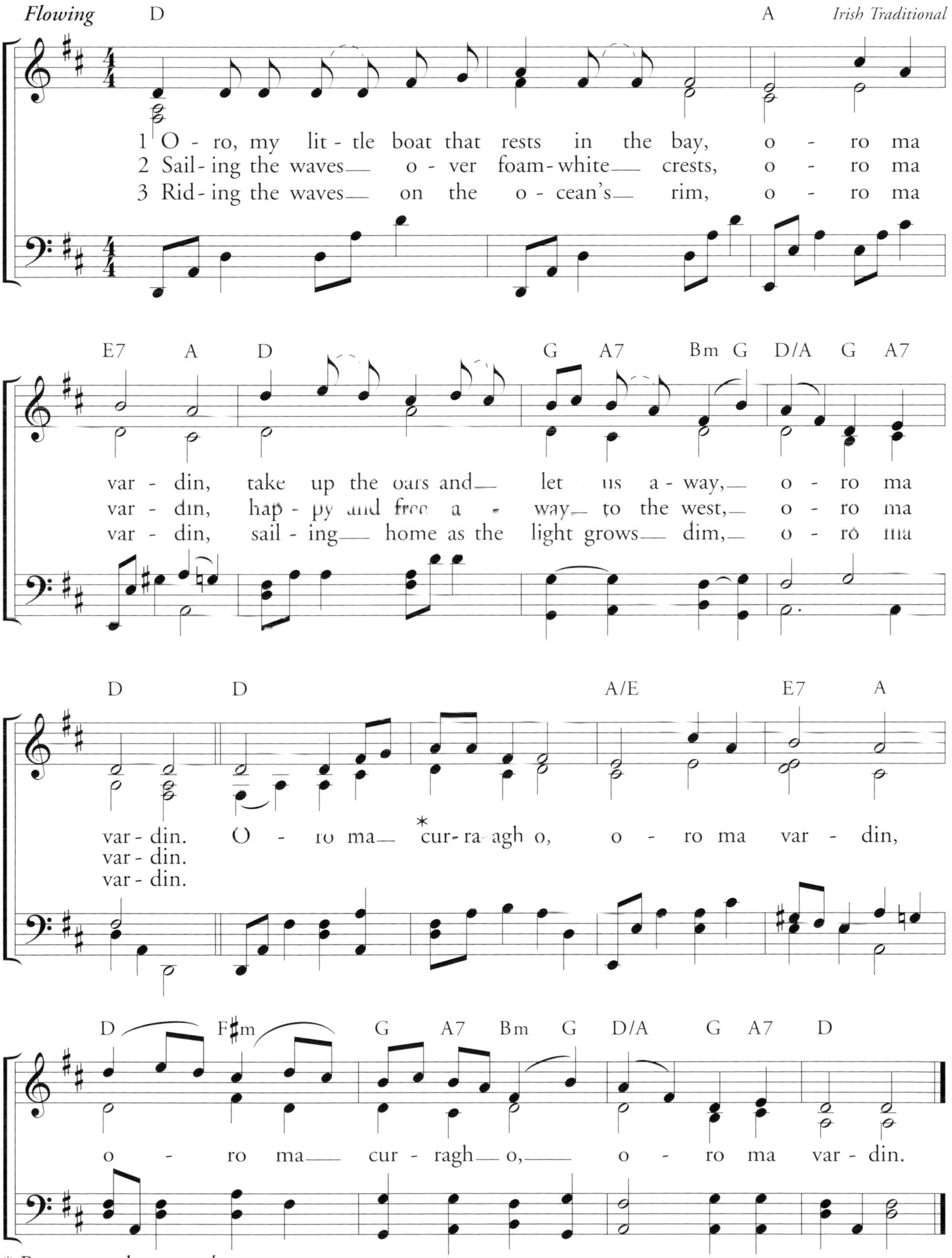

Flowing

Irish Traditional

1 O - ro, my lit - tle boat that rests in the bay, o - ro ma
2 Sail - ing the waves o - ver foam-white crests, o - ro ma
3 Rid - ing the waves on the o - cean's rim, o - ro ma

var - din, take up the oars and let us a - way, o - ro ma
var - din, hap - py and free a - way to the west, o - ro ma
var - din, sail - ing home as the light grows dim, o - ro ma

var - din. O - ro ma *cur - ra - agh o, o - ro ma var - din,
var - din.
var - din.

o - ro ma cur - ragh o, o - ro ma var - din.

* Pronounced: *car-ra-kee-o*

Hush-a-bye, Go to Sleep

From a child's point of view, *anything's* possible – even catching whales!

French Folk Song

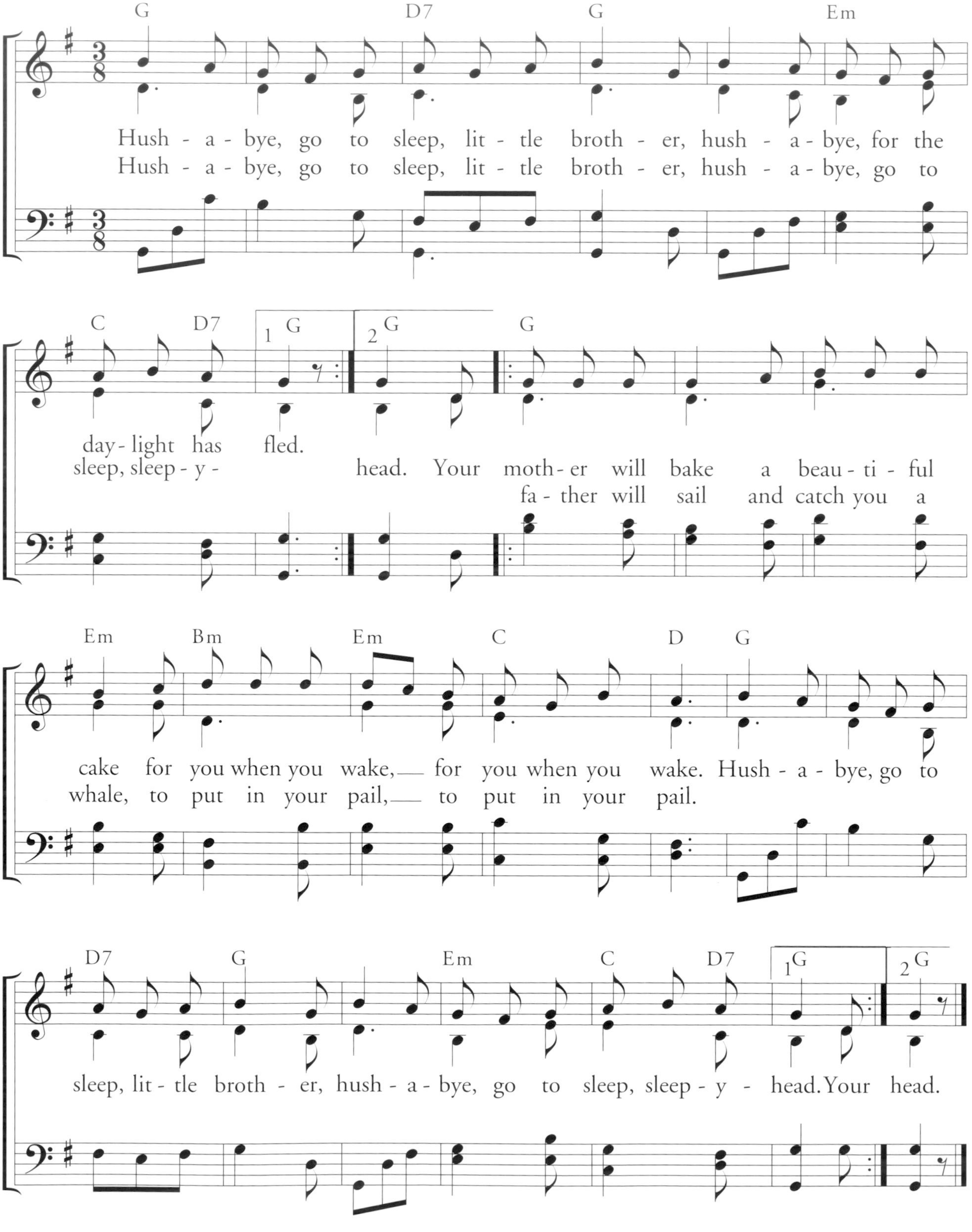

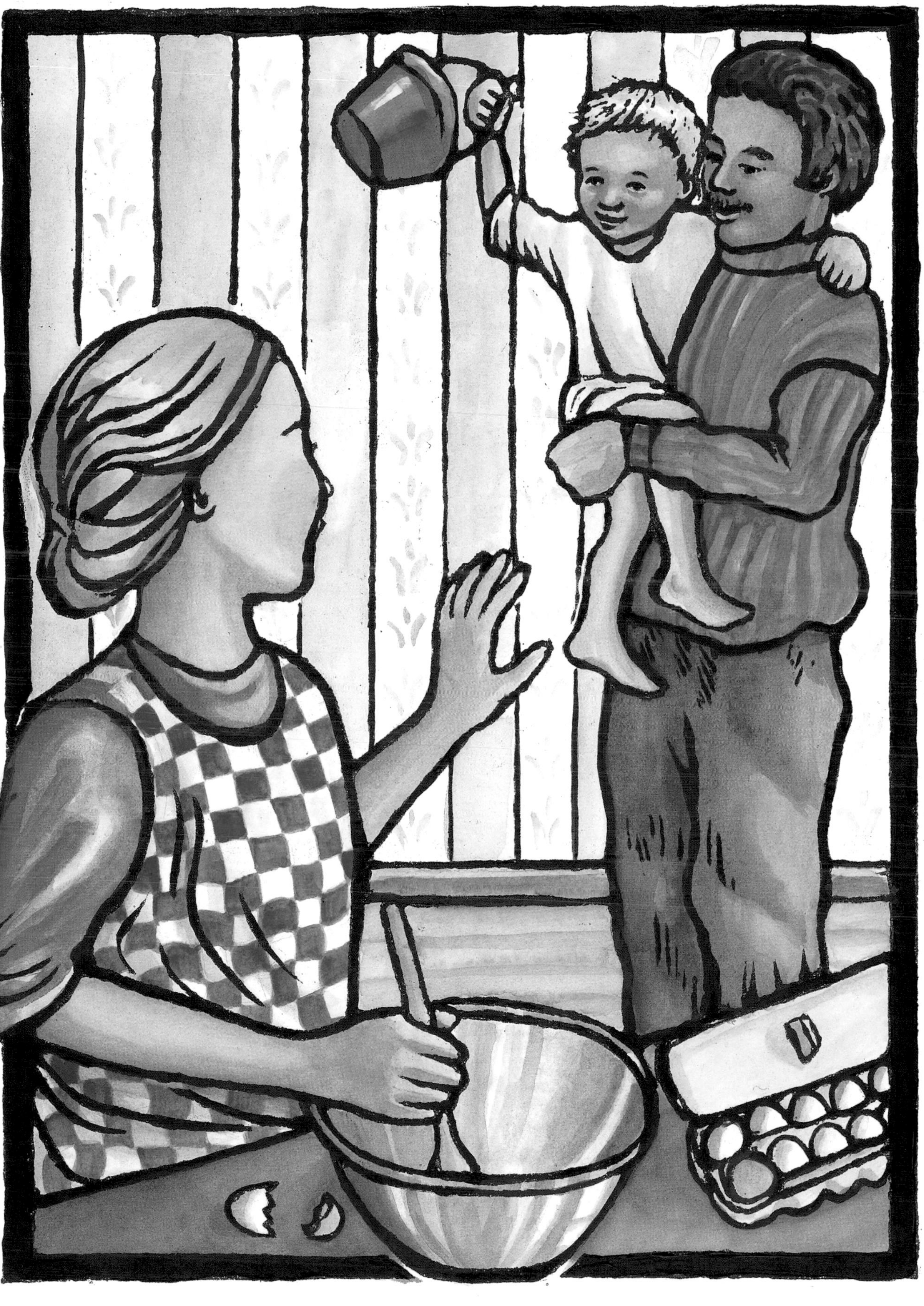

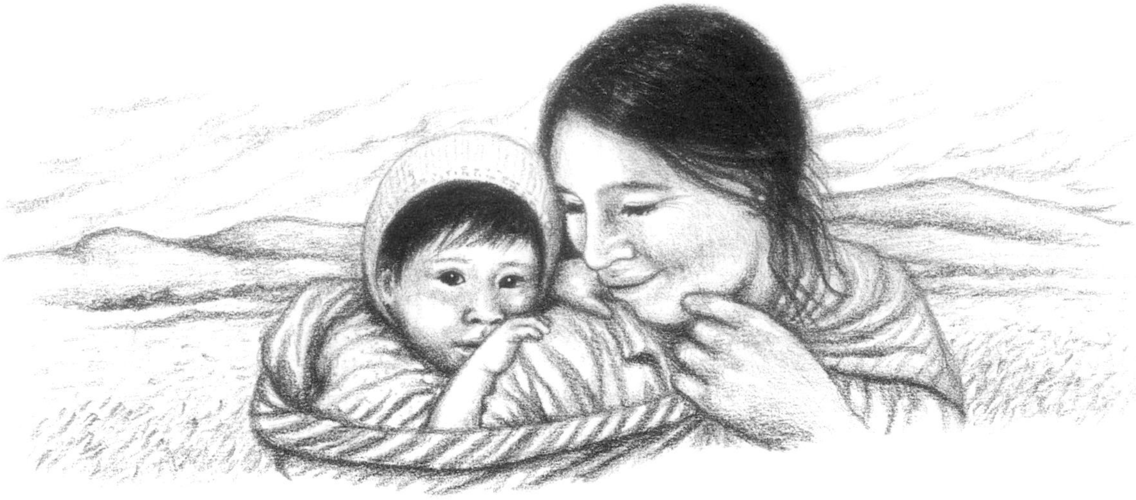

🔊 Arrorro, My Baby

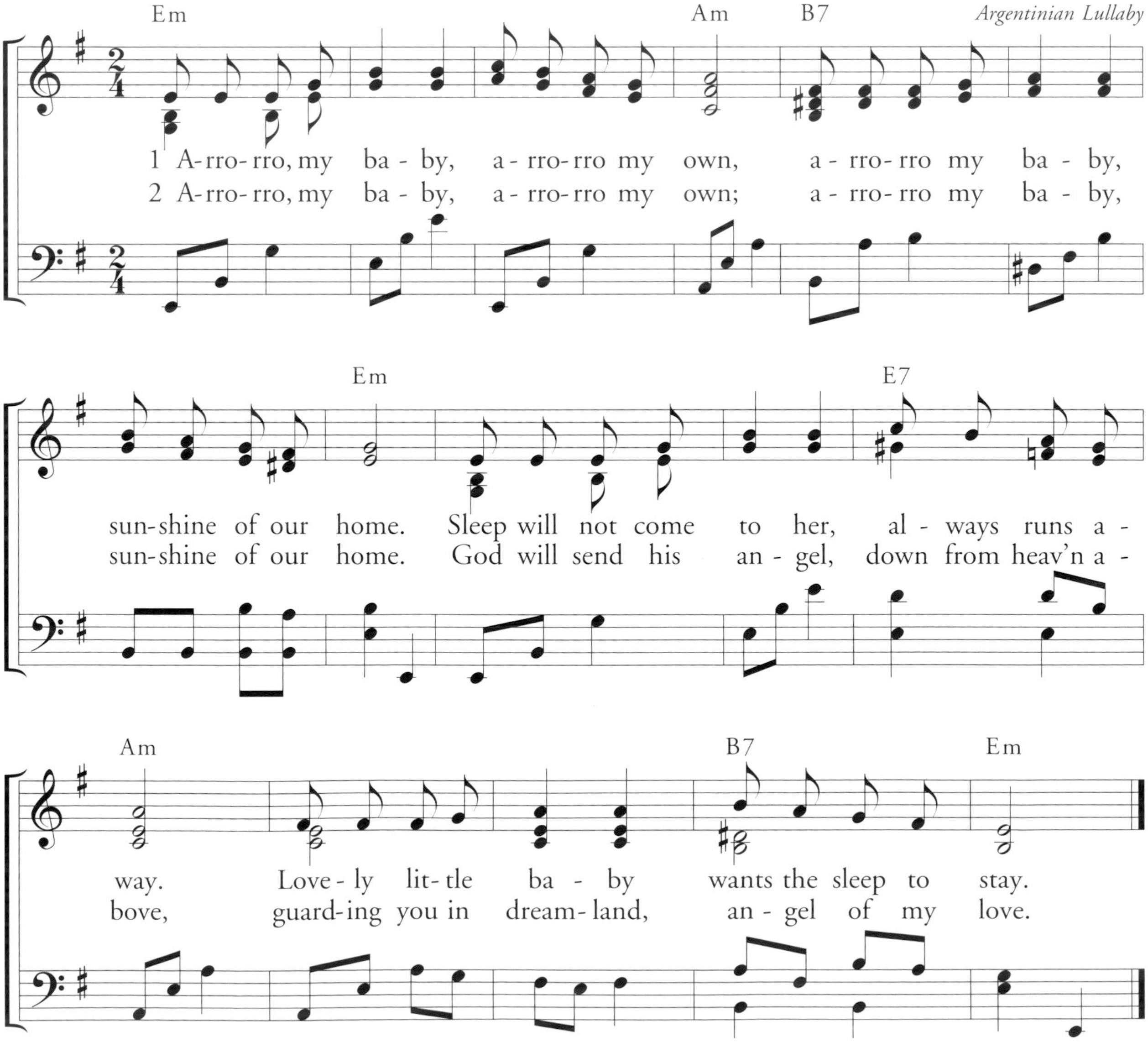

Argentinian Lullaby

Em   Am   B7

1 A-rro-rro, my ba-by, a-rro-rro my own, a-rro-rro my ba-by,
2 A-rro-rro, my ba-by, a-rro-rro my own; a-rro-rro my ba-by,

Em   E7

sun-shine of our home. Sleep will not come to her, al-ways runs a-
sun-shine of our home. God will send his an-gel, down from heav'n a-

Am   B7   Em

way. Love-ly lit-tle ba-by wants the sleep to stay.
bove, guard-ing you in dream-land, an-gel of my love.

Angels Watchin' Over Me

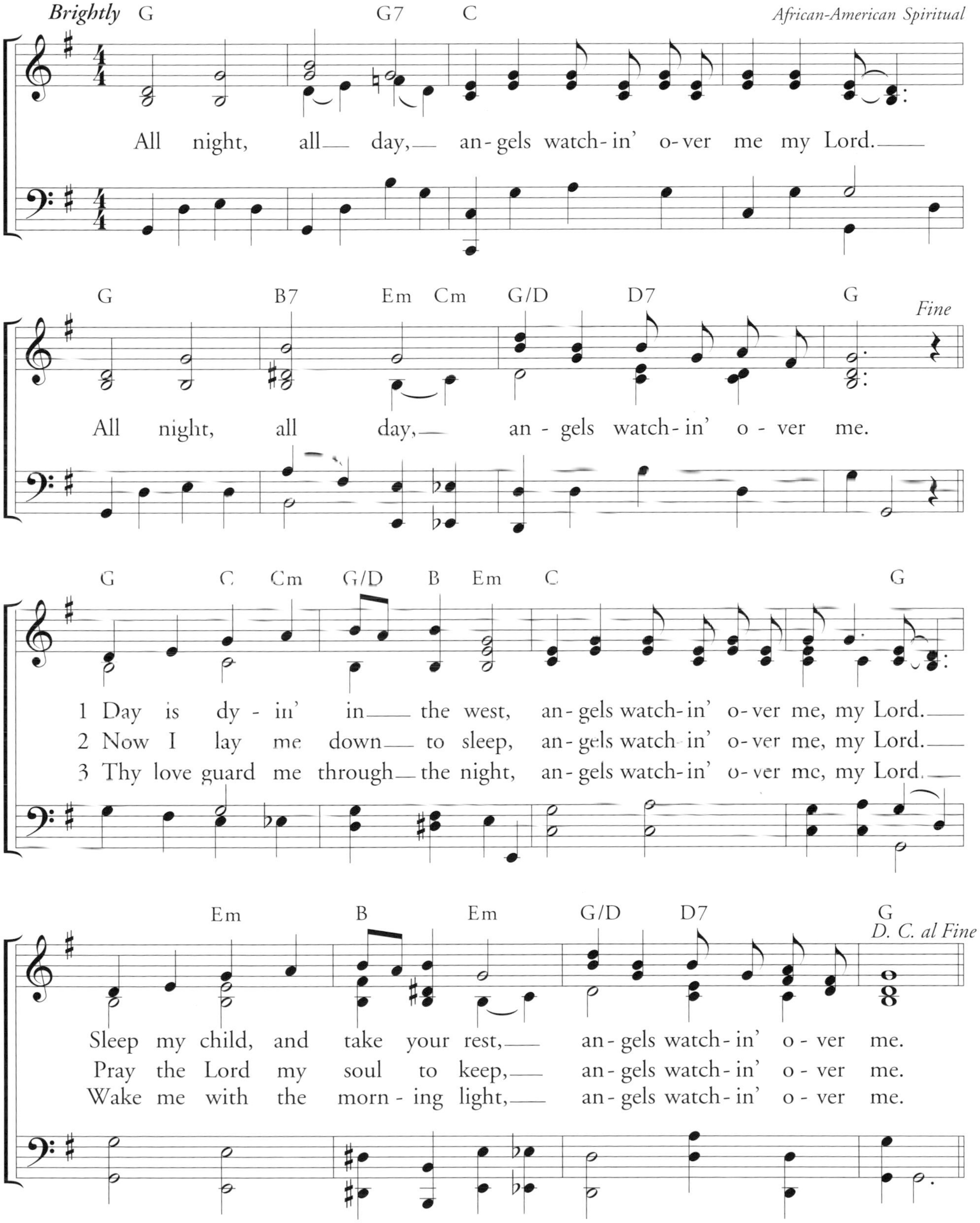

Brightly African-American Spiritual

All night, all day, an-gels watch-in' o-ver me my Lord.

All night, all day, an-gels watch-in' o-ver me.

1 Day is dy-in' in the west, an-gels watch-in' o-ver me, my Lord.
2 Now I lay me down to sleep, an-gels watch-in' o-ver me, my Lord.
3 Thy love guard me through the night, an-gels watch-in' o-ver me, my Lord.

Sleep my child, and take your rest, an-gels watch-in' o-ver me.
Pray the Lord my soul to keep, an-gels watch-in' o-ver me.
Wake me with the morn-ing light, an-gels watch-in' o-ver me.

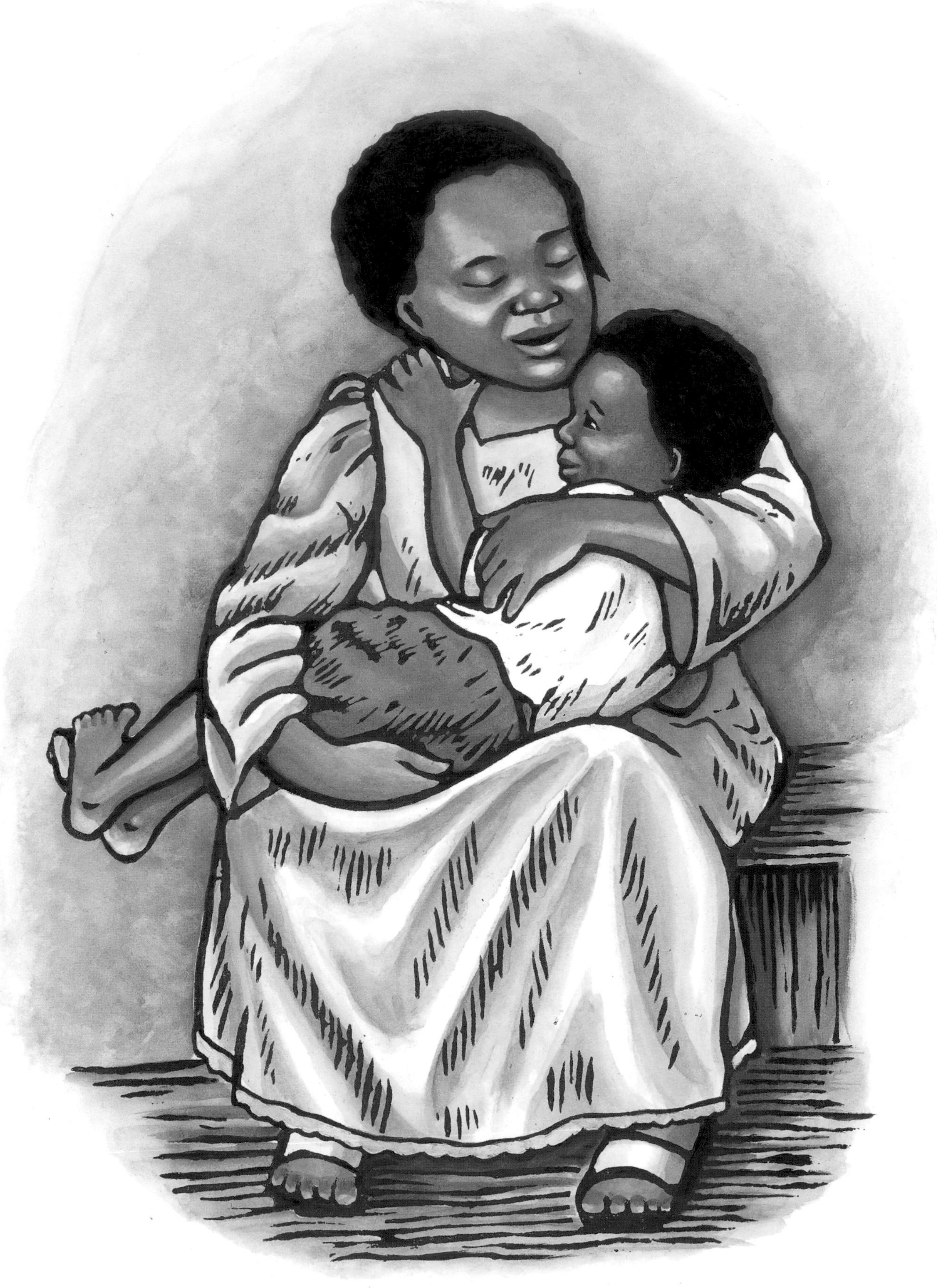

Index of First Lines and Titles